GARY RHODES

GARY RHODES

fabulous food

photographs by Sandra Lane

x

BBC Books

For My Mother

Acknowledgements

A special thank you to Borra Garson, Bill Toner, Wayne Tapsfield, Jane Huffer, the kitchen team at city rhodes, Nicky Copeland, Khadija Manjlai, Frank Phillips, Isobel Gillan, my wife Jenny and my sons Samuel and George for keeping me sane (!) and ahead of everything.

This book is published to accompany the television series entitled *Gary Rhodes*, which was first broadcast in 1997. The series was produced by the Features Department, BBC Television.
Executive Producer: Patsy Newey
Producer: Nick Vaughan-Barratt

Published by BBC Books,
an imprint of BBC Worldwide Limited,
Woodlands, 80 Wood Lane,
London W12 0TT

ISBN 0 563 38385 2

Designed by Isobel Gillan
Photographs by Sandra Lane, © BBC Books
Styling by Mary Norton
Food for photography prepared by Gary Rhodes

Set in Bembo and Gill Sans by BBC Books
Printed and bound in Great Britain by Butler & Tanner Ltd, Frome and London
Colour separations by Radstock Reproductions Ltd, Midsomer Norton
Jacket printed by Lawrence Allen Ltd, Weston-super-Mare

Previous page: Green Tomato *Tarte Tatin* (page 130)

contents

notes on the recipes

1 Follow one set of measurements only; do not mix metric and imperial.
2 Eggs are large.
3 Wash fresh produce before preparation.
4 Spoon measurements are level.
5 A tablespoon is 15 ml; a teaspoon is 5 ml.
6 If you substitute dried for fresh herbs, use only half the amount specified.
7 Mixed-herb tea bags are readily available and can be used as an alternative to bouquets garnis.
8 Unless otherwise stated, 'season' or 'seasoning' simply means seasoning with salt and pepper.
9 I recommend Lindt or Bournville chocolate where recipes call for 'good-quality plain chocolate'.
10 When blind-baking pastry cases, it is best to leave the excess pastry hanging over the rim. Once the pastry is cooked, simply trim off the edges to give a neat even finish.
11 Gas guns can be used to give a crispy sugar glaze to many desserts. It is important to be fully aware of how to operate and use the gun as this is not a conventional kitchen utensil. And, obviously, gas guns should not be used by children.
12 Oven temperatures and cooking times are flexible and may vary according to the equipment and ingredients used.
13 Butter and cream may be reduced, if not excluded, in most savoury recipes.
14 Where a knob of butter is stated, it may be used more than once in the recipe. The exact quantity of butter is left to your discretion – you can use 1 teaspoon or 1 tablespoon, or replace the butter with a trickle of vegetable cooking oil.
15 *Mirepoix* is a term used to mean a general mixture of chopped carrots, onion, celery and leeks.
16 Ingredients are listed with the main ingredient(s) first, followed by the other ingredients in order of use.
17 Always be careful when increasing quantities of ingredients to serve more people, as quite often not all the ingredients will need to be increased by the same proportion. It is best to taste as you add.

introduction

i am often asked where the ideas and recipes come from to put these books together. To be totally honest with you, I'm not quite sure! An idea for a 'new' dish (is there such a thing?) can often come from the oddest and strangest situations. Take Omelette Vesuvius or Baked Alaska as we know it. Was somebody skiing or mountaineering when they thought of this classic dish? The inspiration for the Jaffa Cake Pudding from *Open Rhodes* came from a Saturday-afternoon shopping trip; the Wagon Wheel® Pudding (page 190) came from memories of schoolday tuck shops and, I have to be honest, the Bourbon Biscuits (page 210) came purely from dunking one!

Working in a busy restaurant kitchen spreads thoughts among the whole team, and young chefs often approach me to say they have an idea for a new dish. This automatically inspires me and it pleases me to know that their minds are on the job and that they are also trying to look further than their everyday tastes to create something new. To encourage that inspiration, I want to listen, talk and, with luck, try the dish. Sometimes the idea isn't quite right, but it might have something that sparks off another idea in me, which then develops into something completely different, but is always credited to its originator.

Reading cookbooks is one of my favourite pastimes, not in an effort to find new dishes, but in the hope that reading them will encourage another new idea. I also find myself thinking up new ideas when I'm driving and, as soon as I get to work, I scribble the thought down on paper. Some never develop any further but I'm pleased to say, most often do. I also have a golden rule for any new dishes. If I've had an afternoon with the sous-chef, and a brainstorming session for a menu change, all ideas are listed and put on hold for a few days. This is because, as I'm sure you'll agree, the mind can get a little carried away and totally lose its initial track. Many times we've looked at our ideas three days later and said to each other 'what is that?', pointing to a dish that's never going to work and looks like nonsense. The next row is whose idea it was?! We usually find out!

I remember visiting a smoked-salmon maker (I was about to write 'smoker' but somehow that didn't sound quite right, nor so appetizing!) and dealer in northern Scotland. He has won many awards for the quality of his smoking, giving the salmon a flavour and texture that's an experience to try. One of the stages of his smoking was to marinate the salmon fillets in a mixture of water, black treacle, sherry, black peppercorns, juniper berries and thyme. The balance between those flavours worked so well and left a taste that I hadn't experienced before. The blend played on my mind for some time. I eventually took the majority of those ingredients and turned them into a dressing but, instead of serving smoked salmon with it, I chose fresh salmon. The flavour is immense and has had great success on the menu.

I mentioned driving and ideas coming to me. Could it be the music I'm playing that's at work here? Does Soul give you a warm, sensual feeling towards eating, Jazz a delicate depth, and Country something hearty; and maybe heavy Funk just explodes in the mouth? (I think Pop is take-away and Punk, nouvelle cuisine!) All are part of communication and work together so well.

It's interesting and educational to read a dictionary, looking for the true meanings of words. Often, though, I feel the explanations are quite shallow, and don't communicate enough real information to us. I believe the biggest vehicle for communication we have is food: it brings us all together. Restaurants and dining-room tables are probably the most-used meeting places in the world. It's easy to say, yes, Gary, but we do all have to eat! There's so much more to it than that. One style of cooking and food communicates a totally different message to your friends and partners. I'm sure none of us 'popped the question' over a sausage, chips and beans affair!

Chefs in the kitchen are not just putting flavours together for the sake of it (I hope). There's a link, a sense of communication between tastes and between textures. When dishes are being put together, they are formed with a meaning, to ensure that every taste involved is going to be happy mingling with the others. There really should always be a purpose for any item being on the plate, and I mean in terms of flavour rather than just being decorative.

Looking up the word 'communicate' in the dictionary made interesting reading. It gives quite a few explanations. Speech, writing, gestures, to impart knowledge, and one that stood out for me is: 'to make or have a connecting passage', that is, the kitchen 'communicating' with the dining room. What happened to the food communicating with the eater? The distance between the two rooms is purely a passageway; for me the real communication comes from what you are carrying on plates from one to the other. When the plate is put in front of you, it's the food that is talking to you and that leads me to another word that has a close relationship with cooking: expression.

The first example and, being the first, it means it's the most important current meaning, is the act or instance of transferring ideas into words. How right that is – transferring ideas into words. The ideas are in the cooking; I'm always wanting to create ideas of dishes for the public – the eaters – with the food and flavours. Another explanation for the word expression is 'a look on the face that indicates a mood or emotion'. Cooking should be about trying to tell a story or communicating and, when you look at the dish, it should be alive and talking to you.

I always check people's faces when dishes are presented to them; they are immediately inquisitive and then, I hope, their expression turns into a smile of appreciation and, more importantly, the 'can't wait to taste it' look.

The biggest compliment a chef can receive is when his or her food has stopped or totally changed the direction of conversation. The only line you want to hear then is 'you've got to try some of this' or 'mmmm, delicious'.

In talking about communication and expression, I haven't been referring solely to restaurant and dinner-party food; it applies to all food. The same strength of passion and feeling with me is featured in all the recipes in this book, from a humble bowl of frozen-pea soup through to the more sophisticated roasted *foie gras*. It's quite a strong message!

This book is about trying to take flavours even further and continues my passion for making British cooking amongst the best, if not the best that can be found anywhere. I'm still looking at British classics and trying to put them on a new plane, with more refinement and more exact flavours. I also hope that, somewhere amongst all of these recipes, we'll find a new 'classic', a dish that will be cooked and talked about for years to come. Looking ahead means thinking ahead in place, time and order and, for me, that implies never sitting back, but always trying to cook the next dish better than the last.

I hope you are going to enjoy the dishes and read the personal messages in them; it's been like writing a letter to friends. Make sure you reply by trying them out.

The cookery in this book is definitely about expression and communication. Let's make sure we all keep talking.

Gary Rhodes

STARTERS

starters

We'll start the meal with Warm Champagne Oysters (page 24), followed by a large bowl of Moules Marinière (page 22) and then how about Roast *Foie Gras* (page 42) or Confit of Bacon (page 38)? Sounds like a very tasty meal already and we haven't even looked at the main courses or desserts yet!

All of these dishes are featured in this first chapter, which shows the range of cooking and eating styles that you can achieve without looking much further (but I hope you do!).

I always say that we should never be too strict with our cooking from, or reading of, cookery books. When I hunt for recipes, no matter what type, I look through the whole book and, quite often, have the pleasure of finding, for example, a simple starter that will stand up as a main course. Among all of these starter recipes you will find some interesting flavours, styles and combinations: Potato, Spring Onion and Mozzarella Risotto (page 53), Smoked Haddock and Sorrel Omelette (page 25) and Mussels glazed with Cider Cream Sauce (page 21). There is one, though, that has really made an impact: Escalope of Salmon with Black Treacle, Juniper and Sherry Dressing (page 30). I'm sure you'll all be wondering how salmon and black treacle can complement each another but, I promise you, they do. The black treacle doesn't mask the flavour of the fish but helps to lift all the other tastes.

Here's a sample of some of the other dishes in this chapter: Tuna fish with lemon dressing, Asparagus and leeks, Scallops with a hot mustard sauce, Terrine of duck, pork and chicken liver and Escabeche of red mullet. I'm sure you'll notice the one common ingredient they all have – TASTE!

Frozen-pea Soup

Here's a really quick soup to make. After all, the peas only take about 3 minutes! The soup takes a little longer to finish, but only a few minutes more.

Serves 4–6

450 g (1 lb) frozen peas
1 large onion, finely chopped
A knob of butter
450 ml (15 fl oz) Vegetable
   or Chicken Stock (page 240)
   or alternative (page 243)

A pinch of sugar
150 ml (5 fl oz) single cream
   (optional)
Salt and pepper

Cook the onion in a knob of butter for a few minutes, without letting it colour, until softened. Add the stock and bring to a rapid simmer. Add the peas now and cook on a fast heat for 3 minutes. Once the peas are soft and tender, season with salt, pepper and sugar and then liquidize to a smooth consistency. For an even smoother finish, push the soup through a sieve. For a creamier consistency, add the single cream. The pea soup is now ready to eat, preferably with lots of crusty bread!

Note: A sprig or two of fresh mint can be added to the soup during the cooking of the onion for some extra taste. The soup can also be garnished with fried or toasted bread croûtons and small, crisp-cooked strips of smoked or unsmoked bacon.

Cauliflower Soup *with 'Harry's Bar' Toasties*

Cauliflower soup is pretty self-explanatory, but what are 'Harry's Bar' toasties?

Harry's Bar is a very famous bar in Venice, Italy. It is renowned for its drinks and sandwiches, among many other foods. The toasties are really a Harry's Bar version of the French croque monsieur – a cheese and ham toasted sandwich. The Harry's Bar version is made with Swiss Gruyère, which is turned into a speedy rarebit mix, to give a creamier and more tasty finish. The sandwich is then fried in olive oil for a crispy warm finish.

Both flavours, ham and cheese, go very well with cauliflower, so I decided to make these sandwiches part of the dish. After all, we often sprinkle fried-bread croûtons over soups. Here, you'll be dipping your croûton into the soup!

Serves 4

For the Cauliflower Soup:
1 small cauliflower, trimmed and
  roughly chopped
A knob of butter
1 onion, chopped
1 small leek (white only), chopped
450 ml (15 fl oz) Vegetable
  or Chicken Stock (page 240)
  or alternative (page 243)
150 ml (5 fl oz) single cream or milk
Salt and pepper

For the Filling:
225 g (8 oz) Gruyère, grated
½ teaspoon English mustard
1 teaspoon Worcestershire sauce
A pinch of cayenne pepper
A pinch of salt
1 tablespoon single cream (optional)

For the Toasties:
8 slices of medium white bread
4 slices of ham
Olive oil, for frying

For the soup, melt the butter in a large saucepan and add the onion and leek. Cook for 3–4 minutes, without letting them colour, and then add the roughly chopped cauliflower with the stock. Season with salt and pepper and bring to the simmer. Cover and cook the soup for 15–20 minutes.

Check that the cauliflower has cooked and then add the cream or milk. Blend the soup to a smooth consistency and check the seasoning. If the consistency is a little grainy, simply push the soup through a sieve.

To make the filling for the toasties, the cheese must first be left to reach a warm room temperature. If you try to make this with cheese straight from the fridge, the flavours and textures will not emulsify.

Place all the filling ingredients, except the cream, in a food processor and blitz to a smooth consistency. If the spread appears to be a little thick, add the single cream and blitz again.

Spread the cheese mix onto all the slices of bread. Put a slice of ham on four slices and sandwich with the remaining four slices. Trim off the crusts. These sandwiches can be made well in advance to this point and refrigerated.

To finish the toasties, heat a frying-pan with enough olive oil to coat the base. Once hot, pan-fry the toasties to a crisp golden brown on both sides. This will warm the cheese spread and give it a melting consistency that goes well with the ham and crisp bread. Once all the sandwiches are fried, cut them into soldiers and offer one or two pieces per portion.

Note: These quantities are quite substantial enough for a main course, so if you just want a snack make half the quantity of toasties.

The soup can also be spiced up with a touch of English or Dijon mustard.

Roast Mushroom Soup

This is a basic recipe with only a handful of ingredients, but it certainly has lots of flavour. The twist in the taste comes from the roasting of the mushrooms. The soup could be made without roasting at all, by chopping the mushrooms and stewing them with the onion and potato instead. However, the mushrooms become very watery and lose their good, strong taste.

I like to save one or two of the roasted mushrooms and chop them for the garnish, along with some chopped tarragon or parsley.

Serves 4–6

750 g (1½ lb) flat mushrooms
2 tablespoons cooking oil
2 onions, finely chopped
1 large potato, peeled and cut into
   a rough 1 cm (½ in) dice
A knob of butter

600 ml (1 pint) Vegetable
   or Chicken Stock (page 240)
   or alternative (page 243)
300 ml (10 fl oz) single cream
   or milk
Salt and pepper
Chopped fresh parsley or tarragon,
   to garnish (optional)

Pre-heat the oven to 220°C/425°F/Gas Mark 7.

First wipe the mushrooms clean, rather than washing them. (If you wash them, they tend to absorb too much water.) Heat a roasting tray or an ovenproof frying-pan and add the cooking oil. You can now season the mushrooms and then add them whole and fry them on a high heat to colour them well. Once they are coloured on one side, turn the mushrooms over and colour again. They should now be placed in the oven for 8–10 minutes.

Cook the onions and potato in butter, without letting them colour, until softened. Add the stock and bring to the simmer.

Roughly cut up the mushrooms, saving one or two for garnishing, and add them to the soup, together with any residue left in the roasting or frying-pan. Bring the soup back to the simmer and add the single cream. Season with salt and pepper.

Cook for 5–6 minutes and then remove from the heat.

Liquidize to a smooth finish. The soup can also be pushed through a sieve to give an even smoother consistency. Bring back to the simmer and add the sliced or chopped roasted mushrooms to garnish. Taste again for seasoning and add the chopped parsley or tarragon, if using.

Note: If you are using tarragon, add some leaves during the cooking process to give some extra taste. Adding a squeeze of lemon juice once the soup has been liquidized will also enhance the other flavours.

STARTERS

17

Roast Ham and Cep Soup

Ceps are popular and grown all over Europe; they are known as cèpes *in France and* porcini *in Italy. They are one of the best wild mushrooms, packed with flavour, and they need very little else to help them. Ceps can be bought fresh or dried; the dried are a lot easier to find — the fresh ones are only available in season from Summer through to early Winter.*

The roast ham flavour in this soup is quite powerful but the ceps stand their ground and also make a big impression. The raw ham does need to be soaked for 24 hours, to reduce its saltiness. If you buy hock of ham on the bone, buy 1.25 kg (2½ lb) to allow for the weight of the bone. Cooking the ham on the bone does give the stock a wonderfully powerful flavour.

This is a very hearty soup that can stand as a main course, especially with some good crusty bread.

Serves 6–8

900 g (2 lb) piece of raw ham, knuckle or hock
100 g (4 oz) dried ceps
100 g (4 oz) fresh ceps, wiped and sliced
225 g (8 oz) button or cup mushrooms, sliced
2–3 tablespoons cooking oil
Chicken Stock (page 240) or alternative (page 243) or water, if necessary
A knob of butter

150 ml (5 fl oz) double cream
Salt and pepper
1 tablespoon chopped fresh flatleaf or curly parsley

For the *Mirepoix*:

1 onion, chopped
2 carrots, chopped
2 celery sticks, chopped,
1 leek, chopped
Fresh thyme sprig
A knob of butter

Soak the ham in plenty of fresh water for 24 hours. Cover the dried ceps with 1.2 litres (2 pints) of cold water and leave them to soak for 3–4 hours. Then pre-heat the oven to 190°C/375°F/Gas Mark 5.

Heat the oil in a roasting pan and add the ham. Cook it until golden, turning it from time to time, on top of the stove. Then transfer to the oven and roast for 45–50 minutes. This gives you a half-cooked or perhaps three-quarters-cooked roast ham, having all of the roasted flavours.

While the ham is roasting, soften the *mirepoix* of vegetables and thyme with butter in a large, deep saucepan. Add the roasted ham and strain the water from the soaked ceps into the pan. Top up the pan with more water or some chicken stock, for extra flavour, so that it virtually covers the ham. Bring to the simmer and cook for a further 45 minutes and then remove from the heat. The ham will now be totally cooked and flake easily.

Leave to rest for 15–20 minutes.

Remove the ham from the stock. The stock can now be reduced by simmering to about a third to a half to give you a richer, tastier stock.

Add the soaked mushrooms to the finished stock. Fry the fresh cep and button or cup mushrooms in the butter and also add to the stock with all their cooking juices. Add the cream and bring to the simmer. Taste and reduce, if necessary, to increase the depth of flavour.

Season with salt and pepper. Remove any skin from the ham, shred the meat and add it to the soup. You may well find you have too much ham: if so, I suggest you use it for some delicious ham and cheese 'toasties' (page 14)!

Add the chopped parsley and the soup is ready.

Note: If fresh or dried ceps are unavailable, simply replace with an extra 225 g (8 oz) button or cup mushrooms.

'Main Course' Whole Chicken and Vegetable Soup

This soup is entitled main course because that's exactly what it could be. It could also become a creamy casserole. What I love about this dish is the way in which it creates its own stock – packed with flavour from the chicken and the vegetables.

Many other ingredients can also be added – spaghetti, macaroni, rice, tomatoes, basil and more!

Serves 6–8

1.5 kg (3 lb) oven-ready chicken
2 large onions, cut in large dice
3 carrots, diced
4 celery sticks, diced
1 large potato, diced

1 medium leek, diced
A handful of frozen peas
25–50 g (1–2 oz) butter
85–150 ml (3–5 fl oz) single cream
 (optional)
Salt and pepper

Season the chicken and place it in a deep saucepan; cover it with cold water. Bring to the simmer and skim any impurities from the surface. Cover the pot loosely and leave to simmer for an hour, skimming from time to time.

Add the onions, carrots, celery and potato. Return to the simmer and continue to cook for 20 minutes until all the vegetables are cooked and tender. Remove the chicken from the stock and, when it is cool enough to handle, break it into pieces and pull the meat into strips (remove and discard the skin and bones).

Bring the soup base to the boil and allow it to reduce to increase the flavour. Once a good strong flavour has been reached, add the leek and cook for 2 minutes before adding the frozen peas. Return the soup to the boil and cook for a further 3 minutes. Now add the butter with the cream, if using. Add the strips of chicken and check for seasoning. It is now ready to serve.

Mussels glazed with Cider Cream Sauce

These mussels are served out of their shells. Glazed in a nice, small starter bowl or serving dish, what you'll have are fresh mussels, lots of leeks and good cider-cream sauce glaze. Nothing could be a better accompaniment than a glass of good wine.

If you want to turn this into a main course, take a fillet of cod or salmon, poach it, sit it on a bed of spinach and then glaze it with the mussel and cider sauce.

Serves 2

750 g (1½ lb) live mussels, scrubbed, washed and 'beards' removed

2 small leeks, 1 cut in 1 cm (½ in) dice, 1 roughly chopped

300 ml (10 fl oz) Fish Stock (page 241) or alternative (page 243) or water

A knob of butter

½ onion, roughly chopped

A few fresh tarragon leaves (optional)

1 star-anise (optional)

300 ml (10 fl oz) dry cider

150 ml (5 fl oz) double cream

1 egg yolk

Salt and pepper

Blanch the diced leek in the fish stock or water for a minute until tender. Strain, saving the stock, and leave the leeks to cool.

Melt the knob of butter in a saucepan big enough to cook the mussels in. Add the onion, the other roughly chopped leek, tarragon (if using) and star-anise. Cook for a few minutes until the onion is tender. Increase the heat and add the mussels. Stir the mussels in the pan and then add the cider and reserved stock. Bring to the boil, while stirring the mussels. After a few minutes, the mussels will begin to open. Discard any that don't open. Strain the mussels through a sieve into a large, clean pan, saving only the cider and mussel stock. Bring the stock to the boil and reduce by two-thirds by simmering gently. While the stock is reducing, take the mussels from their shells and keep them warm in a little of the stock.

Add half the double cream and return to the boil. The sauce may well need to reduce further by a quarter in volume. It is ready when it just coats the back of a spoon. Add the reserved cooked diced leeks and mussels and warm through.

Lightly whip the remaining cream. Pre-heat the grill to hot.

Add a knob of butter to the sauce with the egg yolk. Do not allow the sauce to boil or the egg will 'scramble'. Fold in the whipped cream and check the seasoning. Spoon the mussels, leeks and sauce into serving bowls or plates and glaze under a pre-heated grill. After a minute or two, the cider sauce will have glazed to a lovely golden brown.

Note: For the ultimate glaze, the sauce is better bound with a tablespoon of Quick Hollandaise Sauce (page 235) or a whisked *sabayon* of egg yolk and cider, both folded in with the whipped cream.

Moules Marinière

I love eating large bowls of mussels, with some good bread to mop up any juices. Moules Marinière *is a French classic that, for me, stands as a complete dish. I have added one or two extra flavours but they are optional, so you can keep this dish as simple as possible.*

Serves 2–3

1 kg (2¼ lb) live mussels, washed, scrubbed and 'beards' (the threads that hang from the shells) removed

50 g (2 oz) butter

2 heaped tablespoons chopped fresh shallots or onions

1 heaped tablespoon finely diced carrots (optional)

1 heaped tablespoon finely diced celery (optional)

1 garlic clove, crushed

1 heaped tablespoon finely diced leek (optional)

2 glasses of white wine

3 glasses of Fish Stock (page 241) or alternative (page 243) or water

1 star-anise (optional)

85 ml (3 fl oz) double cream

A squeeze of lemon juice

Salt and pepper

1 tablespoon mixed chopped fresh herbs e.g. parsley, tarragon, chervil

Melt 15 g (½ oz) of the butter in a saucepan and add the shallots or onions, carrots, celery and garlic. Cook for a few minutes, until beginning to soften, and then add the diced leek, if using. Cook for a further minute, remove from the heat and leave to one side.

Place the mussels in a large saucepan on a medium–high heat and add the white wine and fish stock or water with the star-anise, if using. Cover with a lid and cook for 30 seconds, then stir for 3–4 minutes. During this time, the mussels will open. Once all are opened (any that don't should be discarded) lift the mussels from the pan into serving dishes and keep warm. Strain the cooking liquor through a fine sieve onto the cooked vegetables. Bring to the boil and reduce by a third. Add the cream and whisk in the remaining butter with a squeeze of lemon. Season with salt and pepper and add the chopped mixed herbs. Pour the finished liquor over the mussels and serve.

Note: *Moules Marinière Royale* is another favourite, with a name I've taken from the famous Kir drink: Kir is a glass of white wine flavoured with *cassis* (blackcurrant liqueur). *Kir Royale* is made with champagne. So, for *Moules Marinière Royale*, just replace the white wine with champagne.

Warm Champagne Oysters *with*
Smoky Cabbage

Eating oysters the classic way, raw with a squeeze of lemon or Tabasco sauce, and accompanied with a glass of champagne is certainly a favourite of mine. But I also really enjoy eating warmed, cooked oysters, which take on an even more tender texture. All of the extras, champagne, lemon and Tabasco, are being used in this dish, so you are not missing a thing! The same idea can be used with other fish and shellfish – scallops, langoustines, prawns or salmon, for example.

Serves 2

10 rock oysters, opened and all
  juices saved
275 g (10 oz) finely shredded
  savoy cabbage
Butter for frying, plus 25 g
  (1 oz) butter
4 shallots or 1 onion, finely sliced
4 rashers of smoked streaky bacon,
  very finely diced

1 glass of champagne
1 teaspoon white-wine vinegar
A small pinch of caster sugar
2–3 tablespoons double cream
A squeeze of lemon juice
A drop or two of Tabasco sauce
Salt and pepper

Once all the oysters have been opened, wash the shells and save for serving the oysters in.

The cabbage can be prepared in advance. Heat a frying-pan and add butter. Fry the shallots or onion for 3–4 minutes until completely tender and beginning to caramelize. Season with salt and pepper and remove from the pan. Fry the bacon for 4–5 minutes, allowing its fat content to cook out, leaving you with fine, crisp bacon. Add the bacon to the shallots. Wipe the pan clean and melt another small knob of butter. Fry the cabbage (which can be blanched in boiling water for 1 minute to give a richer colour) for 4–5 minutes, allowing a slight golden tinge amongst the deep green.

Mix together the cabbage, shallots and bacon and season with salt and pepper. You can do this beforehand and then fry to reheat all together, or cook it at the last minute.

To make the sauce, boil the champagne with the vinegar and sugar until reduced by three-quarters. Add the oyster juices and cream and bring to the simmer. Add the lemon and Tabasco and whisk in the 25 g (1 oz) of butter. Season with salt and pepper. The sauce is now ready. If you have an electric blender, blitz the sauce for a few seconds, just before serving, to make it lighter in taste and consistency.

Warm the oysters in a knob of butter and season. To serve, divide the cabbage between the oyster shells, sit the oysters on top and spoon the sauce over.

Note: If making a larger quantity, some fish stock can be used to produce more sauce. If you're wondering why I'm working with five and not the traditional six oysters per portion, it is because the extra garnish more than makes up for the sixth oyster!

Smoked Haddock and Sorrel Omelette

Eggs and smoked haddock are a great combination but the eggs are normally in the form of poached eggs and not omelettes. Here, the haddock is poached in a little water and butter. This creates a good smoky fish stock; the haddock is then broken into the omelette. The stock isn't wasted either – I make a cream sorrel sauce to go with the finished dish.

For another classic flavour, add a spoonful or two of cooked spinach to the sauce and blitz it to a smooth cream to give a wonderful finish to this dish.

Serves 2

6–8 eggs, depending on size
100–175 g (4–6 oz) natural
   smoked haddock
A knob of butter
6 sorrel leaves

A squeeze of lemon juice
6 tablespoons double cream
50 g (2 oz) cooked spinach
   (optional)
Salt and pepper

Put the haddock fillet in a small, buttered pan with a knob of butter and half-cover with water. Break and add 2–3 leaves of sorrel. Add a squeeze of lemon juice, cover with foil or a lid and bring to the simmer. Cook for a few minutes until tender. Leave to stand for 1–2 minutes. Remove the haddock and break it into flakes. Take one or two tablespoons of liquor and drizzle it over the fish. This will keep it moist and warm.

Reduce the cooking liquor by half and add the cream. Bring to the boil and cook for 1 minute. Check for seasoning and add salt, pepper and lemon juice to taste. If using spinach, add it to the sauce and return to the simmer. Blitz to a purée in a blender or processor and strain through a sieve to give a green spinach-cream sauce.

To make the omelette, heat a 15 cm (6 in) omelette pan. Crack the eggs, enough for one portion at a time, and beat with a fork. Add a twist of pepper. It is very important never to add salt until the last second as salt breaks eggs down and they become watery.

Shred the remaining sorrel leaves and add half to the egg. Put a knob of butter in the pan and, once it begins to bubble, pour in the omelette mix. This can now be stirred in the pan with a fork, not allowing it to stick, set or turn golden on the base. A really good omelette, where the eggs are just set in a pan of butter, should have no colour at all!

Once the eggs are setting but still moist on top, stop stirring and sprinkle the haddock flakes over. Hold the pan at a slight angle and tap it so the omelette slides towards the front of the pan. Fold it over. Fold in the other side and turn the omelette onto a plate. Repeat to make the second omelette. The omelette will have an oval shape; make it neater by covering it with a clean cloth and shaping it. Pour the spinach sauce around and serve at once.

Note: If you are not using spinach in the sauce, add one or two extra shredded leaves of sorrel just before serving.

Seared Scallops *with Hot Mustard Shallot Sauce*

This dish is one of my favourites. The flavour from the scallops alone is sensational, with a hint of bitterness from the searing, and with the 'hot' sauce and a very creamy mashed potato to go with it, it's unbelievable. That's a pretty big statement to make and the only way to prove it is for you to try it!

Serves 4

12 scallops, trimmed and
   cleaned of roe
225–350 g (8–12 oz) Mashed
   Potatoes (page 140)
50–85 ml (2–3 fl oz) single cream

1 quantity Hot Mustard Shallot
   Sauce (page 246)
1 tablespoon cooking or olive oil
A knob of butter
Salt and pepper

The mashed potatoes should be loosened with single cream: the consistency should be very soft but still holding its own weight. If, after adding the cream, the mash still seems to be too firm, add either more cream or milk. Check the seasoning.

Warm the mustard shallot sauce.

Heat a frying-pan with the tablespoon of oil. Once hot, sit the scallops in the pan, making sure the maximum heat is maintained, which will ensure the scallops are searing. Season the scallops in the pan and once a good, almost burnt, tinge has caught on the edges, add the knob of butter. Leave for 30 seconds and turn the scallops over. They can now be cooked for a further 30 seconds–1 minute.

To present the dish, either spoon or pipe the potatoes, using a 1 cm (½ in) plain nozzle, at the top of the plate. Spoon 2–3 tablespoons of sauce in front and sit three scallops on top.

Macaroni Cheesecake

This must be the first cheesecake made without cream cheese! It is made the original way with a good Cheddar sauce. So what makes it into a cheesecake? I'll leave you to read the recipe and find out!

Serves 6
350 g (12 oz) dried macaroni
A knob of butter
1 tablespoon olive oil
Salt and pepper

For the Sauce:
25 g (1 oz) butter
25 g (1 oz) plain flour

1 onion, 1 bay leaf and 1 clove
   (optional)
600 ml (1 pint) milk
5 fl oz (150 ml) double cream
   (optional)
1 teaspoon English mustard
   (optional)
225 g (8 oz) Cheddar, grated
Salt and pepper

To make the sauce, melt the butter in a saucepan and add the flour. Cook on a low heat, stirring from time to time, for 8–10 minutes. While the 'roux' is cooking, stud the clove through the bay leaf onto the onion (if using) and place in the milk. Heat the milk slowly, so the flavour of the onion and aromatics will infuse into it. Add the milk to the roux, a ladle at a time, stirring well and bubbling it before adding more. Once all the milk has been added, place the onion in the sauce and simmer gently for 30 minutes. The sauce will now have become very thick. Remove and discard the onion. Add the cream, if using, for a creamier finish.

Add the teaspoon of mustard (more or none if preferred). Sprinkle in the Cheddar, tasting as you add and it melts. Once at the strength you prefer, drain the sauce through a sieve.

While the sauce is cooking, cook the macaroni according to the packet instructions and then drain. Not all of the sauce will need to be mixed with the macaroni for this stage of the dish; add just a spoonful at a time until the macaroni feels completely bound. Set the rest of the sauce aside for later. Season the macaroni mixture with salt and pepper.

Butter 6 x 5 cm (2½ x 2 in) deep rings and sit them on a tray covered in cling film. Spoon the mix into the moulds, pushing it down to pack it in, which will hold the mix together. Refrigerate for at least 30 minutes until completely set.

Pre-heat the oven to 200°C/400°F/Gas Mark 6. Melt a knob of butter with a tablespoon of olive oil in an ovenproof frying-pan. Sit the cakes, still in the rings, in the pan and fry on a low–medium heat to a golden brown. During this cooking time the macaroni will become crisp. Then bake them for 10–12 minutes until heated through. Or remove the cakes from the pan and leave to cool. Once cooled, turn them over and remove the rings. The golden, crisp cakes can now be microwaved for a few minutes, when needed.

To serve the macaroni cakes, warm the remaining sauce (do not boil it or the cheese will separate). Spoon some onto the centre of the plates and sit the cake on top.

The cheesecakes can be served in many different ways. Here are two ideas that both go very well with the cheesecakes and make it complete.

Macaroni Cheesecake *with Roasted Tomatoes and Olive and Chive Dressing*

Serves 4

1½ tomatoes per portion
A knob of butter
4 tablespoons olive oil
2 teaspoons balsamic vinegar (optional)

A few black olives, stoned and
   quartered
1 teaspoon chopped fresh chives
Salt and pepper

Halve and de-seed the tomatoes; cut each half into three. Melt a knob of butter in a hot pan and add the tomatoes. Season with salt and pepper and fry on a hot heat until golden and softened. Remove from the heat. Mix the olive oil with the vinegar, if using. Season with salt and pepper. Add the black olives and chives. Spoon the tomatoes around the cheesecake or sit them side by side and finish by spooning the black olive and chive dressing around.

Wild Mushroom Cheesecake

The wild mushrooms can be girolles, ceps or trompettes de la mort. *If none of these is available, replace them with button or brown-cap (chestnut) mushrooms.*

Serves 4

275–350 g (10–12 oz) wild or
   cultivated mushrooms, washed
2–3 tablespoons olive oil
2 tablespoons sliced Spring onions
1 tablespoon mushroom ketchup
   or essence

3 tablespoons groundnut oil
A squeeze of lemon juice
1 tablespoon sherry or
   red-wine vinegar
Salt and pepper
½ teaspoon chopped fresh parsley
½ teaspoon chopped fresh marjoram

If using cultivated mushrooms, they should all be quartered. Ceps will need to be sliced, *trompettes* halved and girolles left whole or halved if large.

    Heat a frying-pan with the olive oil. Add the mushrooms and Spring onions and sauté for a few minutes. Mix the mushroom ketchup or essence with the groundnut oil, a squeeze of lemon and the vinegar. Season with salt and pepper and add the chopped herbs. Spoon the mushrooms and Spring onions around the plate and finish with the herbed dressing.

Note: Cooked lentils also go very well with the mushroom dressing.

Escalope of Salmon *with Black Treacle, Juniper and Sherry Dressing*

This recipe came to me after a visit to a small town, very far north in Scotland, called Achiltibuie, where I was shown the stages of preparation for Scottish salmon before it's smoked. Well, this came about from one of the early stages when the salmon are soaked in a marinade made from shallots, juniper berries, black peppercorns, garlic, thyme, sherry, black treacle and water. Once the fish has been marinated and smoked, it takes on an amazing flavour. This recipe uses fresh (not smoked) salmon, with one or two changes to the marinade, giving us, instead, a rich dressing. The bitter-sweet flavour of black treacle lifts all of the other tastes.

Serves 4

4 x 1 cm (½ in) thick (100–175 g/ 4–6 oz) slices of fresh salmon
A knob of butter
225 g (8 oz) mixed green salad leaves e.g. rocket, baby spinach
1 teaspoon olive oil, mixed with a few drops of lemon juice
Salt and pepper

For the Dressing:

2 heaped tablespoons finely chopped shallots or onions
10–12 black peppercorns, crushed
15–20 juniper berries, finely chopped
1 garlic clove, crushed
4 tablespoons sherry vinegar
⅓ tablespoon black treacle
3 tablespoons walnut oil
3 tablespoons groundnut or grapeseed oil
A pinch of salt

To make the dressing, mix together the shallots or onions, crushed peppercorns, finely chopped juniper berries, garlic and sherry vinegar. Bring to the simmer and cook until the vinegar has almost completely evaporated. Add the black treacle and oils and bring back to the simmer. Cook for 1–2 minutes and season with a pinch of salt. This dressing can be made hours or even days in advance. It's best kept refrigerated – the flavours will become more dominant as it relaxes – and brought back to a warm temperature before serving.

To cook the salmon, and finish the dish, first heat a frying-pan and season the salmon with salt and pepper. Add the butter to the pan and lay the salmon slices, presentation-side down, in the sizzling butter. Cook for 2–3 minutes on one side only, keeping the fish pink. While the salmon is cooking, spoon the dressing onto four plates. Season and add the olive oil and lemon juice to the green leaves, sitting them on top of the dressing. Place the salmon, presentation-side up, on top of the leaves. The dish is now ready to serve.

Note: This dressing also works well with smoked salmon, trout, mackerel or herrings. Pan-fried scallops sitting on the treacle dressing are also very good.

Spiced Tuna Fish *with Lemon and Tomato Dressing*

For this recipe, I am using fresh tuna fillets. The best size fillet is about 6–7.5 cm (2½–3 in) diameter, giving enough texture and actual fish to balance the spice paste.

Small tuna fillets can also be used, but they should be cut at a fairly acute angle to give the right quantity of 'meat' to spice.

I am also giving a recipe for home-made curry oil, which is an optional extra. This has a warm flavour that works well with this dish and could also be used to spice up salads, vegetables, risottos and more.

Serves 4
450 g (1 lb) fresh tuna fillet,
   skinned and trimmed
A knob of butter

For the Spice Paste:
2 teaspoons yellow mustard seeds
½ green chilli, finely diced
½ teaspoon cumin seeds
¼ teaspoon ground turmeric

For the Dressing:
8 plum or salad tomatoes, blanched,
   skinned and seeded
2 lemons, peeled and segmented
4 tablespoons olive oil
Salt and pepper
1 tablespoon shredded fresh
   coriander

First make the spice paste. Blitz the yellow mustard seeds, chilli, cumin and turmeric in a coffee grinder or mortar and pestle to a spreadable paste (you may need to add a teaspoon of water). Spread the paste over the tuna fillet, covering it completely.

Wrap the fish in cling film and refrigerate for 1 hour to help set and firm the paste. Unwrap and fry the fish in the butter on all sides for 4–5 minutes, which seals the fish and also cooks the spices. It is important not to cook the fish for too long; it should be served raw, with the cooked spices around the outside. Obviously, if you would prefer the fish to be rare or medium-rare, simply cook for 5–6 minutes, moving it around to brown all sides.

The small tuna fillets, being thinner, will need very little time in the pan. Remove the fish and leave to rest at room temperature.

To make the tomato and lemon dressing, first cut the tomato flesh into 1 cm (½ in) dice. The lemon segments can also be sliced thinly. Warm 2 tablespoons of the olive oil and add the tomatoes and lemon. Season with salt and pepper and warm through, allowing the tomatoes just to soften. Add the remaining olive oil with the shredded coriander. Divide the tomato mixture between four plates or bowls. Carve the tuna fish into 3–5 mm (⅛–¼ in) slices and set them, overlapping, on top, allowing two or three slices per portion. The dish is now ready to serve or it can be finished with a tablespoon of curry oil poured around the plate.

Note: It is very important that the tuna fish used is absolutely fresh.

To make a curry oil to accompany the fish, cook 4 tablespoons chopped onion, 4 tablespoons chopped apple, 1 tablespoon medium–hot curry powder, 2 teaspoons ground cumin and salt and pepper in 12 tablespoons grapeseed or groundnut oil, without letting them colour, until softened and translucent. Blitz to a purée in a blender or food processor. Either tie up and hang the purée in muslin or pour into a fine strainer; in either case, set over a bowl. The flavoured oil will begin to drain. If you leave it for an hour or two, you will be left with about 150 ml (5 fl oz) of curry oil.

Red Mullet Escabeche *with Shallots, Orange and Capers*

Escabeche is a Spanish way of preparing fish and meat. The word itself literally means 'pickled' but, before pickling, the main ingredient is cooked. This dish will suit most fish, especially trout, herrings and mackerel, and the fish will take on a lot more flavour if this dish is prepared a few hours in advance.

Serves 4

4 × 225–275 g (8–10 oz) red mullet, scaled, filleted and all pin bones removed

½ cucumber, peeled and seeded

2 shallots, cut into thin rings

1 tablespoon fine capers or chopped large ones

3 tablespoons white-wine vinegar

3 tablespoons water

The juice of 2 large oranges, plus one curl of zest

The juice of 2 large lemons, plus one curl of zest

2 fresh tarragon sprigs

4 tablespoons olive oil

A knob of butter

Salt and pepper

Mix the shallot rings with the capers in a small pan and add the vinegar and water. Bring to the simmer and cook for 1–2 minutes. Drain off the vinegar liquor into another small pan, reduce by a third and reserve. Keep the shallots and capers to finish the dish. Boil the two juices with their zests and one sprig of tarragon in a third small pan. Reduce by half. Once reduced, drain through a sieve onto the reserved reduced vinegar and mix with the olive oil. Pre-heat the grill to hot.

Lay the red mullet fillets (skin-side up) on a buttered and seasoned baking tray. Brush the fillets with butter, season and place under the grill. The fish will take 2–3 minutes, leaving a good, crisp skin. Once cooked, transfer the fish, while still hot, to a shallow, clean dish and pour over the orange-lemon marinade. The fish will start to take on the marinade's flavours. For maximum taste, leave the fish for 3 hours at room temperature. Half an hour before serving, cut the cucumber into thin julienne strips, approximately 7.5 cm (3 in) in length. Mix with ½ teaspoon of salt and leave to soak and drain in a colander for 30 minutes. Taste it for excess salt flavour. If it tastes too salty, quickly rinse it under cold water and dry it well.

To serve the fish, add 2 tablespoons of the marinade liquor to the cucumber and season with a twist of pepper. Tear the remaining tarragon leaves. Put a pile of cucumber towards the top of the plate and set two red mullet fillets either side. Sprinkle the shallot rings, capers and torn tarragon leaves over the fish and around the plate. Finish by trickling with the marinade.

Note: The dressing can be re-warmed to bring the fish back to room temperature.

Use 3 oranges and 3 lemons to give an even stronger flavour to the dish.

Duck, Pork and Chicken-liver Terrine

This terrine recipe is quite something. The ingredients list might appear to be quite frightening as well! It uses four duck breasts, 750 g (1½ lb) chicken livers, a pork fillet and veal kidneys – all for a starter!

The terrine will in fact feed 12 people or maybe even 15. It is the sort of dish that you will make for a large dinner party or, perhaps, at Christmas time for when you have lots of visitors.

I felt I had to share it with you because it is very easy to make; you don't have to create mousses, but more or less just stack the ingredients in the mould. It is exciting to eat, having such a variety of textures and flavours in one slice. The watercress salad, with a port and red-wine dressing to go with it, makes a perfectly rounded dish.

The terrine mould I use for this recipe is a 1.5–75 litre (2½–3 pint) size.

Serves 12–15

4 small duck breasts, skinned
1 pork fillet, taken from behind the
   loin, trimmed of all sinews,
   weighing 275–350 g (10–12 oz)
750 g (1½ lb) chicken livers, trimmed
2 veal kidneys, trimmed of all fat
   and sinews
120 ml (4 fl oz) Madeira
50 ml (2 fl oz) port
50 ml (2 fl oz) brandy
Milk, enough to soak livers
20 thin, rindless rashers of
   unsmoked streaky bacon
Salt, pepper and ground mace

For the Red-wine Dressing:

2 teaspoons Dijon mustard
2 tablespoons red-wine vinegar
4 tablespoons walnut oil
4 tablespoons groundnut oil
1 dessertspoon redcurrant jelly
4 tablespoons port
Salt and pepper
1 bunch watercress, picked and
   washed, or a 75 g (3 oz) bag

Begin two or three days before you want to cook the terrine. It is best to buy the veal kidneys completely cleaned and you can even ask your butcher to mince them for you, using a medium cutter. If you have a mincer, just cut the kidneys into small pieces for now and pour over the Madeira. Stir, cover and refrigerate.

Pour the port over the pork fillet and leave it in the refrigerator. Flavour the duck breasts with the brandy and refrigerate them.

Fresh chicken livers have a slightly bitter flavour. If they are soaked in milk and refrigerated for 2–3 days, along with the other meats, they will be less bitter and simply sweeter to eat.

Turn all the meats in their marinades from time to time.

After 2–3 days, drain the chicken livers from the milk. Pre-heat the oven to 150°C/300°F/Gas Mark 2. Remove all of the marinated meats from the fridge. If necessary, mince the kidneys through a medium cutter. Line the terrine mould with buttered greaseproof paper and then with the rashers of streaky bacon, making sure to leave the ends overhanging so that there is sufficient to cover the top surface once it's filled.

Season all of the meats and livers with salt, pepper and ground mace.

Spoon half the minced kidneys into the base of the terrine, smoothing them out. Sit two duck breasts on top. Put half the chicken livers close together in the mould. Sit the pork fillet along the centre and then continue to lay the chicken livers on top. Sit the two remaining duck breasts over the livers and spoon on the remaining minced kidneys. Fold over the overhanging streaky bacon, to cover the terrine.

Place the terrine in a deep roasting tray and half-fill with hot water. Bake for 35 minutes. Reduce the oven temperature to 130°C/265°F/Gas ½–1 and continue to cook for a further hour.

The terrine should now be cooked, but still slightly pink inside. Check by inserting a skewer or thin, sharp knife: if it's warm when removed, the terrine should be ready. Cook the terrine for a further 20–30 minutes if you feel it needs a little longer or you like it less pink. Once cooked, remove from the oven, lift out of the roasting tray and leave to rest for 20 minutes. Now you can weigh down the terrine to press all of the cooked meats together. Either use another empty terrine dish or wrap a rectangle of firm cardboard, cut to fit the terrine top, in foil and cling film and put directly on top of the terrine's surface. Put some weights, for example, two 500 g (1 lb) bags of sugar or tins of baked beans inside the empty terrine or on top of the cardboard and leave to cool.

Once cold, refrigerate the terrine overnight with the weights in place. In the morning, you have the duck, pork and chicken liver terrine. This can now be turned out and carefully sliced.

For the dressing, whisk together the mustard and red-wine vinegar. Mix the two oils together and gradually whisk them into the mustard and vinegar, as for mayonnaise. Once the ingredients are blended, season with salt and pepper. Warm the redcurrant jelly with the port, melting the jelly to a liquid. Whisk it into the red-wine sauce and adjust the seasoning.

Separate the watercress into generous sprigs. Add two tablespoons of the finished dressing and gently fold in. Arrange the watercress on the slices of terrine. Trickle a further tablespoon or two of dressing around the plate before serving.

Note: To achieve the absolute maximum flavour, the 'meats' should be marinated for 2–3 days in advance.

I like to finish the terrine presentation with a small twist of pepper and a few coarse sea-salt granules sprinkled on top.

Confit of Bacon *with Apple and Celery Salad*

Confit *is the French word for preserving. The most usual use is for a confit of duck − duck cooked and then set in its own fat − which allows it to be kept almost indefinitely. I'm not exactly looking to do that with this bacon. Once you've cooked it, you'll want to eat it − not save it!*

This piece of smoked streaky bacon (unsmoked can also be used) could just be roasted, instead of cooked in a confit, but it will not have the same succulence.

This dish is a good starter or works very well as a Summer main course. The horseradish dressing is my choice, but you can of course improvise or simply use a basic salad dressing. The confit and the horseradish oil can be made well ahead.

Serves 4–6

750 g (1½ lb) skinned and trimmed
   piece of streaky bacon
600–900 ml (1–1½ pints) cooking oil
   or pork fat

For the Dressing:

100 g (4 oz) fresh horseradish,
   grated
½ fresh green chilli, finely chopped
175 ml (6 fl oz) groundnut oil
A squeeze of lemon juice
Salt and pepper

**For the Dressing Garnish
  (optional):**

2 tablespoons horseradish-chilli oil
6 radishes, finely diced
6–8 marinated anchovies
   (not tinned), diced

For the Salad:

2 apples, peeled, cored and
   quartered
4 celery sticks, peeled and
   thinly diced
2–3 handfuls of mixed green
   salad leaves

The 'joint' of streaky bacon must first be skinned and trimmed, leaving a cleaned piece. This is best soaked for 24 hours in cold water, removing excess salt flavour.

Pre-heat the oven to 180°C/350°F/Gas Mark 4. In a small, hot roasting pan, put a drop of the cooking oil or fat and heat on top of the stove. Fry the bacon, fat-side down, to a golden brown. Turn the bacon in the pan and pour on the remaining oil/fat just to cover the bacon, and bring to a soft simmer. Cover and cook in the oven for about 1–1½ hours.

After an hour, check the tenderness of the meat by piercing with a knife or carefully removing it from the fat and pressing it between thumb and forefinger. The meat should feel totally tender; if it's slightly firm, continue to cook for the remaining ½ hour.

Once cooked, if you're using it immediately, remove the bacon; a lot of excess fat will drain off.

Carve it when it's just warm.

The bacon can be preserved in the fat and refrigerated until needed. When ready to use, remove the bacon from the fat and bring back to its original 'just-cooked' status by roasting in the oven (fat-side down) for 15–20 minutes.

To make the dressing, mix all of the ingredients together in a small pan, bar the lemon juice, and bring to the simmer. This can now be left to stand until cool. The oil will take on a horseradish flavour – that's quite a classic combination, working well with the bacon.

Once cool, the horseradish can be left in the oil and kept refrigerated until it is needed; the flavour just gets stronger. Or, if using straight away, strain it and finish with salt, pepper and a squeeze of lemon.

If you're making the dressing garnish, add enough horseradish-chilli oil to flavour and moisten the radishes and anchovies.

For the salad, cut the apple quarters into thin slices. Mix with the celery and green salad leaves and flavour with a trickle of the horseradish-chilli oil.

To serve, spoon some of the radish and anchovy garnish around the plate. Carve the bacon into thin slices and lay them, overlapping, across the middle; five or six slices per portion is plenty. Put the salad on top, drizzle some extra dressing around and serve.

Note: All of the salad oils, garnishes, etc. will work very well with simple, crisp streaky bacon rashers in place of the confit.

Peppered Chicken Livers
on Watercress Toasts

The pepper on the livers and sweet brandied shallots in the dressing are flavours that work so well together.

Serves 4

3–4 chicken livers per portion, previously soaked for 24–48 hours in milk
4 tablespoons fine fresh breadcrumbs
2 level teaspoons crushed black peppercorns
Salt and pepper

4 thick slices of bread
½ garlic clove
1 large bunch watercress, picked, or a 75 g (3 oz) bag
2 tablespoons olive oil
A knob of butter
1 quantity Gravadlax Sauce (page 74), omitting the chopped dill

Remove the chicken livers from the milk. Mix the breadcrumbs with the crushed peppercorns. Season with salt. Cut the slices of bread into discs with a plain biscuit cutter and toast them. Rub each slice with garlic. Season the watercress and add a tablespoon of olive oil.

Heat a frying-pan with the remaining tablespoon of oil and the butter. Roll the livers in the peppered crumbs and pan-fry them until crisp and golden brown. The total cooking time of the livers will be between 3–5 minutes, depending on the size of the livers.

Sit the toasts in the centre of the plates and top with the watercress and chicken livers. Finish by spooning the gravadlax sauce liberally around.

Roast *Foie Gras* on Potato Pancakes with Macerated Grapes

Goose and duck foie gras *are both the most luxurious of livers. They are expensive to buy and not that easy to get hold of, but I wanted to share this recipe with you as it is a dream to eat.*

The other reason I am including it is that other livers can be used for this recipe: pan-fried chicken livers or grilled calves' or lambs' liver will all work very well.

The pancake recipe will give you approximately 8 pancakes: 4 for this recipe and the remaining 4 to enjoy the following day! Other ingredients, such as sweetcorn, or ratatouille, or prawns, or herbs, can also be added to the remaining pancake mixture to give you a completely new dish.

Serves 4

350 g (12 oz) duck *foie gras*,
   cut into 75 g (3 oz) lobes
Cooking oil
6 tablespoons Macerated Grapes
   (page 239)
6 tablespoons *Jus*/Gravy (page 242)
   or alternative (page 243)
Salt and pepper

For the Potato Pancakes:

150 g (5 oz) plain mashed potatoes
1 tablespoon milk
1 tablespoon plain flour
1 tablespoon double cream
   (or extra milk)
1 egg
1 egg white
Salt and pepper

Pre-heat the oven to 200°C/400°F/Gas Mark 6. To make the potato pancakes, simply beat all the ingredients together and season with salt and pepper. You will now have a thick batter.

Heat a frying-pan with a trickle of cooking oil. Season the *foie gras* with salt and pepper and place the lobes in the pan. The livers will colour very quickly so, once they are coloured on one side, turn over and finish cooking in the oven. They will take 3–4 minutes to become tender.

The pancakes should be started while the *foie gras* is frying to ensure everything is cooked together. The pancakes can even be made 10–15 minutes beforehand and kept warm.

To cook the pancakes, heat a tablespoon of oil in another frying-pan and ladle the batter into four discs – they should be about 7.5 cm (3 in) diameter each. Cook on a medium heat for 1–2 minutes until golden and then turn each one over carefully with a spatula. Continue to cook for 1–2 minutes.

Bring the grapes to the boil with 2–3 tablespoons of the macerating liquor. Add the thick *jus* or gravy. Continue to boil and reduce, if necessary, to a rich, glossy consistency. Check for seasoning and add salt and pepper as necessary.

Sit two pancakes in the centre of the plates with the *foie gras* on top. Spoon the macerated grapes and their sauce around and serve.

Spaghettini or Tagliolini *with Roast Tomato Sauce*

A bowl of pasta just bound with a great tomato sauce is easy to make and great to eat. There is no end to the flavours that you can add. I like to use broad beans and black olives in this dish, with a trickle of olive oil and freshly grated Parmesan.

Spaghettini and tagliolini are both quite fine pastas. Spaghettini is just a thinner spaghetti and tagliolini a thinner noodle. If you've never made pasta, have a go but if you're pressed for time use bought – either fresh or dried. And, of course, the everyday spaghetti and noodles can also be used.

Serves 4

For the Roast Tomato Sauce:
900 g (2 lb) ripe plum
   or salad tomatoes
2 tablespoons olive oil
A knob of butter
2 garlic cloves, sliced
10 fresh basil leaves (optional)
Coarse sea salt and black pepper

For the Pasta:
2 quantities Home-made Pasta
   (page 234) or 450 g (1 lb) fresh
   or dried spaghettini or tagliolini
Olive oil
Salt and pepper
A squeeze of lemon juice (optional)
Grated Parmesan (optional),
   to serve

If using home-made pasta, roll it out thinly on a floured or semolina-covered surface. Cut the pasta into 10 cm (4 in) thick strips and roll it through a hand-cranked pasta machine several times. If you do not have a pasta machine, simply roll the pasta on a floured work surface with a rolling pin until you have a 3 mm (⅛ in) thickness. Roll the sheet of pasta carefully into a cylinder and cut into very thin strips with a sharp knife to give you spaghettini, or into 3 mm (⅛ in) wide strips to give you tagliolini. Unroll each slice into strands as you cut, otherwise the pasta will stick together. Dry on a cloth.

Pre-heat the oven to 220°C/425°F/Gas Mark 7. Halve the tomatoes. Heat the olive oil in a flameproof roasting tin or large ovenproof frying-pan. Place the tomatoes in the pan, flesh-side down, and colour to a golden brown with slightly burnt tinges. (You may need to do this in two batches.) Add the butter and turn the tomatoes. Season with a sprinkling of sea salt and black pepper and add the garlic slices. Cook for a few more minutes and then add the basil leaves, if using.

Roast the tomatoes for 15–20 minutes. The tomatoes will have cooked completely and should have a mushy texture. These can now be blitzed in a food processor or liquidiser, to make a smooth sauce. Taste for seasoning. For an even smoother finish, push the sauce through a sieve.

Cook the pasta in boiling, salted water. Fresh spaghettini takes 3–4 minutes, dried 5–6 minutes, fresh tagliolini 2 minutes, dried 5–6 minutes. Drain, once cooked, and season with salt and pepper. Trickle with olive oil and lemon juice, if using. Mix with the tomato sauce, divide into portions and serve, offering grated Parmesan as well, if you like.

Note: Any of the following extra flavours can also be added: broad beans, black or green olives, onions or shallots, chopped fresh tarragon, wild or button mushrooms, bacon or parma ham, chillies, fresh peas.

1 Cook the leeks until tender. Drain and separate the leaves. Line the mould with them, leaving enough overhanging to fold over at the end.

2 Cook the potatoes and pencil leeks separately until slightly overcooked. Drain and season. Put a third of the leeks in the base, then cover totally with half the potatoes.

3 Add the shallots and parsley to the stock. Spoon over half the stock and repeat with more leeks, stock and potatoes.

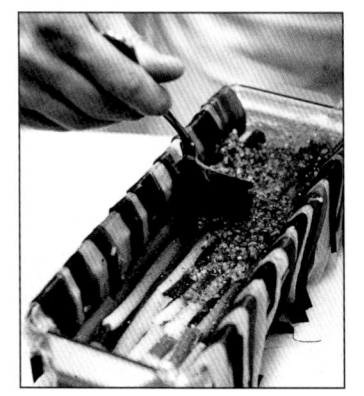

Potato and Leek Terrine

Here's a vegetarian dish that tastes and looks spectacular, using just two very basic ingredients, lifted with a shiny, glossy dressing. I am using a basic Le Creuset terrine mould. This will give 10–12 portions. If you have a smaller terrine mould, simply halve the ingredients.

Serves 12–15

For the Herb Oil:
150 ml (5 fl oz) olive oil
2 bay leaves
1 garlic clove, chopped
A few sprigs of fresh thyme, basil, sage, tarragon and marjoram

For the Saffron Vinegar:
2 tablespoons white-wine vinegar
A pinch of saffron strands
6 tablespoons water
2 teaspoons salt
2 teaspoons sugar
1 teaspoon pepper

For the Terrine:
2 large leeks, split lengthways
900 g (2 lb) new potatoes, unpeeled
1 lemon
30 pencil-thin leeks
600 ml (1 pint) Vegetable Stock (page 240; good-quality stock cubes can be used)
15 g (½ oz) leaf gelatine (approximately 4 leaves), soaked in cold water, or 1 x 11.7 g sachet powdered gelatine
8 shallots or 2 onions, finely chopped
2 tablespoons chopped fresh parsley
Salt and pepper

4 Finish with a final layer of leeks and fold over the overhanging leek leaves. Put a weight on top and refrigerate for 2 hours.

Make the herb oil in advance (a minimum of 24–48 hours will give you a stronger taste). Heat all of the ingredients together and then leave to infuse. Strain before using.

To make the saffron vinegar, heat all of the ingredients together. Leave to stand for 15–20 minutes. Re-heat and then strain through a sieve.

To make the terrine, first line the terrine mould with cling film.

Cook the large leeks in salted, boiling water for 4–5 minutes until absolutely tender. Refresh in iced water. Drain on kitchen paper and separate the layers. Line the terrine mould with these leek leaves, making sure there is enough left overhanging to fold over the filling at the end.

Cook the new potatoes in salted, boiling water with the peel of 1 lemon until slightly overcooked. Once cooked, drain and start to peel while still warm.

While the potatoes are cooking, cook the pencil leeks in salted, boiling water until completely tender. Drain and keep warm.

Reduce the vegetable stock by a third to increase its flavour. Let it cool slightly and then add the gelatine and half the chopped shallots or onions. When just at room temperature, add half of the chopped parsley.

Halve the potatoes lengthways, using a fork to give a more natural break. Season the leeks and potatoes, adding a squeeze of lemon to the softened potatoes. Line a third of the leeks in the base of the terrine. Now sit half the new potatoes on top, totally covering the leeks. Spoon half of the vegetable, shallot and parsley stock on top and repeat with more leeks and then the remaining stock and potatoes. Finish with a final layer of leeks and fold over the large leek leaves. Put another terrine, or some form of weight, the same shape, on top. This will press all of the vegetables together to give a proper terrine texture. Refrigerate for 2 hours.

To finish the dressing, mix the herb oil and the saffron vinegar together (they will not emulsify totally, but the combination of flavours and colours does work well). Stir 3–4 tablespoons of this into the remaining shallots and parsley and check for seasoning.

Turn out the terrine; this should happen quite easily because of the cling film. It is now best to serve it at room temperature. The terrine can be sliced into about 1 cm (½ in) thick portions.

Sit the slices on plates and spoon around a border of the shallots and parsley. To finish, trickle the remaining dressing over the terrine to lift the shine and heighten the flavour.

Note: Once completed, the terrine will keep refrigerated for at least 3–4 days.

Skate, Potato and Leek Terrine

The recipe is more or less identical to the Potato and Leek Terrine with the dressing being exactly the same and the quantity of leeks and potatoes the same. The vegetable stock, however, should be replaced with fish stock or water.

Serves 12

Ingredients for Potato and Leek Terrine (page 46), but replacing the Vegetable Stock with Fish Stock (page 241) or alternative (page 243) or water, and using

only 2 leaves gelatine or ½ x 11.7 g sachet powdered gelatine
750–900 g (1½–2 lb) skate wings on the bone
½ onion, chopped
1 star-anise

Poach the skate in the stock or water with the chopped onion and star-anise. The fish will only take 8–10 minutes. Remove the skate and strain the stock. Reduce the stock by two-thirds and then add the gelatine leaves. This can now be mixed with the shallots and parsley as for the vegetarian recipe. Carefully remove the skate fillets from the bone.

Line the terrine with cling film and large leeks as for the vegetarian terrine.

Line the base with one-third of the pencil leeks, follow with a layer of half the potatoes, spooning some of the fish stock, shallot and parsley mix over. Now carefully place half the skate fillet on top with a drop more stock. Sit more leeks on top, more stock, the remaining fish, more stock, the rest of the potatoes and then a final layer of leeks. Fold over the large leek leaves. Press gently and refrigerate.

The terrine is best eaten at room temperature, presented in the same way as the potato and leek terrine.

Grilled Asparagus and Leeks *with* Parsleyed Eggs

Leeks are known as 'poor man's asparagus', a vegetable to stand in for or replace the lovely green spears. I think leeks are a wonderful vegetable, so I thought I would treat them both as equals.

These don't have to be grilled; simply boiled and rolled in butter or dressing, they will still eat very well. The parsleyed eggs are hard- or soft-boiled eggs, chopped, and flavoured with olive oil, parsley and lemon. A good twist of pepper and a sprinkling of sea salt and you have a complete dish. Another flavour I like to add is Parmesan shavings, melting over the spears.

Serves 4

16–20 thin asparagus spears
16–20 thin baby leeks
3 hard-boiled eggs (boiled for
   6–7 minutes, so slightly soft)
6 tablespoons olive oil
A squeeze of fresh lemon juice

A knob of butter, melted
1 tablespoon chopped freshly cut
   flatleaf parsley
Salt and pepper
Coarsely ground black pepper and
   coarse sea salt granules, to garnish
Fresh Parmesan shavings (optional)

The first job is to prepare the asparagus and leeks. The asparagus should be lightly peeled from half-way down to the base of the spear. Cut about 2.5 cm (1 in) of the base stalk away as this will be tough and stringy. It may be enough to cut off the bases of the leeks and remove one layer; wash away any grit.

Both need to be cooked separately in salted, boiling water. The asparagus will take only 2–3 minutes, still leaving a 'bite'. The leeks will take 4–5 minutes to cook completely. If you are serving them grilled, refresh both in iced cold water. If not, they are ready to serve.

Shell and roughly chop the eggs. Season the olive oil with salt, pepper and lemon juice.

The leek and asparagus spears can now be grilled. This is best done on a ridged cast-iron grill pan or a barbecue, but they can also be pan-fried or coloured under the grill for 3–4 minutes. Heat the grill pan until really hot and brush with oil. Place the asparagus and leeks on top and brush with butter. The grilling will take only a couple of minutes, leaving good grill lines on the vegetables.

To serve, arrange the asparagus and leeks in the classic asparagus fashion, close together in line across the plate (alternating with the leeks) or just dotted about, rustic style. Both can be halved and mixed all over the plate (which makes it look like a lot more!). Add the parsley and chopped egg to the olive oil and lemon dressing and spoon over. Finish with a twist of black pepper, coarse sea salt and Parmesan shavings, if using.

Note: The Parmesan can be placed over the asparagus and leeks before the dressing and melted under the grill.

If thin baby leeks are unavailable, simply use 3 larger ones per serving.

Red-wine Caramelized Lamb's Kidneys
with Creamy Scrambled Eggs

Scrambled eggs are normally just beaten eggs, cooked in melted butter. These, however, take on a different texture. Cream and butter are boiled together before the eggs are added, giving a good creamy finish.

The lamb's kidneys are pan-fried and caramelized at the same time. The flavour is powerful and immense but gently calmed when eaten with the eggs. I like to serve the eggs on crisp toast.

This eats well as a starter, snack or a main course. The scrambled eggs on toast go just as well with crisp bacon for breakfast. If serving as a main course, then a rich jus/gravy/red-wine sauce just trickled around adds an extra flavour to the dish.

Serves 4

8 lamb's kidneys, skinned, trimmed
  and quartered
100 g (4 oz) butter
3 tablespoons red-wine vinegar

1 teaspoon demerara sugar
150 ml (5 fl oz) double cream
8 eggs, beaten
4 thick slices of crusty bread
Salt and pepper

Season the kidneys with salt and pepper. Heat a frying-pan with 25 g (1 oz) of butter and pan-fry the kidneys quickly on a good, fast heat for 2–3 minutes until they're slightly browned. This will seal all the juices in the kidneys. Add the vinegar and sugar and allow to reduce for a minute. This will very quickly caramelize around the kidneys, giving them a rich shiny glaze.

While the kidneys are cooking, make the creamy scrambled eggs. In a separate pan, boil the cream with the remaining butter and pour in the seasoned, beaten eggs. Stir the eggs, to give an even scrambling. Meanwhile, toast the bread. Check the eggs for seasoning before serving on the toast. The kidneys can be spooned over or around the toast.

The dish is now ready to serve.

Potato, Spring Onion and Mozzarella Risotto

The book just wouldn't be the same without a risotto somewhere! Risottos in general have become so popular, with almost unlimited flavours and variations to choose from. This one is slightly different, having mashed potato added to create a more-than-creamy texture.

Serves 8 as a starter or 4 as a main course

225 g (8 oz) arborio risotto rice
2 bunches of Spring onions
50 g (2 oz) butter
1 onion, finely chopped
1.2 litres (2 pints) Vegetable
  or Chicken Stock (page 240)
  or alternative (page 243)

2 large potatoes, cut in 5 mm
  (¼ in) dice
100 g (4 oz) Mashed Potatoes
  (page 140)
2–3 tablespoons grated Parmesan
  (optional)
25 g (1 oz) per portion coarsely
  grated Mozzarella
Salt and pepper
Good olive oil, to serve

Shred the Spring onions finely, separating the white from the green. Blanch the green Spring onion in boiling water until tender, then strain.

Melt the butter in a saucepan and add the chopped onion with the shredded whites of Spring onion. Cook without letting them colour for a few minutes until softened. Add the rice and continue to cook for a few minutes. While the onions and rice are cooking, heat the stock. Add the stock, a ladle at a time, stirring the rice continuously. Once the rice has absorbed the stock, add another ladleful and continue to cook and stir; repeat until the rice is tender. This process will take 20–30 minutes.

While the rice is cooking, boil the diced potatoes until tender.

To finish the risotto, add the mashed potatoes and Parmesan, if using, to lift all the flavours, with the diced potatoes and greens of Spring onions. Check the seasoning and add salt and pepper to taste; add a little more stock, if necessary, to give a looser, creamier consistency.

Add the Mozzarella and let it melt into the risotto or – as I like to do – serve the risotto in bowls and sprinkle the Mozzarella on top. Put the bowls under the grill to melt the cheese for a few seconds. Now just trickle with olive oil and serve.

Note: You could add half the Mozzarella to the risotto and use the remainder to sprinkle over the top.

You can also add an extra 25–50 g (1–2 oz) butter to enrich the flavour of the dish.

MAIN COURSES

MAIN COURSES

Welcome to main courses, often seen as the most important part of the meal. I've broken this chapter down into sections: fish, poultry and meat, and vegetarian dishes and vegetables. With all of the dishes featured in these categories there's room for change. You should not be over-strict in keeping to the recipe, especially if you feel like chopping, changing and swapping! And if the results are better – send me the recipe!

There are also lots of main courses that don't really need an accompaniment, that is, a vegetable served just out of habit to fill the plate. Vegetables should also stand as complete dishes on their own – sitting proudly on the table, with flavour simply oozing out of the dish.

I'll leave you to read on. Enjoy your meal and don't forget to leave some space for a pudding – coming up next!

fish

*f*ish is such a wonderful food to cook: nothing in terms of flavour or time needs to be overdone. Anything that is served with fish I think of as the pickle that goes in your cheese sandwich: it's there to spice up the flavour and excite the tastebuds, but the taste of the Cheddar should always win through. Different ways of cooking fish also give, obviously, a different feel and taste. Scallops, for example, just can't be eaten any better than when seared in a hot pan and allowed almost to burn at the edges, while ensuring they have a moist medium-rare centre. They can also be steamed and poached, but the meat then has a totally different texture and won't give off that caramelized, natural sweetness that is just sensational to eat.

Among all of these recipes you'll find almost every cooking method possible for fish; deep-frying, pan-frying, poaching, steaming, roasting and griddling, all of which means there are plenty of fish for you to try and taste, and I'm sure you'll find one of them, for once, will catch you!

Happy fishing!

Steamed Smoked Haddock on Spinach
with a Warm Poached Egg, glazed with a Sweet Pepper Béarnaise Sauce

Smoked haddock on spinach, with a warm poached egg, is a great dish we all know on its own. Finishing it with the sweet pepper béarnaise sauce lifts it to entirely new heights.

Béarnaise sauce is similar to hollandaise, which is made with egg yolks, clarified butter, vinegar and seasoning. The béarnaise version is flavoured with tarragon, which gives it a more powerful finish. To speed things up, you could use a packet of béarnaise or hollandaise sauce.

The sweet red peppers are cooked and then puréed. This purée, added to the béarnaise, is delicious. Peppers and tarragon have always worked well together and, when glazed over the poached egg and smoked haddock, they are even better!

Serves 4

4 x 175–225 g (6–8 oz) smoked
    haddock fillets, skinned (preferably
    naturally smoked)
450 g (1 lb) fresh spinach, stalks
    removed
A knob of butter
2 tablespoons water
4 poached eggs (see Note)
Salt and pepper

For the Pepper Purée

2 red peppers, seeded and cut into
    1 cm (½ in) rough dice
1 tablespoon olive oil
1 garlic clove
Salt and pepper

For the Béarnaise Sauce:

175 g (6 oz) butter, melted
3 shallots or 1 onion, roughly
    chopped
½ teaspoon crushed black
    peppercorns
3 tablespoons white-wine vinegar
1 heaped tablespoon chopped fresh
    tarragon leaves, stalks reserved
3 egg yolks
50 ml (2 fl oz) double cream, lightly
    whipped
Salt and pepper

First make the béarnaise sauce. To make a reduction for the sauce, mix together the shallots or onion, black peppercorns and vinegar (plus any tarragon stalks) in a small pan and bring to a simmer. Reduce by three-quarters, which takes 1–2 minutes. Add a tablespoon of water, strain and leave the liquor to cool. The butter should be left to stand once melted. This will separate the solids from the butter oils, leaving you with clarified butter.

Mix the egg yolks with the reduced liquor in a bowl over simmering water. Whisk together until a 'sabayon' is achieved. This is the stage when the yolks are thickening and approaching a softly whipped, creamy consistency.

Remove from the heat and continue to whisk until at room temperature. The warm clarified butter can now be ladled in very slowly, whisking continuously until you have a thick sauce and all the butter has been added. Season with salt and pepper and then strain through a sieve. Add the chopped tarragon and keep in a warm place.

To cook the peppers, heat the olive oil in a pan. Add the peppers and garlic and cook on a moderate heat for 8–10 minutes until the peppers have softened. Season and blitz to a purée in a food processor. Push the purée through a sieve to remove any skin.

Melt a small knob of butter with the water and bring to a fast simmer. Add the spinach and cook for a few minutes until softened and tender. Season with salt and pepper and pour off any excess liquid.

Put the four portions of haddock on buttered and peppered greaseproof paper. Steam them over a pan of boiling water covered with a lid for 5–6 minutes. The cooking time will differ, depending on the thickness of the fillets. The maximum time will be no more than 10 minutes.

To serve, mix the béarnaise sauce with the sweet-pepper purée. Gently fold in the whipped cream. Divide the spinach between four bowls or plates. Sit the steamed fillets of smoked haddock on top.

Pre-heat the grill. Warm the poached eggs for 1 minute in boiling water. Sit one on top of each haddock portion. Spoon over the sweet-pepper-béarnaise-sauce, covering the egg and fish, and then glaze under the grill to a golden brown. The dish is now ready to serve. Any remaining sauce can be offered separately.

Note: For the perfect poached egg, fill a small saucepan with two-thirds water and one-third malt vinegar. The vinegar reacts with the egg white and draws it around the yolk. Salt should not be added because this tends to break down the egg-white consistency. Bring the water and vinegar mixture to the boil and stir. Now crack 1 egg at a time into the centre of the water and poach for 3–3½ minutes. The eggs can be poached in advance and plunged into iced water immediately. To re-heat, simply plunge into boiling water for 1 minute.

A hint of Dijon mustard in the béarnaise sauce will fire up the flavours even more.

Crispy Salmon *with Sweet-pepper and Tomato Sauce*

I normally use a home-made tomato coulis sauce for this, which is simple enough to make, but for this recipe I'm making it even simpler. For the base I'm using passata, a sieved tomato sauce. It's just pure tomatoes and easily available in all supermarkets. Mixing it with all of the other flavours and lots of fresh tomatoes gives you a powerful tomato flavour. The salmon is cooked using a method that will give a crackling finish to the salmon skin.

New or boulangère potatoes with some good, buttered spinach eat very well with this dish.

Serves 4

4 x 175–225 g (6–8 oz) salmon fillet
    portions, scaled, skin left on
2 tablespoons olive oil
4 large shallots or 1 onion,
    finely chopped
1 teaspoon green peppercorns
300 ml (10 fl oz) passata
4 tomatoes, blanched, peeled
    and seeded

½ x 400 g (14 oz) tin or 210 g
    (7½ oz) jar of sweet red peppers
1 lemon, peeled, segmented and sliced
1 dessertspoon fine or ordinary
    capers, chopped
A knob of butter
Salt and pepper
1 teaspoon chopped fresh parsley
1 heaped teaspoon chopped
    fresh tarragon

For the sauce, warm a tablespoon of olive oil and add the chopped shallots or onion in a medium pan. Cook on a moderate heat for 1–2 minutes until softened. Add the green peppercorns with the passata. Bring the sauce to the simmer and cook for 2–3 minutes.

Cut the tomato flesh and tinned peppers into 5 mm–1 cm (¼–½ in) dice. Add the sliced lemon segments, capers, diced tomato and sweet red pepper. Bring back to the simmer for 1 minute and season with salt and pepper. The sauce is now ready. Save the parsley and tarragon until just before serving (if added too early, the herbs will lose their colour). Keep the sauce warm while you cook the salmon.

First, I like to score the skin of the salmon carefully, making 3–4 incisions. This helps to release any fat, leaving you with crispier skin. Season the salmon with salt and pepper.

Heat the remaining tablespoon of olive oil in a frying-pan. Place the salmon, skin-side down, in the oil on a moderate heat. Leave the fish for a good 5–6 minutes, not moving the pan around but checking the skin is not burning. The skin will now be just crisp and turning golden. Add the butter and turn the salmon and finish cooking for 2–3 minutes. The salmon will be lovely and tender with a pink finish.

Add the parsley and tarragon to the sauce. Spoon it onto the plates and put the crisp salmon, skin-side up, in the centre.

Note: For a thicker, chunkier tomato-pepper sauce, just use 150 ml (5 fl oz) passata.

Parsleyed Cod *with Roast Potatoes and Mustard Butter Sauce*

I have changed this classic cod and parsley combination to give a purée of parsley mixed with spinach, which is spread over the fish, so that the parsley flavour comes through in every bite. This dish is a complete meal: the roast potatoes and sea kale finish it off perfectly.

The pig's caul is only available by order from your butcher. It works like a net to hold the parsley purée in place. If it's unavailable, wrap the cod in buttered foil and steam it instead of pan-frying and roasting. Or leave the parsley purée off the cod, pan-fry the cod and put it on top of the warm purée.

The reason I am using the two varieties of parsley is to put the flavour from the flat parsley, which has a stronger taste, into the curly parsley, which has a better texture.

Serves 4

4 x 175–225 g (6–8 oz) portions of
    cod fillets, skinned and boned
½ bunch of fresh flatleaf parsley
½ bunch of fresh parsley
100 g (4 oz) spinach, cooked
225 g (8 oz) pig's caul (crépine)
1 tablespoon cooking oil

A knob of butter
Salt and pepper

To serve:
1 quantity of Curly Kale (page 148)
1 quantity of Mustard Butter Sauce
    (page 237)
1 quantity of Banana Roast Potatoes
    (page 138)

Pre-heat the oven to 200°C/400°F/Gas Mark 6. The two parsleys should be plunged into salted, boiling water for 2–3 minutes until cooked and tender. Drain in a colander and refresh with cold water. Once cold, squeeze out any excess water and blitz in a food processor with the cooked spinach to a smooth purée. Season with salt and pepper.

This purée can now be spread 3 mm (⅛ in) thick on the presentation (skinned) side of the cod. Then wrap in the pig's caul. Refrigerate to set and firm.

To cook the cod, warm a frying-pan with a tablespoon of cooking oil. Put the cod portions in, parsley-side down, and add the butter. Cook and colour for 3–4 minutes until golden with the rich green coming through. Turn the fish over and transfer to an ovenproof dish, if necessary. Complete by cooking in the oven for 8–10 minutes.

While the cod is cooking, warm the curly kale in a little butter and season it. Warm the mustard sauce and add one or two spoonfuls to the curly kale. The banana roast potatoes should be crisp and golden with tinges that are almost burnt.

Once the cod is cooked, remove it from the pan and put it at the front of the plate. Make a small pile of roast potatoes, allowing four pieces per portion, and add a few spoonfuls of curly kale. Pour the mustard sauce over and around the kale and serve.

Note: I also like to serve a trickle of fish *jus* (page 64), omitting the fennel, with this dish.

Steamed Fillet of Cod *with a Coriander Butter Sauce and Ratatouille Cake*

Steaming cod gives you the pure, natural flavour of the fish, which in this dish is complemented by the coriander butter sauce and the zesty flavours from the ratatouille cake.

Serves 4

4 × 175–225 g (6–8 oz) cod fillet
   portions, skinned
Plain flour
Cooking oil, for deep-frying
Mashed Potatoes (page 140)
1 quantity of Coriander Butter
   Sauce (page 237)
Salt and pepper

For the Ratatouille Cake:

½ small aubergine
1 medium courgette
2 red onions, chopped,
   or 1 large Spanish onion
1 red pepper
3 tomatoes, blanched, skinned
   and seeded
Olive oil
A knob of butter
1 garlic clove, crushed
Salt and pepper

For the Fennel *Jus* (optional):

1 small fennel, diced
1 small onion, diced
A knob of butter
1 star-anise
1–2 teaspoons red-wine vinegar
   (cabernet sauvignon vinegar is
   preferable because it has a much
   thicker and richer consistency),
   (optional)
1 glass of red wine
150 ml (5 fl oz) Fish Stock (page
   241) or alternative (page 243)
Salt and pepper
A squeeze of lemon juice,
   if needed

For the ratatouille, all of the vegetables and tomatoes need to be cut into 5 mm (¼ in) dice and kept separate. Fry the onions in olive oil and butter with the crushed garlic and season with salt and pepper. Cook the onions for a few minutes until softened and slightly golden. Remove the onions from the pan. Return the pan to the heat and fry the courgette, red pepper and aubergine in the same manner, without the garlic. These can now all be mixed together and seasoned again.

If you don't want it immediately, leave the cooked vegetables to cool and keep them refrigerated until needed. If heating from cold, just warm it with the tomatoes in a drop more olive oil. If using immediately, add the tomatoes and warm through.

If you are making the *jus*, melt the butter with the onion and fennel in a saucepan and cook, without letting them colour, with the star-anise for a few minutes. Add the vinegar, if using, and reduce until almost dry. Add the red wine and reduce by three-quarters. Meanwhile also reduce the fish stock by three-quarters. (Using the fish stock will completely change the finished sauce, giving you a much fuller flavour.) Add this to the red-wine mixture and cook for 5–10 minutes and then strain through a sieve. This fennel *jus* may well need more seasoning with salt, pepper and a squeeze of lemon juice to help lift all the flavours.

The cod fillets can be bought already skinned and boned if you wish, but I like to remove the skin myself and serve it as part of the dish. Lightly flour it and deep-fry until golden and crisp. Leave to drain on kitchen paper and sprinkle with salt.

Season the fillets with salt and pepper and place them on squares of buttered greaseproof paper. Steam the fillets over a pan of boiling water covered with a lid for 8–12 minutes, depending on the size and thickness of the fish. The cod will begin to feel firm to the touch but it will still just 'give' in the centre. This will give you beautifully cooked, translucent flakes.

To make the ratatouille cakes, I use small, buttered individual ring moulds 6–7.5 cm (2½–3 in) in diameter and 5 cm (2 in) deep. Set them slightly to one side of the serving plates. Pipe some mashed potato approximately 1 cm (½ in) deep into each mould. Spoon some of the ratatouille into the top of the mould, pushing down to ensure the cake will keep its shape.

Lift off the moulds and put the fried cod skins, if using, on top of each ratatouille cake. Sit the cod next to the cake and spoon over some of the coriander butter sauce. Pour a little fennel *jus*, if using, around the cake.

Note: You can make the coriander butter sauce 20–30 minutes in advance and simply heat and whisk it (an electric hand-blender works very well) at the last minute, adding the chopped fresh coriander just before serving.

Seared Scallops *with Home-made Pasta, Spring Onions and Maltaise Sauce*

Scallops are sweet to eat and taste even better if seared with almost burnt edges to give a crisp, bitter-sweet finish. The 'home-made' pasta can of course be replaced with a dried or ready-made variety.

Serves 4

16–20 large, fresh scallops, cleaned
  and trimmed of roe
1 quantity of Home-made Pasta
  dough (page 234) or dried or
  ready-made spaghetti/tagliolini
1 bunch of Spring onions
Olive oil

A knob of butter
6 tablespoons Orange Oil
  (page 238, optional) or olive oil
8 tablespoons Carrot Butter Sauce
  (page 237, optional)
1 quantity of Maltaise Sauce
  (page 235), to serve
Salt and pepper

If using home-made pasta dough, roll out the pasta thinly on a floured or semolina-covered surface. Cut it into 10 cm (4 in) thick strips and roll it through a hand-cranked pasta machine several times, then cut it through the 'spaghetti' attachment. Place the spaghetti on a tray covered with a cloth and leave it to relax and dry for 30 minutes. If you do not have a pasta machine, simply roll the pasta with a rolling pin until you have a 3 mm (⅛ in) thickness. Roll the sheet of pasta carefully into a cylinder and cut thin strips with a sharp knife. Unroll each slice into strands as you cut, otherwise the pasta will stick together. Dry on a cloth. Cook the fresh pasta in salted, boiling water for 3–4 minutes until tender or follow the packet instructions for the dried pasta. Strain in a colander and leave to cool.

Slice the Spring onions at an angle. Heat a frying-pan and a small saucepan. Add a few drops of olive oil to the frying-pan and, when hot, sear the scallops. While the scallops are colouring, melt the butter and fry the Spring onions for 2–3 minutes, without letting them colour. Season with salt and pepper. The scallops should now have a rich, dark tinge on the edges and be golden in the centre. Turn the scallops in the pan, seasoning them with salt and pepper. The total cooking time of the scallops will be 2–3 minutes, 4 minutes maximum.

Warm the pasta in 2 tablespoons of orange or olive oil and a knob of butter. Season.

To serve, sit a pile of pasta at the top of each plate with a good spoonful of Spring onions on top of each. Spoon 2 tablespoons of the carrot butter sauce, if using, over each pile. Sit the scallops in the front and trickle a tablespoon of orange oil on each portion. Hand the maltaise sauce separately.

Note: If you do not have the time to make the orange oil and carrot butter sauce, simply serve with the maltaise sauce mixed into the pasta at the last moment.

The carrot butter sauce could also be the one to use on its own and, for a sharp orange flavour, add 50–85 ml (2–3 fl oz) of strongly reduced juice.

Steamed Turbot *with Potato Gnocchi Tartare and French Beans*

Turbot is one of the best fish that you can buy and eat. The quality of the fish is amazing with a firm but succulent texture. It is quite expensive but, if you get the chance to spoil yourself, buy some and try it.

Other fish will also work with this recipe – halibut, salmon, cod and sea trout in particular.

Serves 4

4 × 175–225 g (6–8 oz) portions of turbot fillet, with skins

275 g (10 oz) fine French beans

A knob of butter

1 quantity Gnocchi Tartare (page 134)

1 tablespoon grated Parmesan

1 quantity Basic Butter Sauce (page 236)

Salt and pepper

Coarse sea salt (optional)

The French beans should be trimmed at the stalk end only. This leaves the fine points still attached, giving a better presentation. Cook the beans in salted, boiling water without a lid for 2–4 minutes until tender. They can also be cooked while the turbot is steaming if you wish. Drain them once tender, season with salt and pepper and roll them in a small knob of the butter.

To steam the fish, place the fillets, flesh-side down, on buttered and seasoned greaseproof paper or foil. Now steam the fillets over a pan of boiling water covered with a lid for 6–8 minutes, depending on the thickness of the fish.

While the fish and beans are cooking, pan-fry the gnocchi tartare in butter for a few minutes until golden brown. Once cooked, sprinkle with the Parmesan and roll the gnocchi around in it to coat them. Warm the butter sauce and the dish is ready to serve.

To serve, put a pile of the seasoned French beans onto each plate at six o'clock and the gnocchi at the top. Pour the warmed butter sauce over and around the French beans. Remove the skin from the turbot fillet, sprinkle it with a few coarse sea-salt granules and place the fish on top of the beans. The dish is ready!

Grilled Mustard Halibut *with Warm* *Pickled Potatoes*

The pickled potatoes are just new potatoes, cooked, skinned and then marinated while still warm in a fresh mixed-herb pickling liquor. I like to overcook the potatoes slightly so that when steeped in the pickling liquor and then eaten the soft, creamy centres help balance the whole taste.

The halibut (more or less any fish can be used for this recipe) is just brushed with a mustard butter and grilled: few ingredients, lots of taste – always a good combination.

Serves 4

4 x 175–225 g (6–8 oz) halibut fillet
    portions
450–750 g (1–1½ lb) hot, very
    well-cooked new potatoes, peeled
    and halved
1 tablespoon butter
1 heaped teaspoon Dijon mustard
Salt and pepper
Plain flour, for dusting

For the Pickling Liquor:

4 tablespoons white wine
4 tablespoons white-wine vinegar
A few black peppercorns
1 star-anise (optional)
4 round shallots, sliced into rings
1 large garlic clove, finely chopped
The juice of 1 lemon
6–8 tablespoons olive oil
1 teaspoon chopped fresh chives
1 teaspoon chopped fresh tarragon
½ teaspoon chopped fresh parsley,
    basil or chervil

Heat the wine and vinegar together with the black peppercorns, star-anise, if using, and shallot rings. Reduce by a third, which should take 3–4 minutes. Add the garlic while still warm. Pour this over the warm new potatoes with the lemon juice and leave to marinate for 20–30 minutes.

Mix the butter with the mustard. Season the halibut fillets with salt and pepper and then lightly dust them with flour on the presentation side. Sit the fillets on a buttered baking tray and brush each one with the mustard mixture.

Don't cook the fillets until the potatoes have been marinated. Put the fish under the grill on a medium heat and cook for 8–10 minutes until golden and only just firm. (If the fish is quite thin, 6 minutes may well be enough.)

Add the olive oil and chopped herbs to the potatoes and lightly warm. Spoon the pickled potatoes onto the serving plates with the grilled mustard halibut.

Note: This dish goes very well with a simple green or watercress salad.

Confit of Sea Trout *with Caramelized Shallots, Lemon, Olives and Capers*

The word confit *comes from the French word meaning 'to preserve'. Most things that are cooked in the confit style are cooked in their own fat and preserved in it. Sea trout doesn't have its own fat to cook in, but it cooks beautifully when poached slowly in goose fat or a flavoured oil. The oil keeps all of the natural juices in the fish and it certainly doesn't leave a greasy, oily finish.*

Goose fat is the best to cook it in but for this recipe I am using a flavoured oil. Should the confit method put you off this dish, just pan-fry or grill the sea trout which will still give you great results.

Serves 4

4 x 175–225g (6–8 oz) sea trout
    fillet portions, skinned and boned
12 large shallots, cut into 1 cm
    (½ in) dice
5 tablespoons olive oil
A knob of butter
1 teaspoon soft brown sugar
    (optional)
1 large lemon, peeled, segmented
    and sliced
12–16 pitted black olives, quartered
1 tablespoon of fine capers
1 tablespoon chopped fresh chives

Mustard Hollandaise Sauce
    (see Quick Hollandaise Sauce,
    page 235), to serve
Salt and pepper

For the Flavoured Oil :

600 ml (1 pint) groundnut or
    cooking oil
300 ml (10 fl oz) olive oil
1 lemon, quartered
A pinch of sea salt
A few black peppercorns, crushed
½ bunch of fresh tarragon
1 bay leaf
1 star-anise

To make the flavoured oil, mix all the ingredients together in a pan. Bring to the simmer and then remove from the heat. Leave to infuse for a few hours. After the oil has infused, pour it through a sieve and discard the infusing ingredients. The oil is now ready to use.

You can make the mustard hollandaise 20–30 minutes in advance.

For the garnish, the shallots first need to be caramelized. This can be achieved by placing them in a saucepan with a tablespoon of the olive oil and cooking them slowly until they reach a rich, deep, golden caramel flavour and colour. The natural juices and sweetness of the shallots have now caramelized. This will take 8-10 minutes. To speed up the process, simply heat a frying-pan with the tablespoon of olive oil and add the shallots with a knob of butter. Fry to a quick golden brown and add a teaspoon of soft brown sugar. This will instantly caramelize, giving you rich, tasty shallots. Season with salt and pepper.

Add the sliced lemon segments, black olives and capers to the remaining 4 tablespoons of olive oil. This 'dressing' should not be too oily. All of these flavours work together, giving off lots of tastes that will neither mask one another nor overpower the sea trout.

Heat the flavoured oil till it is just warm. Salt the sea trout fillets and put them in the oil. They will take 10–12 minutes to cook slowly, keeping the fish pink inside. After the first 5–6 minutes, check the sea trout in case the temperature of the oil is too high. It is then best to check every 2–3 minutes. Lift out of the oil and leave to drain slightly.

To serve the dish, add the chopped chives to the shallot dressing and spoon over the plate, spreading it out evenly. Place the sea trout in the centre and spoon the mustard hollandaise over the sea trout.

The dish is now ready to eat.

Note: For an extra flavour in the dish, I like to spoon a couple of tablespoons of the fennel *jus* (from Steamed Fillet of Cod with a Coriander Butter Sauce and Ratatouille Cake, page 64) around the plate.

Open Cod Hash

Everyone's usual idea of a hash is corned beef fried with potatoes and onions. That's exactly what I'm going to do with this cod hash: it's composed of fried potatoes, Spring onions and chunks of cod. It could also be made in the classic way, using mashed potatoes and then frying the whole thing as a cake.

Serves 4

750 g (1½ lb) cod fillet, skinned and
    cut into 2.5 cm (1 in) chunks
450 g (1 lb) new potatoes in skins
1 large bunch of Spring onions

2–3 tablespoons olive oil
A knob of butter
Plain flour, for dusting
Salt and pepper

Boil the new potatoes for 25–30 minutes; this will overcook them, with the outside beginning to crumble. Once cooked and while still warm, peel the potatoes and cut in half. Slice the Spring onions into 1 cm (½ in) thick slices. The potatoes can now be fried in 1 tablespoon of hot olive oil and a knob of butter. Fry until golden and beginning to break up. Season with salt and pepper. The Spring onions can also be fried quickly in a tablespoon of oil, making them tender with only tinges of golden brown and maintaining the rich green and white colours. Season the cod cubes and roll them very lightly through the plain flour.

Heat the remaining oil and another knob of butter in a hot pan and fry the cod pieces for 5–6 minutes. This will give them a good colour and still leave a moist, flaky interior. All of the ingredients can now be mixed together and served. The fish will break up: don't worry about this.

Note: The fish is best fried a handful or two at a time. This will prevent the pan from becoming too cold and stop the fish stewing and flaking.

This can be finished with a trickle more olive oil and some lemon juice. The Basic Butter Sauce on page 236 can also be poured over.

Other flavours can be added, such as tomatoes or sweet peppers. Or try a sprinkling of Cheddar across the top, which you then brown under a hot grill.

The softness of the overcooked potatoes is one of the real winners in this dish – they create creaminess and help to bind simply because they have been overcooked. Fresh herbs could be added, such as tarragon or parsley. A good tartare sauce also goes very well with the hash.

This recipe can also be used for a corned-beef hash. Just replace the cod with a tin of corned beef.

Grilled 'Crunchy' Salmon *with*
Gravadlax Sauce

Gravadlax is basically salmon that has been marinated or cured with equal quantities of salt and sugar, flavoured with brandy, dill and pepper. After a few hours or days, you have gravadlax (if you are thinking of making any, it is 25 g (1 oz) salt and 25 g (1 oz) sugar per 450 g (1 lb) of fish).

This dish isn't gravadlax but what I have done is to take those flavours and turn them into a sauce. The salmon itself is mock-grilled with a skewer or trussing needle (it can be pan-fried or cooked directly under the grill instead) and then sprinkled with coarse sea salt and finished under the grill. The sea salt gives a crunchy finish, which balances with the sweet, brandy-flavoured dressing.

Serves 4

4 x 175–225 g (6–8 oz) fillet
   portions of salmon, skinned
Plain flour, for dusting
A knob of butter, melted
Salt and pepper
2 teaspoons coarse sea salt

For the Sauce:
1 egg yolk
4 teaspoons Dijon mustard

2 tablespoons white-wine vinegar
8 tablespoons olive oil
4 tablespoons groundnut or
   vegetable oil
A knob of butter
½ teaspoon demerara sugar
2 tablespoons finely chopped
   shallots or onions
50 ml (2 fl oz) brandy
1 heaped teaspoon chopped fresh dill
Salt and pepper

To make the mayonnaise-style sauce, mix the egg yolk, mustard and vinegar. Mix the two oils and slowly whisk them into the mustard and vinegar.

Melt the butter and the sugar, add the shallots and cook without colouring them for 2–3 minutes. Add the brandy and reduce for 2–3 minutes until almost dry. Allow to cool to room temperature. Add the shallots to the sauce with the dill. Season with salt and pepper.

To cook the salmon, heat some skewers or trussing needles on an open flame (or use a ribbed grill pan). Season the salmon and lightly dust the skinned side with plain flour. Use the hot skewers to mark the flesh or sit the salmon, skinned-side down, on the grill pan for 4–5 minutes by turning it round by 45° half-way through to give an attractive crisscross 'grilled' effect.

Sit the finished salmon, grill-marked side up, on a buttered baking tray. Brush with butter and sprinkle over the sea salt. Cook the salmon under a pre-heated grill. The salmon will take 8–10 minutes to gain a good, golden, crunchy finish. If using a grill pan, turn the fish over once marked, cook for 4–5 minutes maximum and sprinkle with the sea salt. Serve with the sauce.

Note: A good green salad and lemon wedges will go very well with this dish or perhaps some fresh spinach or peas with new potatoes.

The gravadlax sauce also goes well with smoked salmon or cold, poached fresh salmon.

Whole Roast Mackerel *with Red Onion and Tomato Salad*

The mackerel is best bought already cross-cut filleted with the central bones to both fillets removed. This basically means the fish is filleted before being gutted and cut along either side of the backbone and then the main 'carcass' is removed. The fish is then gutted and any remaining bones are removed and rinsed.

I like to make a spicy garam masala butter with which to stuff the fish. So, while it is roasting the butter is melting and giving the fish a rich, spicy taste. Garam masala is a mixture of spices used to flavour Indian curries. It can be bought already made, but I am going to give you the recipe (as featured in Open Rhodes*) to make your own.*

Serves 4

4 × mackerel, filleted as above

100 g (4 oz) butter

1 heaped tablespoon finely chopped
  shallot or onion

1 × heaped teaspoon garam masala
  (see below)

1 pig's caul (crépine, optional)

2 tablespoons olive or cooking oil

For the Garam Masala:

2 tablespoons coriander seeds

2 tablespoons cumin seeds

1 teaspoon cardamom pods

2 bay leaves

1 tablespoon black peppercorns

2 teaspoons cloves

½ teaspoon grated nutmeg

¼ teaspoon ground mace

¼ teaspoon ground ginger

**For the Red Onion and
  Tomato Salad:**

8 plum or salad tomatoes

2 red onions, sliced

2 tablespoons olive oil

2 tablespoons groundnut oil

1 teaspoon balsamic vinegar

A squeeze of lemon juice

A pinch of ground cumin (optional)

1 tablespoon water

1 tablespoon chopped fresh
  coriander

Salt and pepper

For the garam masala, dry-roast all of the ingredients except the nutmeg, mace and ginger, in a dry frying-pan over a medium heat until they colour and become aromatic. Leave to cool. Add the remaining spices and grind to a powder in a coffee grinder or blender. This can now be kept in an air-tight jar until needed.

To make the butter, melt 15 g (½ oz) and add the shallot or onion, with a heaped teaspoon of garam masala. Cook without letting the shallot or onion colour for 3–4 minutes; allow to cool. Mix with the remaining 85 g (3½ oz) of softened butter.

FISH

To stuff the mackerel, divide the spicy butter between all four. Fold the fillets together into a whole fish (bar the head). These can now be seasoned and wrapped in pig's caul to hold the fillets together or wrapped in buttered foil. The fish are best refrigerated for half an hour before roasting. This will set the butter, holding the fish together.

Pre-heat the oven to 200°C/400°F/Gas Mark 6. To roast the mackerel, heat some olive or cooking oil in a frying-pan that can be used in the oven or a flameproof roasting tray. Pan-fry the fish (in foil, if using) for 2–3 minutes on each side, allowing them to colour, before roasting for 12–15 minutes in the oven.

To make the salad, blanch the tomatoes in boiling water for 8–10 seconds and then plunge them into iced water. Remove the skins and slice into rings. Make the dressing by mixing the olive and groundnut oils together and flavouring with the balsamic vinegar, a squeeze of lemon juice and salt and pepper. I also sometimes add a pinch of ground cumin to the dressing. Loosen the dressing slightly with the tablespoon of water. Season the tomato and onion slices and build the salad up in layers, putting some dressing and chopped coriander between each layer. These salad 'cakes' can be built in individual pie or flan rings on the presentation plates.

Put the roasted mackerel on the plates. Pour any cooking juices from the foil if used over the fish and serve.

Note: Mackerel fillets can be used in this recipe; simply grill them and serve with the butter melting over, alongside a tossed tomato and red onion salad.

Monkfish Fritters 'à la Scampi' *with Roast Tomato Relish*

Monkfish, when cut into fingers and either breadcrumbed or battered and deep-fried, takes on a scampi-like texture and image. It is a very meaty fish and has a succulent flavour.

This recipe can also be used to cook Dublin Bay prawns, king prawns or just chunks of fish. The roast tomatoes are my chunky replacement for tomato sauce. They give a good, fresh tomato flavour, spiced to sharpen your taste buds.

Serves 2
350–450 g (12 oz–1 lb)
   monkfish fillet
Salt and pepper
A squeeze of lemon juice

For the Batter:
175 g (6 oz) self-raising flour
Salt
1 egg
150–300 ml (5–10 fl oz) lager
   or beer
Oil, for deep-frying

For the Roast Tomatoes:
6 plum or salad tomatoes, cut into
   six wedges and seeded
1 tablespoon olive oil
½ garlic clove, crushed
A pinch of English mustard powder
A knob of butter
1 tablespoon white-wine or
   malt vinegar
½ teaspoon demerara sugar
Salt and pepper
1 lemon, halved or cut in wedges
Fresh parsley or watercress sprigs

Trim and cut the monkfish fillet into fingers 5 x 1 cm (2 x ½ in), season with salt and pepper and a squeeze of lemon juice.

To make the batter, sieve together the self-raising flour and salt into a bowl. Whisk in the egg and lager or beer. Heat a domestic fat fryer to 180–190°C/350–375°F. Lightly dust the monkfish fingers with flour and dip them into the batter. This is best achieved by lifting them with a cocktail stick. Carefully place the fingers in the hot fat and fry in batches if necessary until golden. Lift from the fat and sprinkle with salt.

While the fish is cooking, heat the olive oil in a frying-pan. Once hot, drop the tomatoes in and fry for 30 seconds to 1 minute before adding the garlic and mustard powder. Also add the butter and continue to fry, giving a golden brown edge to the tomatoes. After 3–4 minutes, the tomatoes should have softened. Add the vinegar and sugar and quickly reduce for 2–3 minutes. Season with salt and pepper and the roast tomato relish is ready.

To serve, sit a pile of monkfish scampi on each plate with a spoonful or two of the roast tomatoes. Garnish with lemon wedges or halves and perhaps a sprig of parsley or watercress.

Note: The relish can be given more heat with a dash or two of Tabasco sauce.

Other dips that go very well with this dish are soured cream mixed with lemon juice and chives, or guacamole (see below), which is a Mexican relish.

Guacamole

The main ingredient for guacamole is avocado, which is spiced up with chillies and other flavours. Guacamole should be used almost immediately as after a while the avocado will begin to discolour. Chopped red and green peppers can also be added and lemon juice can be used in place of lime. Here's a recipe for two generous portions:

Serves 2

2 ripe avocados, peeled, halved and
   stoned
The juice of 1 lime
2 shallots or ½ onion, finely chopped
1 fresh green chilli, seeded, if wished,
   and finely chopped
2 tomatoes, blanched, skinned and
   seeded
1 garlic clove, crushed
1 tablespoon chopped fresh
   coriander
Salt and pepper

Chop the avocado and fork in the lime juice. Add all the remaining ingredients and season with salt and pepper.

poultry
and meat

*t*his is a section for meat-lovers, with most dishes carrying a British influence. I've used a lot of the traditional methods and styles with twists and influences from here and there to help them along.

On the poultry side, there are chicken, duck and pigeon dishes, with chicken appearing in two roasts. One is a pot-roast, creating its own stock as it roasts in the large pot. The other is just a roast chicken-leg with bacon; well, it's not quite *just* that; it's prepared, boned, stuffed, wrapped, roasted and on page 86, you'll find it!

I've also featured home-made pies, which give a great sense of achievement and pure culinary satisfaction when eaten. The Steak and 'Kidney Pie' (page 118) is, for me, an incredibly exciting dish, along with the Slow-honey-roast Duck (page 82) and Braised Pig's Trotters (page 96). Steak and kidney pie is a British classic with all of the flavours working under one (pastry) roof. With my version, the kidney pie is a completely separate item, flavoured with a mixture of caramelized onions and cream. Sitting next to it you have the piece of steak, slowly braised until melting. Hence the title – Steak and 'Kidney Pie'.

The slow-honey-roast duck is just as tasty, with a rich honey glaze caramelizing the whole bird. There are also recipes for Four-hour Lamb (page 109), Tournedos of Pork (page 106), Rabbit Carbonara (page 89), Boiled Brisket of Beef (page 121) and lots more.

Pot-roast Chicken *with Mushrooms,*
Peas and Mint

Pot-roasted chicken, presented on the table still in its cooking pot, is a mouth-watering sight. The semi-roasted, poached chicken will just be golden in the pot, with the finished sauce around.

Wild mushrooms, which will give the end result an even more 'earthy' taste, could be used instead of the button or chestnut mushrooms. Chestnut mushrooms are rich brown in colour and are so named because of their nutty flavour.

Serves 4

1.5–1.75 kg (3–4 lb) chicken
2 tablespoons olive oil
A knob of butter
1 onion, roughly chopped
2 celery sticks, roughly chopped
1 garlic clove
4–5 fresh mint leaves
900 ml (1½ pints) Chicken Stock (page 240) or alternative (page 243) or water
Salt and pepper

For the Sauce Garnish:

225 g (8 oz) fresh peas, cooked (frozen can be used)
225 g (8 oz) button or chestnut mushrooms
150 ml (5 fl oz) double cream
50 g (2 oz) cold butter, cubed, plus a knob of butter
6 fresh mint leaves, finely shredded
Salt and pepper

Pre-heat the oven to 200°C/400°F/Gas Mark 6. Season the chicken with salt and pepper. Heat the oil and butter in a frying-pan and cook the chicken for 4–5 minutes until golden brown.

Sit the chicken in an earthenware braising pot or casserole dish. In the same frying-pan, lightly fry for 4–5 minutes the onion, celery and the stalks from the sauce garnish mushrooms, along with the whole glove of garlic and mint leaves. Add to the chicken. Heat the chicken stock or water and pour it into the pot. Cover and place in the oven. The chicken will now take an hour to cook. During this time, baste the bird now and then with the cooking liquor.

Prepare and cook the peas and mushrooms for the sauce while the chicken is pot-roasting. Cook the peas in rapidly boiling, salted water until absolutely tender. This will take 10–15 minutes for fresh and 3–5 minutes for frozen. Once they are cooked, refresh immediately in iced water. Quarter the mushroom caps, season and shallow-fry in a knob of butter for a few minutes until golden brown and tender.

After an hour, check that the chicken is cooked by pressing the thigh/drumstick between forefinger and thumb. The flesh should give and feel tender when pressed. Remove the chicken and cover with foil to keep warm. Strain the cooking liquor through a sieve and reduce it by half; this will take 8–10 minutes. Add the cream and simmer for 3–4 minutes.

To finish the sauce, add the peas and mushrooms and warm through for a few minutes. Add the cubed butter and stir in. Check for seasoning. The sauce should still have a fairly loose consistency. At the last minute, add the shredded mint.

Slow-honey-roast Duck

The flavours from this dish remind me of the taste found in Chinese pancakes with Spring onions and cucumber. The duck is so tender and gives a very full flavour, which makes you just want to eat more and more of it. I think that's exactly the 'problem' you are going to find here: you just won't be able to stop wanting more! For this reason, it's best to allow half a duck per person!

Serves 2

1.25–1.5 kg (2½–3 lb)
   oven-ready duck
5 heaped tablespoons clear honey

1 teaspoon crushed white
   peppercorns
1 dessertspoon coarse sea salt

Pre-heat the oven to 160°C/325°F/Gas Mark 3. The duck-breast skin should first be scored four or five times, just cutting into the skin itself. Put the duck in a small roasting tray. Sprinkle the peppercorns over the duck with the salt, pushing the salt onto the skin. Spoon the honey over the duck, making sure it is completely covered. Place the duck in the oven.

After the first half hour, baste the duck with the honey and duck residue in the roasting tray. Leave to slow-roast for a further 30 minutes. The salt sprinkled over the duck will draw the excess water and fat from the skin itself and this will obviously collect in the roasting tray. After the second half hour, remove the duck from the roasting tray and carefully, from one corner, pour off as much excess fat as possible; it will be sitting on top of the honey in the tray. Replace the duck in the tray, baste with the honey residue and return to the oven. The duck can now be left to slow-roast, basting every 15 minutes for a further hour.

The duck has now been slowly cooked for 2 hours. Remove the duck once more from the tray and again pour off any excess fat. Baste the duck with the honey and return to the oven.

During the last half hour of cooking, baste the duck every 5–10 minutes. The honey will now have reduced and become very thick, glazing the duck even more. After the 2½ hours are up, remove the duck from the oven and tray. If any excess honey seems to be still a little thin, simply boil it in the tray and reduce it to a thick, coating consistency. Pour over the duck and leave to rest for 15 minutes.

Remove the legs along with the breasts, making sure they are left whole. Sit the breast and leg, for each portion on the plates, spooning over a tablespoon of honey and any residue. The slow-roast duck will be well done throughout; the meat will have become very tender and moist, just crumbling nicely as you eat it.

Note: You may well find that after 2 hours the duck is completely roasted, tender and glazed.

I like to simply serve a good green salad, trickled with olive oil and a squeeze of lemon with this dish.

Another favourite is to serve with the Mashed Potato Sauce (page 140). The potato sauce helps balance the richness of the honey.

Red-wine Mallard *with Buttered Greens*

Mallard is a wild duck which is in season between September and the end of January. It is the largest of the wild duck family, feeding two people per bird. Other wild 'ducks' in the same family are wigeon and teal. You may have to order mallard in advance from your butcher.

This recipe can be made using an 'oven-roast' duck, but the cooking times will be longer.

Serves 4

2 mallard, legs removed
1 bottle of red wine
Cooking oil
1 carrot, roughly chopped
1 onion, roughly chopped
½ leek, roughly chopped
Fresh thyme sprig
1 bay leaf
2 juniper berries, lightly crushed
　(optional)

150 ml (5 fl oz) Chicken Stock
　(page 240) or alternative
　(page 243)
300 ml (10 fl oz) Veal or Beef
　Jus/Gravy (page 242) or
　alternative (page 243)
750 g (1½ lb) Spring greens, stalked
　and shredded 1 cm (½ in) thick
A knob of butter
2–3 tablespoons water
Salt and pepper

The mallard legs can be marinated in half a bottle of red wine for 24 hours beforehand if you wish to guarantee a good strong flavour from them.

Pre-heat the oven to 200°C/400°F/Gas Mark 6.

Warm a trickle of cooking oil in a large saucepan and add the chopped vegetables, thyme, bay leaf and juniper berries. Cook for 10–15 minutes, allowing the vegetables to colour. Add the red wine from the duck legs and the remaining half bottle and boil rapidly until reduced by three-quarters. To help increase the duck flavour of the sauce, the main carcass of the ducks can be removed. This will leave the duck breasts still sitting on the bone, but with no carcass beneath them. Chop the carcasses from both ducks into small pieces and fry for a few minutes in a little oil until golden. Add the fried carcass pieces to the red-wine reduction. The duck legs can now also be coloured in oil and added to the reduction.

Add the chicken stock and *jus*/gravy to the pan and bring to the simmer. Braise the legs in the pre-heated oven for 45 minutes–1 hour. The duck legs will now be totally tender. Remove the legs and strain the sauce through a fine sieve. Bring the sauce back to the simmer, skimming off any excess fat and cook until it is reduced to a coating consistency. The flavour will have a combination of strong red wine and duck. Season to taste with a little salt and pepper.

Lay the remaining double breasts, skin-side down, in a heavy-based, ovenproof frying-pan and fry over a high heat until golden. Turn the breasts over and roast in the oven for 20–25 minutes. This will give you wonderful pink duck still sitting on the bone.

Remove from the oven cover with some foil and leave to rest somewhere warm for 10–15 minutes.

While the duck is resting, cook the greens. Melt the butter with 2–3 tablespoons of water. Bring to the boil and add the shredded greens. Season with salt and pepper and cook, stirring, on a medium heat for a few minutes until tender. Also, return the duck legs to the finished sauce and warm through.

To serve, put a spoonful of greens at the top of a plate or bowl and sit a duck leg next to it. Cut the duck breasts off the bone by following the direction of the carcass. Carve each breast into three and then lay the slices at the front of the plate. Pour the finished sauce over and around and serve.

Note: The cooking of the duck legs and finishing of the sauce can be done 24 hours in advance. Then just re-heat the legs for 10–15 minutes in the warming sauce. If buying from a local butcher, I am sure they will remove the legs and take out the central carcass (and chop it) for you, leaving the two breasts of each duck still attached to the bone. This guarantees a tender finish and the shape of the duck is not lost.

1 Cut either side of the thigh bone and around the knuckle at the top of the thigh. Scrape towards the drumstick and cut knuckle, leaving a single bone.

2 Skin the legs. Mix together the ingredients for the butter. Divide between the 4 legs, filling each empty thigh.

3 Place a bacon rasher on the drumstick end and fold round the leg. Continue with more rashers until all the legs are covered. Fry and then roast.

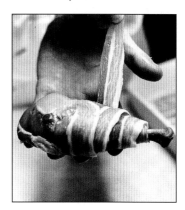

Roast Chicken and Bacon *flavoured with*
Tarragon, Garlic and Lemon

The title 'roast chicken' may be a little deceptive when in fact all it's going to be is a roast chicken leg! That's one of the features of this dish that makes it so exciting. Once you've tried it, you'll be amazed at just how good a roasted chicken leg can be. For this recipe, I'm boning out the thigh bone, which will leave me space to fill with the flavoured tarragon butter. This melts as the chicken roasts and leaves a wonderful flavour in the chicken.

Serves 4
4 legs of chicken
12–16 rashers of green
   (unsmoked) streaky bacon
Cooking oil

For the Butter:
75 g (3 oz) butter, softened
2 tablespoons chopped fresh tarragon
2 small garlic cloves, crushed
2 tablespoons finely chopped
   shallots or onions
The finely grated zest of 1 lemon
Salt and pepper

For the Sauce:
A knob of butter
½ onion, roughly chopped
2 garlic cloves, crushed
1 bay leaf
2 glasses white wine
The juice of 1 or 2 lemons
300 ml (10 fl oz) Chicken Stock
   (page 240) or alternative
   (page 243)
150 ml (5 fl oz) double cream
Salt and pepper

Pre-heat the oven to 200°C/400°F/Gas Mark 6. To make the sauce, melt the butter and add the onion, crushed garlic and bay leaf. Cook without colouring for 3–4 minutes. Add the white wine and reduce until almost dry. Add the juice of 1 lemon and reduce by half. Add the chicken stock and reduce by two-thirds. Pour on the double cream and bring to the simmer. Simmer gently for 10–15 minutes. Strain through a sieve and season with salt and pepper. To make the sauce fuller and sharper, add another squeeze or two of lemon juice. The sauce is now ready.

First remove the bone from the thigh part of each leg. Cut either side of the bone and then cut around the knuckle showing at the top of the thigh. Scrape down the bone to the joint connecting the thigh with the drumstick. Now simply break or cut at the knuckle. This will leave you with a single 3–5 cm (1½–2 in) bone in the drumstick. Skin the legs.

For the butter, mix together the softened butter, tarragon, garlic, shallots or onions, lemon zest and seasoning. Divide the flavoured butter between the four legs, filling the empty thigh. Now wrap the chicken legs in the streaky bacon. Start by placing a rasher of streaky bacon on the drumstick end of the leg. Fold the rasher round and round the leg, slightly overlapping as you do to keep the bacon in place. Continue covering the leg with the rashers, starting where the last rasher finished. You will need 3–4 rashers to cover each leg. Once completely covered, pierce with a cocktail stick to hold the bacon in place.

Warm a roasting tray on a medium heat with a trickle of cooking oil. Add the legs to the pan, cooking and colouring the bacon all the way around until crisp. This is best achieved by colouring over a medium heat. Place the chicken legs in the oven and roast for 15–20 minutes. During this time, the bacon will become even more golden and crisp. Leave to rest for 5–6 minutes before carving.

Carve three slices through the thigh part of the joint and sit the slices, overlapping, on the plates. The drumstick can be presented standing up, revealing its bone behind the slices. To finish, just pour some of the cream sauce around.

Note: This dish goes very well with buttered spinach as featured in the photograph on page 87. To cook buttered spinach, pick and de-stalk and wash the spinach several times to remove any grit. Heat a knob of butter and a tablespoon or two of water to boiling point and add the washed spinach. Cook on a fast heat for a few minutes until tender. Season the spinach with salt, pepper and grated nutmeg.

Rabbit Carbonara

I've chosen rabbit as an alternative to the obvious chicken but the recipe can be made replacing the rabbit legs with four chicken breasts, so please don't be put off if you don't like rabbit. The flavour of rabbit is richer and stronger, which is why I have chosen to use them. I must have seen literally hundreds of different recipes for carbonara sauces. This is mine; it's simple to make and extremely tasty to eat.

Serves 4

4 rabbit legs
350 g (12 oz) fresh or dried noodles
  or spaghetti

For the Sauce:

600 ml (1 pint) Chicken Stock
  (page 240) or alternative
  (page 243)
1 onion, finely chopped
1 garlic clove, crushed

2 tablespoons olive oil
100 g (4 oz) smoked or unsmoked
  streaky bacon, cut into thin strips
150 ml (5 fl oz) double
  or whipping cream
50–75 g (2–3 oz) Parmesan, grated
2 tablespoons chopped fresh flatleaf
  or curly parsley
A squeeze of lemon juice (optional)
Salt and pepper
A trickle of good olive oil, to serve

Poach the rabbit legs in the chicken stock for 20–25 minutes until tender. Remove the legs and reduce the stock to 150 ml (5 fl oz). Cook the onion and garlic in a tablespoon of olive oil for a few minutes without letting them colour. Fry the bacon separately in the remaining olive oil until crisp (or just cook it with the onions). Add the reduced stock and the cream and bring to the simmer. Cook for a few minutes. Add the bacon, if cooked separately. Season with salt and pepper.

Cook the noodles or spaghetti in salted, boiling water, following the packet instructions, if dried. If fresh, they will take 4–5 minutes.

Meanwhile, take the meat from the rabbit legs off the bone. Shred it into strips. Add the rabbit to the sauce to warm through.

As soon as the noodles are cooked, drain in a colander. Season and mix with the rabbit sauce. Add a tablespoon or two of grated Parmesan with the parsley. A squeeze of lemon juice will lift all of the flavours. Divide between bowls, finishing each with a trickle of olive oil.

Note: Mushrooms can also be added to the recipe and a good twist of pepper at the end will really fire up the dish.

Roast Wood Pigeon *with Sautéed* *Red-wine Potatoes*

Wood pigeons have a strong, almost beefy flavour so a good red wine always goes well with them. The potatoes are flavoured with red onions and then caramelized in red wine – the flavour is so good. I also like to sauté the potatoes in goose fat for a very rich flavour. You can of course sauté the potatoes in butter, which is almost as good.

The pigeons are going to be roasted on the breast bones. The rest of the carcass and the legs are going to be removed, chopped up and turned into a 'game' sauce.

Serves 4

4 large wood pigeons
4 potatoes, boiled in their jackets
Cooking oil
5 red onions, sliced
1 carrot, chopped
1 bay leaf
Fresh thyme sprig
¾ bottle of red wine
600 ml (1 pint) Chicken Stock
　　(page 240) or 300 ml (10 fl oz)
　　Veal *Jus*/Gravy (page 242) or
　　alternative (page 243)

50–75 g (2–3 oz) cold butter
50 g (2 oz) butter or goose
　　or duck fat, for frying the potatoes
　　and onions
1 teaspoon demerara sugar
50 ml (2 fl oz) brandy or Armagnac
　　(optional)
1 tablespoon chopped fresh flatleaf
　　parsley
Salt and pepper

Pre-heat the oven to 200°C/400°F/Gas Mark 6. Remove the legs from the birds and detach the breasts on the bone from the rest of the carcass. Chop the legs and the discarded parts of the carcass into small pieces and brown them in a drop of cooking oil in a large, deep frying-pan or saucepan. Add one of the onions, the carrot, bay leaf and thyme and cook for 10–15 minutes or until all have taken on some colour.

Add two-thirds of the wine and boil rapidly until reduced by three-quarters. If using chicken stock in place of *jus*/gravy (which is what I shall be using), add it now and simmer for 20 minutes before starting the final reduction. Now increase the heat and boil rapidly. Once the liquid is reduced to 150 ml (5 fl oz), you will have a good, rich, strong pigeon stock. Now you can whisk in the 50–75 g (2–3 oz) of cold butter, cut in small cubes, to give a red-wine butter sauce. If using veal *jus*/gravy instead, add to the sauce and simmer very gently for 20–30 minutes. It will not need the final reduction by rapid boiling. Strain the sauce through a fine sieve into a clean pan.

Peel the cooked potatoes and cut into 5 mm (¼ in) thick slices. Classic sauté potatoes should start to break down as they are fried: this gives them a much better crumbly texture. Pan-fry the potato slices in some of the goose or duck fat or butter over a medium-high heat until golden and beginning to crisp. Season with salt and pepper.

Meanwhile, pan-fry the remaining onions in the remaining butter or duck or goose fat, in a separate pan on a high heat until slightly softened and coloured. Add the remaining third of the wine and reduce until almost dry. Add the demerara sugar, which will caramelize quite quickly. Mix together the potatoes and onions and keep warm.

The pigeons can now be roasted. Season them with salt and pepper and cook, skin-side down, with a drop of cooking oil on top of the stove in a roasting pan or heavy ovenproof frying-pan. Finish the pigeons in the oven, breast-side up, for 15 minutes. This will keep the breasts nice and pink. Another 10 minutes will make them well done.

Once cooked, remove them from the oven, cover with foil and allow to rest somewhere warm for 5–6 minutes. Remove the breasts from the bone and sprinkle the pink side with the Armagnac or brandy (if using). The flavour will be absorbed by the meat, which will be wonderfully enhanced. Leave to stand for a further 5 minutes. Meanwhile, reheat the sauce and finish the sautéed onions and potatoes with the chopped parsley. Spoon some onto each plate and add the pigeon breasts (two per portion) either sitting at the front or on the top of the plate. Pour the butter sauce or gravy around and serve.

Note: The French Bean Purée (page 156) goes very well as a vegetable with this dish; you could put the breasts on a pool of purée, offering the sauté potatoes separately.

Other game – pheasant, teal, grouse, etc. – will all work with this recipe.

Escalopes of Pork *fried with a Sage, Garlic and Anchovy Crust, served with Apple Mashed Potatoes*

If you are not a big fan of anchovies, you can leave them out of this recipe. I prefer to use marinated anchovies which are a totally different 'kettle of fish' from the tinned variety. The tinned variety can be used but you'll only need about a quarter of the quantity – they are a lot, lot stronger and saltier.

Next is the apple mash. Apple and potato are both favourite flavours of mine, as you probably know by now! A ready-made apple sauce can be used instead of cooking your own but it is best to select one that isn't too sweet. The combination of the pork with the apple works very well, as indeed does the mash!

Serves 4

4 × 175–225 g (6–8 oz) pork fillets
   or pork loin portions
50 g (2 oz) butter
2 shallots, finely chopped or ½ onion
100 g (4 oz) fresh white
   breadcrumbs
8–10 fresh sage leaves, chopped
8 marinated anchovy fillets or
   4 tinned ones (optional)
2 garlic cloves, crushed
Plain flour, for dusting
1 egg, beaten

2 tablespoons olive oil
Salt and pepper
A squeeze of lemon juice

For the Potatoes:
750 g (1½ lb) Mashed Potatoes
   (page 140)
4 Granny Smith or
   Golden Delicious apples
A knob of butter

To make the apple mashed potatoes, peel, quarter and core the apples. Cut the apple quarters into six or eight. Melt the butter and add the apples. Cook on a medium heat until the apples are completely cooked, soft and translucent. Push the apple through a sieve or purée it in a liquidizer and then mix it with the mashed potatoes. The ratio between the two is really up to you – it's a question of adding and tasting. I find between a quarter and a third of apple to potato works well but if you prefer more simply add more.

Trim the pork fillet or pork loin portions so they are totally fat-free. Both can be found prepared and cut in most supermarkets. Put the portions between sheets of cling film and bat them out to escalopes 5 mm (¼ in thick) with a heavy saucepan or rolling pin.

Melt a knob of butter with the shallots or onion and cook for 2–3 minutes until softened but without colour. Leave to cool. Once cool, mix into the breadcrumbs with the sage, anchovies (if using) and garlic. Season with salt and pepper. Season the pork, dust with plain flour and pass it through the egg. The pork can now be coated in the breadcrumbs; make sure the escalopes are all well covered on both sides.

Heat a frying-pan with the olive oil. Add a knob of butter and put the escalopes in the pan. Cook them on a medium heat for 4–5 minutes on each side until they have a crisp, golden finish.

Serve the apple mashed potatoes on the plates with the escalopes or in a separate bowl. To finish, heat a knob of butter in the frying-pan until it bubbles to a nut brown. Add a squeeze or two of lemon juice and pour over the pork.

Note: Chicken breasts can also be tenderized into escalopes and finished as for the pork.

Four-hour Pork – *pressure-cooked in two!*

Trying to cook a 4-hour dish in 2 hours would normally put you under a lot of pressure. But with this recipe, that's exactly what I am going to do!

I'm using a pressure cooker. I have been amazed at how good these machines are. You put all the ingredients in and, in under 2 hours, the dish is virtually done! If you don't have one, this dish really is a four-hour pork. Just cook the dish in the oven at 150°C/300°F/Gas Mark 2 for 4 hours; either way, the meat simply melts and falls off the bone.

Serves 4–6

1.5–1.75 kg (3–4 lb) joint of
   shoulder or leg of pork
100 g (4 oz) prunes,
   stoned and quartered
4 apples, peeled, cored and
   cut into eighths
2–3 strips of orange zest
1 bay leaf
2 potatoes, peeled and quartered

2 onions, roughly chopped
2 cloves
600 ml (1 pint) beer
300 ml (10 fl oz) Chicken Stock
   (page 240) or alternative
   (page 243) or water
½ teaspoon demerara sugar
A knob of butter
Salt and pepper
1 tablespoon chopped fresh parsley

The pork joint can be cooked as it is with the skin left on or the skin can be removed, scored, salted and roasted separately for 30–40 minutes at 200°C/400°F/Gas Mark 6 to make crackling. If you want to do this, re-tie the pork joint into shape.

Place all of the ingredients, bar the butter and the chopped parsley, in the pressure cooker and bring to the simmer. Fit the lid on top, set the pressure weight and adjust the heat as required. Cook for about 1½–2 hours on a fairly low heat but still at full pressure and then turn off the heat. Leave to stand for at least 15 minutes to allow the steam to be released before removing the lid. Remove the succulent, overcooked joint and allow it to rest for 10 minutes.

The cooking liquor may need to be skimmed to remove excess fat. The apples and potatoes will have almost broken down, thickening the liquor. Add the butter and carefully stir in. Remove the orange zest. You now have a sauce that has nothing but flavour. Season with salt and pepper and add the chopped parsley.

You can now literally break the pork into portions and put them in bowls or on plates. Spoon the sauce over and serve. This dish has a very rustic look about it, but it has immense flavour and is so easy that it relieves a lot of 'pressure' in your kitchen!

Note: Check the pressure-cooker manufacturer's instructions for detailed instructions on pot-roasting joints of this size.

Braised Pig's Trotters

Pig's trotters are an unusual but sensational dish. Filling them with a pork sausage and black pudding stuffing and serving them with mashed potatoes and gravy gives them a traditional English touch. If you try these once, I can assure you'll be excited and delighted by the results! Ask the butcher to prepare them for you and you could also get him to mince the pork belly, which gives the stuffing the right fat-to-meat content.

Serves 4

4 pig's back trotters, boned
Mashed Potatoes (page 140)

For the Stuffing:

350 g (12 oz) pork belly, minced
175 g (6 oz) black pudding, cut into
   1 cm (½ in) dice
2 large onions, chopped
1 garlic clove, crushed
A knob of butter
A pinch of ground mace
1 egg
2 tablespoons white breadcrumbs
1 dessertspoon chopped fresh sage
A dash of Worcestershire sauce
Salt and pepper

For the Cooking Liquor:

A knob of butter
1 onion, roughly chopped
1 carrot, roughly chopped
1 leek, roughly chopped
Fresh thyme sprig
1 bay leaf
1 glass white wine
2 glasses Madeira
600 ml (1 pint) Chicken Stock
   (page 240) or alternative
   (page 243)
300 ml (10 fl oz) Beef or Veal
   Jus/Gravy (page 242) or
   alternative (page 243)
Salt and pepper

Pre-heat the oven to 160°C/325°F/Gas Mark 3. For the cooking liquor in a casserole dish or saucepan, melt a knob of butter with the chopped vegetables, thyme and bay leaf. Cook without letting them colour for 1–2 minutes before adding the white wine. Boil rapidly until reduced by half. Add the Madeira and reduce by half again. The stock and *jus*/gravy can now be added with the boned trotters. Bring to the simmer, cover, place in the oven and braise for 2½–3 hours. After 2½ hours, check the trotter skin for tenderness. If pinched, it must tear very easily. If slightly firm, cook for the remaining half hour.

    Once cooked, remove the trotters and sit on individual, buttered foil strips, skin-side down.

    Strain the cooking liquor through a fine sieve and if necessary boil rapidly until reduced to a sauce consistency.

    As it is reducing, the sauce may need to be skimmed of any excess fat. It should be rich in colour with a glossy finish. Season with salt and pepper. The sauce can also be lifted with an extra dash of neat Madeira. Set aside while you finish the trotters.

For the stuffing, cook the chopped onions and crushed garlic in the butter without letting them colour for 5–6 minutes or until softened. Leave to cool. Mix the onions into the minced pork belly with the black pudding. Season with salt, pepper and ground mace. Beat in the egg and then add the breadcrumbs and chopped sage. Check the seasoning and finish with a dash of Worcestershire sauce.

Once the trotters have cooled to room temperature, roll some of the stuffing into a sausage shape. Sit this on the trotter, adding enough to make the trotter resemble its original shape. Fold over the remaining skin and roll in the foil, twisting either end to help maintain a good cylindrical shape. Refrigerate the trotters for 1–2 hours to set. They will keep very well, refrigerated, for 2–3 days.

To finish and serve the trotters, steam the trotters over a pan of boiling water for 15 minutes. Carefully unwrap them. An alternative method is to sit them in a roasting tray with 5 mm (¼ in) of hot water from the kettle and bake them at 190°C/375°F/Gas Mark 5, also for 15 minutes. Spoon or pipe through a 1 cm (½ in) plain tube, some creamy mashed potatoes at the top of the plate. Sit the trotter in front. Now just pour the reduced, finished sauce over the trotter and serve.

Pan-fried or Grilled Liver *with Young Sprouting Cabbage and Gorgonzola Rarebit*

Rarebit was never going to escape from this book! There are so many different cheese flavours that can be used. This recipe can be made with Stilton or Roquefort – I just can't ignore them.

The liver I'm going to use is calves', which is obviously the very best but also the most expensive. Lamb's liver will also go very well. The greens and Gorgonzola go very well with pork too; a good pork roast served with them is delicious.

Serves 4

4 x 175–225 g (6–8 oz) thick slices
  of calves' or lamb's liver
Plain flour, seasoned
A trickle of cooking oil
A knob of butter
Salt and pepper

For the Cabbage:

750–900 g (1½–2 lb) young
  sprouting cabbage, or savoy
  cabbage, or Spring greens

25 g (1 oz) butter
225 g (8 oz) Gorgonzola Rarebit
  (page 233)
Salt and pepper

For the Sauce:

2 tablespoons sherry vinegar
1 teaspoon demerara sugar
150 ml (5 fl oz) thick Jus/Gravy
  (page 242) or alternative
  (page 243)
Salt and pepper

Wash the young sprouting cabbage, keeping the leaves intact with their stalks which cook very tender. If using savoy cabbage or Spring greens, just cut into wide strips. Cook in salted, boiling water for 2–3 minutes or until tender. Drain. If you want to cook the cabbage in advance, refresh it in plenty of cold water and re-heat it in the microwave when you are ready. Season the cabbage with salt and pepper and add the butter. Mix thoroughly. You can now serve it separately in a vegetable dish with the Gorgonzola rarebit just golden and melting over or put individual portions on the serving plates, mould the rarebit into 5 mm (¼ in) thick discs and lay them on top, so they melt over the cabbage when grilled. If using savoy cabbage or Spring greens, it is best served glazed in a separate vegetable dish.

For the sauce, quickly boil together the sherry vinegar and sugar until slightly reduced and then add to the *jus*/gravy. Bring to the simmer and season with salt and pepper.

Pre-heat the grill to high. For the liver, dust the thick liver slices in the seasoned flour. Heat a frying-pan or grill pan with a trickle of cooking oil. Put the liver in the pan and add the butter. For thick liver slices, cook for 2–3 minutes, turn over and cook for a further 2 minutes. For thin slices, cook for 1–2 minutes on each side. Meanwhile, slide the cabbage under the grill to colour. Season the liver, put next to the glazed cabbage (if presenting on plates) and either serve the sauce separately or trickle over or around the liver.

Rib Steak 'au Poivre' *with* *Sweet Brandy Butter*

Steak au poivre has many variations: one of these is the type of steak you use (fillet, sirloin, T-bone, chateaubriand or rib). The other variation depends on your choice of pepper for the au poivre *– crushed black peppercorns or green peppercorns in a brandy cream sauce. This one is going to be a combination of both. The rib will be smothered with the crushed black peppercorns and the brandy is used in the butter along with sweet white wine, shallots or onions, parsley and mustard.*

One of the advantages of cooking a rib is that it is a joint of meat for two people. The weight of the meat is 750–900 g (1½–2 lb) and that includes the rib bone as well! Consequently, the steak will be 3–5 cm (1½–2 in) thick. If a 225 g (8 oz) sirloin steak is being cooked, the strong flavour of the crushed peppercorns may take over because of the size of the meat. With the thick rib, the flavour is totally different. You have the peppery outside with the rich, almost sweet, flavour of the beef to look forward to. When you are eating the rib with the tasty butter just melting over the taste is really quite sensational. Remember that the rib is for two people so, although it sounds so good, you really will have to share it!

I like to serve a good watercress or green salad with the steak, accompanied by either Mashed Potatoes (page 140) or chips.

Serves 2
750–900 g (1½–2 lb) rib steak, on
  the bone, trimmed
2 tablespoons black peppercorns
2 tablespoons olive oil
A knob of butter
Salt

For the Sweet Brandy Butter:
2 tablespoons finely chopped
  shallots or onions

50 ml (2 fl oz) brandy
4 tablespoons sweet white wine,
  or dry white wine with a pinch
  of sugar
75 g (3 oz) butter, softened
2 teaspoons chopped fresh parsley
1 teaspoon Dijon or English mustard
  (optional)
Salt and pepper

To make the sweet brandy butter, warm the shallots or onions with the brandy and then boil until reduced and almost dry. Add the wine and reduce until almost dry. Leave to cool. Once cold, mix into the butter with the parsley and mustard, if using. Season with salt and pepper.

Crush the peppercorns, not too finely, in a mortar and pestle, coffee grinder or with the back of a knife. Shake the crushed peppercorns in a sieve to release the powdered pepper, which will make the peppered flavour too strong. Press the crushed peppercorns into each side of the meat – be quite firm. Season with salt.

Heat the olive oil in a frying-pan and, once hot, add the meat. It is important now not to fry too quickly, otherwise the steak will burn before it is cooked. Also, I only like to turn the meat once. This ensures a good, crusty finish and that the peppercorns are cooked.

For a medium-rare to medium steak, it is best to turn the steak after 8–10 minutes. This may seem a long time to cook it, but a rib on the bone does take quite a time to cook. Once turned, add the butter, which will turn to a good nut-brown as the steak continues to cook. The steak will now take a further 8–10 minutes and during that time you should spoon over the cooking juices to baste the meat.

Once cooked, leave the meat to rest somewhere warm for 6–7 minutes before carving. This will relax the meat, giving it a more tender finish. Spoon the brandy butter on the rib, leaving it just to melt over before serving; or re-heat the rib-cooking pan with all the residue still in the pan. Add some of the brandy butter, stirring it into all the other flavours and then pour it over and around the steak to serve.

One-piece Irish Stew

I featured Irish stew in my first book Rhodes Around Britain. *That was done in the good old-fashioned way with everything in one pot and just ladled up and ready! This method gives you the same flavours but in a totally different form.*

Chumps of lamb are joints of lamb that come in pairs at the rear of the saddle. They are usually cut into chump chops but I prefer to use them as individual joints for roasting, braising or stewing. With all fat and sinew removed (ask your butcher to do this), they can be tied into joints.

This whole recipe may appear long-winded, but I promise you it really is very simple and easy. Basically, it is just boiled meat with one potato and three veg – I'd call that a traditional British dish, wouldn't you?

Serves 4

For the Lamb:

4 lamb chumps, trimmed of all fat
A knob of butter
2 carrots, roughly chopped
1 large onion, roughly chopped
2–3 celery sticks, roughly chopped
2 garlic cloves, finely chopped
1 bay leaf
Fresh thyme sprig
900 ml (1½ pints) Chicken Stock
   (page 240) or alternative
   (page 243) or water
A few lamb bones (optional)

For the Garnish:

4 small onions
100 g (4 oz) butter
1 small savoy cabbage
4 carrots, peeled
½ teaspoon sugar
2 large potatoes, peeled
1–2 teaspoons roughly chopped
   fresh flatleaf parsley (optional)
Salt and pepper

To cook the lamb, melt a knob of butter in a large pan and add the chopped vegetables, garlic, bay leaf and thyme. Cook for 5–6 minutes until slightly softened. Add the lamb chumps and top with the chicken stock or water. Because of the slow-cooking method, the chumps will create their own stock if cooked in water. A few extra lamb bones can also be added to increase the flavour. Using chicken stock rather than water will obviously leave you with a stronger broth.

Bring to the simmer and continue to simmer, covered, for 1½ hours. The stock may need skimming from time to time to remove any impurities.

Once cooked, remove the meat and keep warm. Strain the cooking liquor through a sieve and discard the vegetables. Taste the stock for strength and reduce it to increase the flavour and thicken the consistency.

All the vegetable garnishes can be prepared and cooked while the lamb is braising. I prefer to cook these separately from the stew to give a better finish to the dish.

For the onions, pre-heat the oven to 200°C/400°F/Gas Mark 6. Melt a knob of butter in a frying-pan. Put the onions in the pan and cook for 4–5 minutes until golden brown on the presentation side. Transfer the onions to a braising dish and fill to half-way up the sides with some of the braising liquor from the lamb or some extra chicken stock. Cook them in the oven for 30–35 minutes until completely tender. They can just be reheated in the liquor when needed.

For the cabbage parcels, peel the outside leaves from the cabbage, wash and remove the stalks leading through the centre of the leaf. Cook four large or eight small leaves in salted, boiling water for 2–3 minutes until completely tender. Refresh in iced water. Quarter the centre of the remaining cabbage and remove all the stalks. Shred the cabbage leaves very finely. Melt another knob of butter with 2–3 tablespoons of water in a saucepan and add the shredded cabbage. Cook on a medium heat for 3–4 minutes until tender. Season with salt and pepper and allow to cool.

Once it's cool, divide the mix into four balls and wrap each one in the cooked leaves. These can now be wrapped tightly in cling film to maintain a good ball or parcel shape. To re-heat, steam them over boiling water for 5–6 minutes or microwave for 1–2 minutes on full power.

For the carrots, place in a small saucepan, barely covering them with cold water. Add a knob of butter, sugar and a pinch of salt. Cover and bring to the simmer, cooking them for 10–12 minutes until they are tender. Remove the lid and reduce the cooking liquor with the carrots until a buttery syrupy consistency is achieved. The carrots are now glazed with their own cooking liquor. To re-heat, toss in a little water and butter over a low heat.

For the potatoes, halve the peeled potatoes lengthways. Each piece can now be cut into barrel shapes with a sharp knife, or leave them as half-potatoes. Boil them in salted water until tender but still keeping their shape. Melt a knob of butter. Once the potatoes are cooked, brush with melted butter.

We now have the lamb and the garnishes ready.

Sit the vegetables at the top of the plate and the chump of lamb at the front. Add the remaining butter to the reduced cooking liquor and also the chopped parsley. Spoon the sauce over the lamb and serve: one-piece Irish stew!

Cornish-pasty Pudding

This steamed version of the traditional favourite is lovely to eat; the beef cooks with potatoes, onions and swedes in its own juices with a touch of stock to help it along.

All it needs then is a good spoonful of mustard to go with it and the dish is complete. Some jus/gravy (page 242) can also be offered separately.

Serves 4

For the Suet Pastry:
450 g (1 lb) plain flour
25 g (1 oz) baking powder
275 g (10 oz) dried suet
1 tablespoon dried English mustard
    (optional)
300 ml (10 fl oz) water
A pinch of salt

For the Filling:
450 g (1 lb) beef chuck or skirt,
    sliced into very thin strips
1 large potato, peeled and sliced
1 small swede, peeled and sliced
1 large onion, sliced
A knob of butter
150–250 ml (5–8 fl oz) Beef Stock
    (page 242) or alternative
    (page 243)
Worcestershire sauce
Jus/Gravy (page 242, optional)
Salt and pepper

Sieve the flour, baking powder and salt together. Mix the suet and mustard powder, if using (the mustard fires up the flavour of the pastry and the rest of the pasty), and add to the flour mix. Add the water and work to a good suet dough. Before rolling, allow the dough to rest for 20 minutes.

Butter a 1.2-litre (2-pint) pudding basin. Roll out three-quarters of the dough and line the mould, making it at least 5 mm–1 cm (¼–½ in) thick. Roll the remaining quarter of the dough into a circle to cover the pudding.

Season the meat, vegetables and onion separately with salt and pepper. Melt the butter and trickle it over the vegetables. The meat can now be layered between individual layers of the swede, potatoes and onions. Once the suet pudding bowl is filled, mix a few shakes of the Worcestershire sauce with the beef stock and pour over.

Brush water around the edge of the pudding and cover with the lid. Press to seal all around and then cover with buttered foil, pleating it to leave room for rising. The pudding can now be steamed for 2 hours. Once it's cooked, remove from the steamer and leave to rest for 10 minutes before turning out. If gravy is being served, pour it over or offer it separately.

Note: Fresh chopped thyme can be added to the mixture with a pinch of ground mace and cayenne pepper to spice up the filling.

Tournedos of Pork *with Caramelized Apple and Mashed Potato Sauce*

Another tournedos dish with exactly the same concept as the lamb on page 122. Of course you'll not be needing a whole leg of pork – that would give you at least 40 portions! I buy 1.5 kg (3 lb) of pork meat from the leg. This can be broken down and prepared as for the lamb recipe. This recipe also illustrates exactly what I feel about British dishes: working with classic British flavours and then turning them into something even more special by enhancing their flavours. Pork with apples and mashed potatoes is a classic. Here's a 'new' classic.

Serves 8

1.5 kg (3 lb) leg of pork meat, boned
   and skin removed
225 g (8 oz) pig's caul (crépine) or
   15–18 rashers of smoked
   streaky bacon
10 fresh sage leaves, chopped
A knob of butter
Salt and pepper

For the Sauce:

600 ml (1 pint) Jus/Gravy (page 242)
   or alternative (page 243)
300 ml (10 fl oz) apple juice
A squeeze of lemon juice

For the Garnishes:

4 Granny Smith apples
A knob of butter
A sprinkling of caster sugar
1 quantity Mashed Potato Sauce
   (page 140)

To prepare the pork, cut and prepare it in exactly the same way as for the lamb (page 122). Remove all sinews, cut the lean meat into strips and mince the trimmings. Instead of adding cumin, just add salt, pepper and the chopped sage. Arrange the meat strips and farce as for the other recipe, roll into a cylinder and wrap in pig's caul, foil or bacon rashers. Refrigerate, cut and tie as for the lamb and the tournedos are ready.

Pre-heat the oven to 200°C/400°F/Gas Mark 6. The sauce can be kept very simple. Just reduce the apple juice by two-thirds and then add the *jus*/gravy. Add a squeeze of lemon juice, if you like, to sharpen the apple flavour.

Peel the apples and remove the cores. Cut through the middle, trimming off the ends to give you 1–1.5 cm (½–¾ in) thick slices.

Season the pork tournedos with salt and pepper and sauté in butter on all sides until nicely browned. Finish cooking in the oven for 12–15 minutes. This will leave the pork still moist in the centre. Leave to rest for 5–6 minutes.

While the pork is cooking and resting, pan-fry the apples in butter until golden and tender. This will take 5–6 minutes. Once cooked, sit them on a tray, wider-side up, and sprinkle with caster sugar. Caramelize under a hot grill.

To serve the dish, spoon some warmed mashed potato sauce on the top half of the plate. Place the apples towards the front with the pork tournedos sitting at the side. Trickle the pork apple gravy around and serve. You can also serve this with pork crackling (see Note below) as shown in the picture on page 107.

Note: It is best to reduce the apple gravy to a good, thick consistency, so it easily coats the back of a spoon. Any pork skin can be cut into thin strips and well salted. Bake in a pre-heated oven (180°C/350°F/Gas Mark 4) for 30–40 minutes. This will remove all excess fat, and leave you with pork crackling. These can be salted and left to cool. A few to eat with the tournedos are lovely. A glass or two of Madeira, reduced into the sauce, will make the sauce even stronger.

A stronger pork flavour for the sauce can be achieved by taking 450 g (1 lb) of chopped pork bones and roasting them with onions, leeks, celery, sage leaves and garlic. Once golden brown, add 600 ml (1 pint) of chicken stock and cook for 1–2 hours. Reduce by three-quarters and add to the *jus*/gravy. Continue to simmer gently for 20–30 minutes and strain through a sieve. Now reduce the apple juice, add to the gravy and the sauce is ready.

Four-hour Lamb

I'm sure you all know by now how much I love slow-cooking methods. Waiting 4 hours for this leg of lamb is worth every minute!

Pierre Koffman, one of the most talented and famous chefs in the UK and Europe, featured this recipe (or one very similar) in one of his books. I tried it, loved it and now I'm just passing it on. It's that good.

This recipes uses a leg of lamb, which will feed eight people generously.

Serves 8

For the Vegetable *Mirepoix*
2 onions, diced
2–3 carrots, diced
1 leek, diced
2–3 celery sticks, diced

For the Lamb:
1 leg of lamb
Fresh thyme sprig
1 bay leaf
65 g (2½ oz) butter
100 g (4 oz) garlic, tied in muslin
1 bottle of white wine
Cooking oil
900 ml (1½ pints) Chicken Stock
   (page 240) or alternative
   (page 243)
Salt and pepper

Pre-heat the oven to 180°C/350°F/Gas Mark 4. Soften the *mirepoix* vegetables, thyme and bay leaf in 15 g (½ oz) of butter in a deep ovenproof braising pan. Once softened, add the bag of garlic cloves and the white wine. Bring to the boil and reduce the wine by three-quarters. While the vegetables and wine are cooking, season the leg of lamb and brown all over in a hot frying-pan with the cooking oil. Once coloured, put the lamb in the braising pan. Add the chicken stock and top with water, so the lamb is half-covered. Return to the simmer and cover with a lid. Cook the lamb in the oven for 4 hours. I like to turn the lamb over after 2 hours, so it cooks evenly.

After 4 hours, remove the lamb which will now be very tender. Leave to rest. Strain and reduce the liquor by half or more. Taste the stock for strength: a really good, strong stock will give a better finish to the sauce. About 300 ml (10 fl oz) of well-reduced stock should be plenty. Take the almost puréed garlics from the bag and press them to a smooth paste. Add this paste as a thickener to the sauce and then whisk in the remaining 50 g (2 oz) butter. The sauce is now finished. Carve the lamb or break it into chunks. Spoon over the sauce and serve.

Note: Vegetables that go well with this dish are Mashed Potatoes (page 140), roasted carrots, Turnip Purée (page 152) or peas.

'Piece' of Beef Braised *with a Rich Glaze (and more!)*

The 'piece' is a cut of beef taken from the chuck steak, which you can get from the butcher. Chuck is normally sold diced and used for stews and pies. The texture is reasonably soft and open. This means that, while braising or stewing, the meat is absorbing all of the sauce it is being cooked in. Consequently, you end up with very tender meat, which can be carved with a spoon. Closer and firmer cuts, such as topside or sirloin, stay firm and all the pores close during cooking, so although they become tender they are also quite dry to eat.

This dish is served with roasted onions filled with turnip purée. To lift the flavours of the purée, I've added some diced bone marrow, purely an optional extra, but a good one. You can of course leave the onions as they are and omit the turnip purée from the recipe.

Serves 6

6 x 225 g (8 oz) chuck joints,
    trimmed of all sinews and tied
A knob of butter
Salt and pepper

For the Vegetable *Mirepoix*:

1 onion, roughly chopped
1 carrot, roughly chopped
½ leek, roughly chopped
2 celery sticks, roughly chopped
A knob of butter

For the Sauce:

4 tomatoes, roughly chopped
1 bottle of red wine
900 ml (1½ pints) Beef Stock, not
    too strong (page 242; good-quality
    stock cubes can be used) or water
6 onions, halved through middle,
    skins left on
A knob of butter
300 ml (10 fl oz) *Jus*/Gravy
    (page 242) or alternative
    (page 243)
25–50 g (1–2 oz) bone marrow
    (optional), soaked in water for
    24–48 hours
350 g (12 oz) Turnip Purée,
    (page 152)
Salt and pepper

Pre-heat the oven to 190°C/375°F/Gas Mark 5. Cook the vegetable *mirepoix* in a braising dish with a knob of butter for 5–6 minutes until beginning to colour and soften. Add the tomatoes and continue to cook for a further 5–6 minutes. Add the red wine and bring to the boil. The wine can now be left to boil and reduce by three-quarters. This will give a powerful red-wine flavour to the finished sauce. Add the beef stock or water and bring to the simmer.

Heat a frying-pan. Season the mini chuck joints with salt and pepper. Add a knob of butter to the pan and fry the joints, sealing them on all sides. Lift the beef from the pan and place in the braising dish. Return to the simmer and cover with a lid. Place the pot in the oven and leave to braise, turning the meat every half hour or so for 2–2½ hours.

While the meat is braising, caramelize the onions. Sit the onions, flesh-side down and skins left on, in a roasting tray with a knob of butter. Cover with foil and place in the oven, with the beef. After half an hour, remove the foil. This will have helped create steam and lightly softened the onions, releasing their natural juices. For the next 40–45 minutes, the juices will begin to caramelize while the onions are roasting. After the cooking time, pierce with a knife to check they are tender. If not, then cook for a further 20–30 minutes. Once tender, the onions should have caramelized to a golden brown with tinges of burnt colour.

After 2 hours, lift one of the joints from the pan and check for tenderness. The beef must really be overcooked to be at its best. When you are testing the meat, it should start to break away with just a little pressure. If not ready, return it to the oven for a further 30 minutes. The meat can sometimes take up to 3 hours.

Once cooked, remove the joints from the stock, cover and keep warm. Strain the stock and bring to the boil, reducing by at least half to two-thirds. Once reduced, add the finished *jus*/gravy. This will thicken the cooking liquor, giving you a good sauce consistency. Season with salt and pepper. At this stage I like to take 150 ml (5 fl oz) of the sauce and reduce it further to a very thick, shiny consistency – it also becomes very sticky! This I use to brush the meat before serving, giving it the most incredible shiny finish.

The bone marrow really is an optional extra. If using, it needs to have been soaked in cold water for 24–48 hours. This cleans the marrow, giving you an almost pure white finish. Divide the marrow into 5 mm (¼ in) pieces and quickly warm in a knob of butter. Heat the turnip purée and add the bone marrow. Remove the skins of the onions. I like to remove some of the centre of the onions and spoon in some of the turnip purée. Spoon the purée into the onions. Sit the 'pieces' of beef on top and drizzle the heavily reduced glaze over. The remaining sauce can be offered separately.

Note: The 'pieces' of beef can be served with the garnish of your choice, so the stuffed onions become an extra to the basic recipe. Good Mashed Potatoes (page 140) and spinach are delicious with it!

Home-made Individual Pies

This is an introduction to a combination of flavours that has unlimited variations and could become a complete book on its own. Making individual pies is a lovely bonus for the eater, who breaks through the crisp pastry to find a delicious filling. But they don't have to be individual at all; one large pie (approximately 25 cm/10 in in diameter) presented at the table is also very exciting. Cooking the fillings in pie dishes with just a pastry topping will also work, so feel free to adapt these recipes to suit you.

This first recipe is for the quantity of pastry needed to line and top four moulds. After that you have some recipes and ideas for fillings, which are all cooked and finished separately before moulding.

Makes 4 Pies
750 g (1½ lb) Shortcrust pastry, or
Rich Shortcrust Pepper Pastry
(page 224)

225 g (8 oz) Quick Puff Pastry
(page 225), rolled and cut into
11 cm (4½ in) circles
1 egg

The metal pastry rings I use for this recipe are 10 cm (4 in) in diameter and 7.5 cm (3 in) high. The rings should first be buttered. Sit them on a greaseproof-paper-lined baking tray. Roll out the shortcrust pastry and cut out four 10 cm (4 in) circles. Sit one in the base of each ring. Roll the remaining pastry and cut it into strips wide enough to line the sides of the rings. If you are making one large pie, cut out one 25 cm (10 in) disc of pastry and one wide strip for the sides. Once in place, press the pastry along the bottom edge, so that it makes a good seal with the base and then all the way around the sides, so it comes a little above the ring to provide an edge to join to the puff pastry lid. Line each mould with greaseproof paper or foil and fill with baking beans or rice. Leave to rest in the fridge for 20 minutes. Bake blind for 15–20 minutes at 200°/400°/Gas Mark 6, cooking them to a light golden colour. This will guarantee a crisp finish.

Make the filling of your choice (see pages 113–117) and allow it to cool completely.

To finish the pies, pre-heat the oven to 200°C/400°F/Gas Mark 6. Pack the filling into the baked pastry case. Save any excess sauce from the filling to serve with the pies. Brush egg around the edge of the pastry and sit the puff pastry lids on top, pressing to seal the two. Brush the lids with egg for a glazed finish. Cook the pies for 40–45 minutes. This will cook the puff pastry while heating the pie filling. Sit the pies on a plate or in large bowls, remove the pastry rings and pour any excess sauce from the filling around. The pies are ready to serve.

Note: One large pie will take 1–1¼ hours to cook. A filled pie dish with just a pastry lid will also take approximately 1 hour.

Hot Pork Pie

This idea is based on traditional cold pork pies. Cold pork pies have quite a spicy finish, so I decided to take those flavours and turn them into a hot dish.

Serves 4

4 pastry cases (see page 112)

For the Stew:

900 g (2 lb) diced shoulder of pork

2 onions, roughly chopped

1.2 litres (2 pints) Chicken Stock
   (page 240) or alternative
   (page 243)

Fresh thyme sprig

A few fresh sage leaves

¼ teaspoon mace

¼ teaspoon mixed spice

¼ teaspoon English mustard powder

A knob of butter

Salt and pepper

For the Sauce:

Pork cooking liquor (once pork has
   been stewed)

300 ml (10 fl oz) double cream

A squeeze of lemon juice

Salt and pepper

For the Onion Mix:

4 onions, sliced

A knob of butter

½ teaspoon chopped fresh thyme

½ teaspoon chopped fresh sage

¼ teaspoon mace

¼ teaspoon mixed spice

¼ teaspoon English mustard powder

Salt and pepper

Place all the stew ingredients in a saucepan and bring to the simmer. Stew gently for 50–60 minutes until the pork is tender. Lift the pork from the stock and keep it covered. Strain the stock and reduce it by half to two-thirds, giving you a good, strong-flavoured pork reduction. Add the double cream and bring to the simmer. Cook for 5–10 minutes until it coats the base of the spoon, before adding a squeeze of lemon juice and seasoning with salt and pepper. The sauce is ready.

For the onion mix, cook the onions in the butter, without letting them colour, for 5–6 minutes, with the herbs and spices. Once softened, season with salt and pepper and leave to cool.

Mix together the cooked pork, onions and a few spoonfuls of the sauce to moisten. Check for seasoning. Spoon the mixture into the cooked pastry cases and cover with the lids as instructed on page 112. These can now be baked and served with the remaining sauce poured around.

Note: When filling the pie moulds, the pork and onions could be layered alternately, just spooning a little sauce between each layer. The spices used give you a flavour very similar to the traditional pork pie, but with a completely different, hot texture.

Chicken and Leek Pie

This recipe can be made with just chicken breasts or boned chicken legs. A combination of both can also be used.

Serves 4

6 chicken breasts, skinned and
    cut into 2.5 cm (1 in) dice
2 medium leeks, cut into 2.5 cm
    (1 in) pieces
4 pastry cases (see page 112)
A knob of butter
2 onions, diced

1 garlic clove, crushed
600 ml (1 pint) Chicken Stock
    (page 240) or alternative
    (page 243)
300 ml (10 fl oz) double cream
Salt and pepper
A squeeze of lemon juice

In a saucepan, melt the butter and fry the chicken for 2–3 minutes. Add the onions and continue to cook for another 3–4 minutes. Add the garlic, chicken stock and seasoning. Bring to the simmer and cook for 15–20 minutes until the chicken is tender. While the chicken is cooking, plunge the leeks into salted, boiling water and cook for 2–3 minutes until tender. Drain and leave to cool.

Lift the chicken and onions from the stock and strain the stock through a sieve. Reduce the stock by two-thirds and then add the cream. Bring to the simmer and reduce to a coating-sauce consistency. Season and flavour with a squeeze of lemon juice.

Once all has cooked, mix the chicken with the leeks and moisten with half of the sauce. Divide between the pastry cases and finish and cook as instructed on page 112. The remaining chicken sauce can be warmed and poured around the pies before serving.

Note: Mushrooms can also be added to give the pie another flavour.

Bacon and Spinach Pie *with Mustard and Broad Bean Sauce*

This recipe has two options – the bacon confit used in the salad on page 38, just sliced and layered with the spinach (that's the best version); or buy some streaky or green (unsmoked) back bacon pieces and shallow-fry or boil them and then layer them. The sauce is the same for either version.

Serves 4

4 pastry cases (see page 112)

For the Pie Filling:

900 g (2 lb) Confit of Bacon (page 38)

900 g (2 lb) spinach, picked and washed

2 onions, sliced

A knob of butter

Salt and pepper

For the Sauce:

2 shallots or ½ onion, finely chopped

1 garlic clove, sliced

2–3 rashers of smoked streaky bacon, chopped

A knob of butter

250 ml (8 fl oz) white wine

600 ml (1 pint) Chicken Stock (page 240) or alternative (page 243)

150 ml (5 fl oz) double cream

English mustard, to taste (optional)

175 g (6 oz) fresh or frozen broad beans

Salt and pepper

To make the sauce, cook the shallots or onion, garlic and streaky bacon in butter for 5–6 minutes, until softened. Add the wine and reduce until almost dry. Add the chicken stock and reduce by two-thirds; this should take 8–10 minutes. Add the double cream and cook for 10–15 minutes. Season the sauce and strain it through a sieve. Add ½ teaspoon of English mustard and taste for quantity and strength. If you prefer more, simply add it to taste.

With the sauce I like to drop in cooked fresh broad beans a minute or two before serving. To cook the broad beans, drop into salted, boiling water and boil for 6–7 minutes until tender. Refresh in iced water before removing their outer skins and adding to the sauce. If using frozen broad beans, simply defrost, shell and add a minute or two before serving.

For the confit of bacon and spinach pie: cook the sliced onions in the butter for 3–4 minutes until soft and slightly golden. Add the washed spinach leaves. Season with salt and pepper and cook for 3–4 minutes, stirring to ensure even cooking. The spinach can now be left to cool.

Carve the confit into thin, 7–10 cm (3–4 in) slices. Lay 2–3 slices in the base of the pie dish and then top with some spinach and onion mix. Repeat the bacon slices and spinach until all the mixture is used between the moulds. Spoon 2 tablespoons of the sauce into each pie and cover.

Bake as instructed on page 112. Heat the remaining sauce with the cooked broad beans and pour around each pie.

Note: The cooking time can be between 3 and 10 minutes for broad beans, depending on their size.

Variation: If you don't have the bacon confit, buy 900 g (2 lb) green back or streaky bacon, remove the rind and cut into 1 cm (½ in) dice. When cooking the shallots or onion for the sauce, add the bacon pieces. Continue to the point of adding the stock – you will need an extra 300 ml (10 fl oz) of stock to cover the bacon. Water can also be used. Bring to the simmer and cook for 30 minutes until the bacon is tender. Remove the bacon pieces and reduce the stock by two-thirds. Finish the method as for the main recipe opposite. The spinach and bacon can now be layered in the pastry cases with a spoonful or two of the sauce added to moisten. Cover and bake as instructed on page 112. Serve the finished sauce (with or without broad beans!) poured around the pies.

Home-made Pie Extras

You now have three solid recipes for pies which are all excellent. I do prefer to use cooked ingredients rather than cooking pies or puddings from raw. This means you have time to get the consistency and the amount of sauce just right before baking. The other bonus is being able to make the filling and sauce a day or two in advance, refrigerating them and then using them for pies when needed. Here are a few extra ideas for more pies:

- Any game, such as venison, pigeon or pheasant, can be turned into pies.

- For a vegetarian pie: stack and layer lightly cooked ratatouille and serve with a tomato salad or sauce.

- Don't forget the classic British steak and kidney pie.

The choice is yours!

Steak and 'Kidney Pie'

This most classic of British dishes can be found just about anywhere in the UK. But not like this! That's quite a statement because I've eaten many excellent steak and kidney pies and puddings. The reason is that this dish is a piece of steak (as in the recipe on page 110) served with a separate kidney and onion pie, so the two separate dishes are presented together to create one classic.

The cut of steak and the method of cooking the steak is exactly the same as for the 'piece of beef' recipe (though I am using slightly smaller cuts because they are pies). The kidney pies are very easy to make with the creamed, bittersweet onions coming from the recipe on page 132.

Serves 6

6 × 175 g (6 oz) chuck joints
   (individually trimmed and tied
   pieces of chuck steak)
A knob of butter
Salt and pepper

For the Pies:

225 g (8 oz) Shortcrust Pastry
   (page 224)
8 lamb's kidneys or 225–275 g
   (8–10 oz) veal kidneys cut into
   1 cm (½ in) dice
A knob of butter or trickle of
   cooking oil
½ quantity Bittersweet Onion Tart
   mix (page 132)
1 egg yolk, beaten
225 g (8 oz) Quick Puff Pastry
   (page 225), rolled and cut into
   8–11 cm (3½–4½ in) circles
Salt and pepper

For the Sauce:

A knob of butter
Fresh thyme sprig
3 tomatoes, roughly chopped
1 bottle of red wine
900 ml (1½ pints) Beef Stock
   (not too strong) (page 242;
   good-quality stock cubes can
   be used) or water
3–4 lamb's kidneys, roughly diced
300 ml (10 fl oz) Jus/Gravy
   (page 242) or alternative
   (page 243)
Salt and pepper

For the Vegetable *Mirepoix*:

1 onion, roughly chopped
1 carrot, roughly chopped
2 celery sticks, roughly chopped
   (optional)

To make the sauce, melt a knob of butter with the *mirepoix* of vegetables and the sprig of thyme. Cook for 3–4 minutes until softened and then add the chopped tomatoes. Continue to cook for a further 3–4 minutes.

Add the red wine, bring to the boil and reduce by three-quarters. This should take 5–6 minutes. Now just add the beef stock and bring to the simmer.

POULTRY AND MEAT

While the sauce is being made, season the chuck 'joints' with salt and pepper. Heat a frying-pan with a knob of butter and colour the beef joints on all sides. Add them to the simmering stock. The beef will take approximately 2½ hours to become completely tender: it needs to be slightly 'overcooked'. After 2 hours, check the texture of the meat. When you press the joint, the meat should start to break away very easily; if not, continue to cook for a further 30 minutes (or more).

Once completely cooked, remove the joints and cover with cling film.

To finish the sauce, sauté the roughly diced lamb's kidney in some butter for 3–4 minutes. Add to the beef cooking liquor. Reduce the liquor by half, skimming off any impurities. This will increase the strength and flavour of the sauce with the kidney giving an extra taste. Once reduced, add the *jus*/gravy. Bring to the simmer and then strain through a sieve. You should have a well-flavoured liquor with a sauce consistency. I now like to pour off 150 ml (5 fl oz) and reduce it by at least half again to a very thick, shiny consistency – it also becomes very sticky. This will be used to brush or roll the finished beef joints before serving. It leaves the meat just glistening.

Season the remaining sauce, if needed (if the sauce is too thin but strong in taste, it can be lightly thickened with cornflour or arrowroot).

The pies can be made while the steaks are cooking. Butter six 6–7.5 cm (2½–3 in) tartlet tins. Pre-heat the oven to 200°C/400°F/Gas Mark 6. Roll out the shortcrust pastry, cut into large discs and use to line the tartlet tins, leaving any excess pastry hanging over the edges of the tins. Line with greaseproof paper or foil, fill with baking beans and bake blind for 15–20 minutes. Once cool, remove the greaseproof paper or foil and beans. Slice away any excess pastry to leave a neat finish.

The 1 cm (½ in) diced kidneys can now be pan-fried very quickly in a hot pan with butter or cooking oil. This takes about 3–4 minutes and is just to seal the kidneys. Season with salt and pepper and leave to cool. Once cool, mix some of the bittersweet onion mix with the lamb's or veal kidneys to bind. Spoon some more onion mix into the base of the tartlet mounds and then top with the sautéed kidney mixture.

Now top with more onion mix to leave a good dome shape. Brush around the edge of the pastry with egg yolk and top with the puff pastry, pressing and sealing all around. Leave the pies to rest in the refrigerator for at least 20 minutes. Once set, trim off any excess pastry around the sides. Brush the tops with egg yolk.

To finish the dish, bake the pies for 15–20 minutes until golden. Put the steaks back into the finished sauce to warm through. Remove them and roll or brush with the reduced sticky sauce.

To serve, sit the steaks and pies side by side in bowls or on plates and pour some sauce around.

Note: This dish can be made well in advance – the steaks will then take up to 20–30 minutes to reheat in the sauce. The pies will keep, refrigerated, for 24 hours before being baked.

Boiled Brisket of Beef *and Vegetable Stew*

Brisket is a cut of beef taken from the forequarter. It is normally pickled in brine, which is a combination of salt, saltpetre and water. The beef can be kept in brine for up to 10 days. This will help tenderize the cut. If buying brisket already salted, I suggest it is soaked in fresh water for 24–48 hours to release some of the salt flavour. This goes very well with mashed potatoes.

Serves 4

900 g (2 lb) brisket, soaked
  in fresh water
1 carrot
1 onion
1 bay leaf
2 celery sticks
1 leek
Fresh thyme sprig

For the Vegetable Garnish:

2 onions, cut into 1 cm (½ in) dice
3–4 celery sticks, cut into
  1 cm (½ in) dice
1 small swede cut into
  1 cm (½ in) dice
2 large carrots, cut into
  1 cm (½ in) dice
2 leeks, cut into 1 cm (½ in) dice
A knob of butter
2–3 tablespoons whipping cream
Salt and pepper
Chopped fresh parsley and thyme

Cover the brisket with fresh cold water in a large saucepan and bring to the boil. Once boiling, pour the water off and refresh the beef in cold water. Once refreshed, top up with more cold water, adding the whole vegetables and thyme. Cover and bring to the simmer, skimming away any impurities. The beef will take 2½–3 hours to become totally tender.

While the beef is cooking, prepare the garnish vegetables and cook them separately. Cook the onions and celery in a knob of butter without colouring. Blanch the swede, carrots and leeks in water or some of the brisket cooking-liquor until tender.

When the beef is cooked, drain off two-thirds of the cooking liquor and reduce to 300 ml (10 fl oz). Add the cream and all of the garnishing vegetables. Warm through and season with salt and pepper. Add a knob of butter and stir in. Add the chopped herbs.

Carve the brisket and place the slices in bowls or on plates. I prefer to serve this dish in large bowls and treat the sauce as a beef and vegetable soup. If the 'soup' is too thick, loosen it with more of the stock. Spoon the vegetables and sauce over and serve.

This dish will eat very well with a bowl of Mashed Potatoes (page 140).

Note: You could use whole, fairly small vegetables for the garnish (you will need to cut swede in chunks and celery sticks in half). Simply boil the beef in water and add the vegetables towards the end of cooking, serving them as the garnish.

Tournedos of Lamb *with Snails, Onions and Bacon*

Tournedos is a description usually used for beef fillet steak. Lamb doesn't carry fillets of that size but with this recipe and method the fillet is created from a leg of lamb. The technique breaks down the meat's textures, making it very tender. On top of that, the lamb prepared in this way will give you at least eight portions and, if it's a large leg, up to twelve. Snails are not to everyone's taste, but the snails I am using are French and tinned, not fresh. This makes the job a lot easier and the quality and tenderness is superb. They have a mushroom-like texture and are not chewy at all. They are well worth trying, if not in this recipe then perhaps as the traditional snails with garlic and parsley on hot toast. The tournedos really are worth having a go at and I know you'll agree when you see the results. If you tell your friends they are going to be eating leg of lamb and these turn up, it will be a more-than-nice surprise.

Serves 8–12

1 leg of lamb, boned and all fat removed, weighing approximately 1.5-1.75 kg (3½-4 lb)

225 g (8 oz) pig's caul (crépine) or 15–18 rashers of smoked streaky bacon (optional)

Salt and pepper

A pinch of ground cumin

For the Garnish (for 8 portions):

1 bottle of red wine

600 ml (1 pint) Veal or Beef Jus/Gravy (page 242) or alternative (page 243)

30–35 tinned snails (optional)

450 g (1 lb) small button onions, peeled

225–275 g (8–10 oz) piece of smoked or unsmoked streaky bacon, cut into 1 cm (½ in) dice

50–75 g (2–3 oz) spinach, cooked, per portion (optional)

A knob of butter

Salt and pepper

Separate the boned leg of lamb into individual muscles by breaking apart the membranes which hold them together. The next job is to remove all the sinews, which doesn't take long but is even quicker done by your butcher! This will break down the meat even more, leaving you with absolutely sinew-free, lean pieces of meat. It is important that all sinews are totally removed. This will guarantee the tenderness of the meat.

Once all is cleaned, you will have a few meat scraps. These need to be minced or processed (make sure you have about 100 g/4 oz). Season with salt and pepper and a pinch of ground cumin. This 'farce' will be used to help hold the other cuts together when you start to assemble the tournedos. All of the remaining meat can now be cut into strips, approximately 10 cm (4 in) long and 1 cm (½ in) wide (lamb fingers). Next rinse the pig's caul (crépine), if using, in cold water, to loosen and clean it. Caul is not easy to get hold of so, if you can't find it, simply just use tin foil or lay thin rashers of unsmoked streaky bacon, vertically, side by side, in a line on the foil first.

The lamb finger fillets can now be laid on the caul, foil or bacon and foil. Lay them lengthways (in the opposite direction to the bacon), side by side, which will give you a line of meat approximately 7.5–10 cm (3–4 in) wide and 30 cm (12 in) long. Spread the minced lamb thinly over it until all is used and then roll or hand-shape into a cylinder. Wrap tightly in the caul, buttered foil or bacon and foil and then re-wrap in more foil, twisting at either end to firm the wrap. Leave to set in the refrigerator for 1–2 hours.

Pre-heat the oven to 200°C/400°F/Gas Mark 6. Cut across the cylinder, still in the foil, into tournedos (fillet-steak shapes) 3–5 cm (1½–2 in) deep. This should give you at least eight portions. The portions are not huge but, remember, they do have quite a considerable quantity of garnish to give the flavours a lift. If caul or bacon have been used to wrap the meat, remove the outer foil. These portions must now be tied with two pieces of string. This will guarantee they keep their shape. If only foil has been used, tie string around the outside of the foil. The tournedos are now ready for cooking.

The next step is to make the garnish. I have kept the sauce to its simplest. All you need to do is to rapidly boil the wine until reduced by three-quarters and then add the *jus*/gravy. Cook for 5–10 minutes and it is made. It will take on the flavour of the garnishes that will be warmed through in it to increase the flavour.

The garnishes can be prepared and cooked well in advance. The snails just need to be halved. Pan-fry the button onions in some of the butter on a medium heat. This will colour them slowly while they are becoming tender. Once golden and almost dark (this is the natural caramelizing of their juices and sugars), remove from the pan. Fry the bacon in its own fat and on a medium heat to give the bacon plenty of time to crispen.

Add some melted butter to the spinach and season. Pan-fry or microwave when needed.

To cook the lamb, season with salt and pepper and pan-fry carefully in butter on all sides. Transfer to a roasting tin if you've not used an ovenproof frying-pan and finish in the oven for 8–10 minutes. The lamb will still be pink in the centre (medium). Remove from the oven and leave to relax and tenderize for 4-5 minutes. While the lamb is relaxing, add the garnishes (snails, button onions and bacon) to the sauce and simmer to warm them through and infuse the sauce with their flavour.

To serve, spoon some spinach in the centre of the plates and pour sauce and garnish around. Remove any string and foil from the lamb and sit the tournedos on top of the spinach.

Note: You can add a few black peppercorns, a bay leaf and some chopped shallots or onions to the red-wine reduction to strengthen the flavour. Or, instead of a wine reduction, a good lamb stock can be made by roasting the chopped leg of lamb bones with some carrots, onions, leeks and celery, garlic, thyme and peppercorns, cooking them in about 600 ml–1.2 litres (1–2 pints) chicken stock for a couple of hours and then reducing it by three-quarters. This will give you a good, strong, lamb flavour, which, when added to the *jus*/gravy, will need no wine at all. Just simmer and strain and an excellent lamb sauce is made.

You do not have to stick with this garnish and sauce. A good redcurrant gravy, with sautéed potatoes and Spring greens, is another option.

vegetarian
and vegetables

*V*arious flavours and tastes have been added to some of the vegetables featured in this section to give them a whole new dimension. This always helps make a feature of them and will also help to lift the flavour of a simple roast or other basic main course.

The Lemon-buttered Broccoli (page 149), Spicy Fried Cauliflower (page 155) or French Bean Purée (page 156) lend themselves to many a dish.

As for vegetarian main courses, how does Pasta with 'Pork Stuffing' Sauce (page 136) sound? Not exactly vegetarian, but it is. The sauce simply uses some of the stuffing ingredients; it tastes delicious and is obviously also a great accompaniment to virtually any pork recipe.

The Green Tomato *Tarte Tatin* (page 130) will give you a whole new feeling and taste for green tomatoes, which are normally just thrown into a chutney. The Potato and Onion Torte (page 126) is absolutely packed with flavour and the Hot-pot (page 141) is a dream. It's been put together by taking all of the classic ingredients from Lancashire hot-pot (featured in *Rhodes Around Britain*), bar the lamb, and building them into a potato and vegetable hot-pot cake. Cutting into and through all of these vegatable layers gives you a lot of texture and taste in one bite.

The vegetables can be found in their own seasons throughout the year, so when the curly kale has finished, move on to broccoli, and and then leeks and so on. Swap ideas and techniques from different recipes and apply them to a variety of vegetables, or just keep to a recipe and technique that suits every vegetable: simple and tasty.

Roast Mushroom and Leek Shepherd's Pie

This is an easy vegetarian recipe which becomes almost 'meaty', using the large flat or cup mushrooms. The dish is layered like a lasagne with the mashed potato piped or forked across the top.

Serves 4–6

900 g (2 lb) flat or open-cup
   mushrooms, wiped and stalks
   removed
4–5 leeks, finely shredded
Olive or cooking oil
A knob of butter
1 onion, sliced
750–900 g (1½–2 lb) Mashed
   Potatoes (page 140)

Juice of ½–1 lemon
Salt and pepper
1 teaspoon chopped fresh parsley
   (optional)
1 teaspoon chopped fresh tarragon
   (optional)
1 teaspoon chopped fresh basil
   (optional)

Pre-heat the oven to 230°C/450°/Gas Mark 8.

Heat a frying-pan or roasting tray with a tablespoon or two of olive or cooking oil. Season the mushrooms with salt and pepper and place in the pan or tray. Fry the mushrooms on a high heat, colouring them well. After a minute, turn them in the tray and repeat the colouring (another tablespoon of oil may be needed). Now roast the mushrooms in the hot oven for 5–6 minutes. Once cooked, remove and keep to one side. Because of the fast, hot frying and roasting, the mushrooms will have kept all of their juices, giving a richer flavour.

To cook the leeks, heat a tablespoon of olive oil with the butter and add the sliced onion. Cook on a moderate heat for a few minutes until softened with very little colour. Increase the heat, add the shredded leeks and season with salt and pepper. Stir for 3–4 minutes and the leeks should now be tender.

Using a buttered ovenproof vegetable or shepherd's pie dish, carve the mushrooms into slices and lay in the base of pie dish. Spoon some leeks on top and then repeat with the mushrooms; continue to layer the ingredients until all are used up.

The mashed potato can now be finished with the lemon juice and chopped herbs, if using. Spread it, fork or pipe it on top. Brush with butter and finish under the grill until golden brown.

Note: If using plain mashed potato to top the 'pie', why not finish it with grated Cheddar or with little pieces of Gorgonzola Rarebit (page 233) sprinkled over and grilled.

Potato and Onion Torte or Pie *with* *Mushroom Sauce*

Here's another pastry-based dish that can be made into individual pies or one large one.

If making individuals, I tend to line the 7.5–9 cm (3–4 in) tins with Shortcrust Pastry (page 224) (or the Rich Shortcrust Pepper Pastry on page 224) and blind-bake them before filling and topping with Quick Puff Pastry (page 225). This gives you a combination of two pastries with completely different textures working together. If I'm making one large 'pie', I tend to go for a complete puff pastry finish, although the shortcrust base will also work, to give you that texture combination.

With this dish, I'm serving a mushroom and thyme sauce, which is not essential, but delicious. Its basis is a very tasty mushroom stock, which will give the sauce a powerful mushroom flavour. If you're short of time, use a good-quality vegetable stock cube instead.

Serves 4

225 g (8 oz) puff pastry, rolled into
  18 cm (7 in) and 23 cm (9 in)
  discs, or 4 x 7.5–9 cm (3–4 in)
  shortcrust pastry tartlet cases,
  baked blind, plus 175 g (6 oz)
  puff pastry, rolled into
  4 x 12 cm (5 in) discs
1 egg yolk
A little coarse sea salt (optional)

For the Filling:

4–5 large potatoes, boiled
  in their skins
3 large onions, sliced
A knob of butter
1 teaspoon light soft brown or
  demerara sugar
Salt and pepper

For the Mushroom Stock:

225 g (8 oz) open-cup mushrooms,
  chopped
1 garlic clove, crushed
Fresh thyme sprig
1 tablespoon olive oil
300 ml (10 fl oz) water

For the Sauce:

150 ml (5 fl oz) of reduced
  Mushroom Stock (see above)
3 tablespoons double cream
225 g (8 oz) open-cup, button or
  paris mushrooms (chestnut),
  quartered
50–75 g (2–3 oz) unsalted butter
Salt and pepper
½ teaspoon fresh thyme leaves

Pre-heat the oven to 200°C/400°F/Gas Mark 6. If making individual pies, place the blind-baked tartlet cases onto a baking sheet. If making the large torte, sit the 18 cm (7 in) puff-pastry disc on a greaseproof-paper-lined baking tray.

Peel and slice the cooked potatoes while still warm and season with salt and pepper. Melt a little butter and trickle over. This will be nicely absorbed by the warm potatoes.

Shallow-fry the sliced onions in a knob of butter, allowing them to soften and take on a rich golden colour. Add the teaspoon of sugar and continue to fry. This will give a mild, sweet, caramelized flavour. Season and leave to cool.

Once the potatoes and onions have cooled, sit a layer of the potatoes onto the pastry disc, leaving a 1 cm (½ in) border, or into the base of each pastry case. Spread on some caramelized onions and then another layer of potato. Repeat this process, forming a dome shape with the lasrger torte until all the ingredients or almost all are used up.

Brush around the border of the tart(s) with egg yolk and cover with puff pastry discs. The egg yolk will help seal the pastries together. On individual tarts, just trim any excess pastry away. On the large tart, the border can be pinched and shaped; use a cutter or simply take an 18 cm (7 in) flan or pie tin and cut around to finish. Leave refrigerated to rest for at least 20 minutes before baking.

Meanwhile, make the stock. Fry the mushrooms, garlic and thyme in the olive oil for a few minutes. Add the water and bring to the simmer. Cook for 15–20 minutes and then strain through a sieve, squeezing all of the juices from the mushrooms. Reduce to 150 ml (5 fl oz), doubling the flavour of the stock.

Brush the pie(s) with more egg yolk to obtain an even richer golden colour and, if you fancy a slightly crunchy finish, sprinkle lightly with a little coarse sea salt. Individual pies will take 15–20 minutes to cook and a large pie will need 25–30 minutes.

To finish the sauce and give it a creamier taste, add the double cream to the stock and bring to the simmer.

Pan-fry the mushrooms in a small knob of the butter until tender and season with salt and pepper. Add the remaining butter to the sauce, gently shaking the pan so the butter and sauce emulsify. Add the fried mushrooms and thyme, season with salt and pepper and the sauce is ready.

Serve the smaller pies whole with mushroom sauce poured around; cut the large pie into four portions, offering the sauce separately.

Note: Lots more flavours can be stacked in the pie: ratatouille, spinach and mushrooms are just a few ideas.

Stilton and Spinach Tart or Pie

Stilton isn't the only cheese I am going to use in this recipe. To help the flavours along,
I'm adding a little grated Parmesan.

The difference between a tart and this pie is the pastry. The pie variation in this recipe
doesn't use any pastry at all: all I have done is to layer the ingredients into a lasagne or
vegetable dish. It works very well and you don't have to make any pastry!

Serves 4 as a pie or
6 as a tart
175–225 g (6–8 oz) Quick Puff
 Pastry (page 225), or frozen puff
 pastry, thawed
900 g (2 lb) picked and washed
 spinach
225 g (8 oz) crumbled Stilton
A knob of butter
150 ml (5 fl oz) double cream
1 egg

2 tablespoons finely grated
 Parmesan
Salt and pepper

For the Cream Dressing:
4 tablespoons single cream
A squeeze of lemon juice
2 tablespoons walnut oil
Salt and pepper
1 heaped teaspoon chopped
 fresh chives

Pre-heat the oven to 200°C/400°F/Gas Mark 6. If making tart(s), butter a 23 cm (9 in) loose-based flan ring or four 10 cm (4 in) tartlet tins. Roll out the pastry and line the tin(s), leaving some excess pastry attached. This will prevent the pastry from sinking into the tins(s). Line with greaseproof paper or foil and baking beans or rice. Bake blind for 15-20 minutes. Remove the paper and beans and, once cooled, trim off any excess pastry to leave a neat finish.

If making a pie, go straight on to melt the butter in a large saucepan with 2–3 tablespoons of water. Add the washed spinach and cook on a high heat, stirring for 2–3 minutes. The spinach will become soft, cooked and tender. Once cooked, pour into a sieve or colander and leave to cool. Once cold, squeeze out excess liquid. Season with salt and pepper.

Mix the double cream with the egg and one tablespoon of the Parmesan. The spinach and Stilton can now be alternately layered, spooning some of the cream mix between each layer into either the large flan, the individual tartlets or an ovenproof vegetable or lasagne dish. Sprinkle the remaining Parmesan on top and transfer to the oven. The individual tartlets will take just 15–20 minutes with the larger flan or the pie needing 20–25 minutes.

If it is a tart, whether individual or large, it will eat very well, presented on some green leaves with the single cream dressing, which is made as follows. Warm the single cream. Add the lemon juice and whisk in the walnut oil. Season with salt and pepper. Add the chopped chives and spoon around the tarts. The dish is ready to serve.

Note: The Parmesan can be left out of the cream mixture.

Green Tomato *Tarte Tatin*

Tarte tatin is a French classic associated with apples. The apples are caramelized in butter and sugar and topped with pastry while still in the frying-pan. This is baked and then turned over onto a plate to serve. It looks stunning and the flavour is immense. Yes, you've guessed it, that's more or less exactly what I'm going to do, but on a savoury note with green tomatoes. You will need an ovenproof 20 cm (8 in) frying-pan. Serve with a simple, tossed salad.

Serves 2
(or 1 if you're very hungry)

6 green tomatoes
Olive oil
A knob of butter
1 teaspoon of demerara sugar
100–175 g (4–6 oz) Quick Puff
    Pastry (page 225) or frozen puff
    pastry, thawed
Salt and pepper

For the Dressing or Garnish
(optional)

4 tablespoons olive oil
1 tablespoon balsamic vinegar
Salt and pepper
4 dessertspoons soured cream
A squeeze of lemon or lime juice
A few fresh basil leaves, torn
½ small red onion, finely sliced
A few fresh Parmesan shavings
A little coarse sea salt and coarsely
    ground black pepper (optional)

Pre-heat the oven to 230°C/450°F/Gas Mark 8, or a little lower. Heat the ovenproof frying-pan with a trickle of olive oil. Halve the tomatoes through the middle. Season the tomatoes with salt and pepper and place, flesh-side down, in a circular pattern, totally filling the pan. Increase the heat so the tomatoes are frying and not stewing. After 1 minute, add the knob of butter and sprinkle with the sugar. Continue to fry for a further minute or two, shaking the pan occasionally so that they are evenly coated with butter. The tomatoes will have started to caramelize. Remove the pan from the stove and leave to cool.

Roll out the pastry into a 20 cm (8 in) circle. Put the pastry on top of the tomatoes, pressing lightly to help it take on the shape of the tomato border. Bake the tart for 15–20 minutes until the pastry is crisp and golden. Turn the tart out onto a plate (remember, the handle will be hot!). You will have rich golden caramelized tomatoes looking straight at you. For an even richer, caramelized look, brush with more butter and sprinkle with a touch more sugar. Flash under the grill until it begins to bubble. Cut into two portions.

For the dressing, mix the oil with the vinegar and season. Season the soured cream separately and add the lemon or lime juice. Spoon threads of the sour cream across the plates and repeat with the balsamic dressing.

Sit the tart portions on top or by the side of the dressings and sprinkle with the torn basil leaves, red onion slices and Parmesan shavings. The tart can be finished with a small sprinkling of coarse sea salt and black pepper.

Bittersweet Onion Tart *with Leek, Tomato and Lemon Dressing*

The bittersweet onion tart stands completely on its own as an idea and dish. The pastry is of a shortcrust variety, enriched with the flavour of black pepper to just give it a tasty bite.

The leek, tomato and lemon dressing is a combination of flavours that go very well with the tart. I also like to add mushrooms to the dressing for even more texture.

The tart can be served with a simple tossed salad or, as I suggest in the Note, it goes beautifully with Pan-fried or Grilled Liver (page 98).

Serves 6

1 quantity Rich Shortcrust Pepper
   Pastry (page 225)
6 onions, sliced
A knob of butter
1 teaspoon demerara sugar
Salt and pepper
300 ml (10 fl oz) double cream
2 eggs
A few salad leaves, to garnish

For the Dressing:

3–4 baby leeks, washed and sliced
3 tomatoes, blanched, skinned and
   seeded, cut into 6–8 wedges
12 button or chestnut mushrooms,
   cleaned and trimmed (optional)
4 tablespoons olive oil
Salt and pepper
Juice of 1 lemon

Pre-heat the oven to 200°C/400°F/Gas Mark 6. Butter six 10 cm (4 in) tartlet tins or a 25 cm (10 in), loose-based flan ring. Roll out the pastry and use it to line the tin(s), leaving some excess pastry attached. This will prevent the pastry from sinking into the tin(s). Line with greaseproof paper or foil and baking beans or rice. Bake blind for 20–25 minutes. Remove the paper and beans and, once cooled, trim off any excess pastry, leaving a neat finish.

Fry the onions in the butter over a high heat. This may have to be done in two or three stages, taking into account the quantity of onions being used. Fry until well softened and on the point of being burnt or caramelized, which will take 5–6 minutes. The burnt tinges (and we do want some of the onions burnt) will give us the bitter side to this dish. Once softened and coloured in the pan, add a good sprinkling of demerara sugar to caramelize the onions and add the note of sweetness against the bitter, 'burnt' flavour.

Once all the onions have been cooked, mix together and season with salt and pepper. Reduce the heat to low. Whisk the cream and eggs together and pour onto the onions while still on the stove. Stir for a few minutes until thickened but not scrambled. Remove from the stove and check for seasoning. Taste the mix (it will now be coffee-coloured) for the depth and balance of the bitterness and sweetness. If you feel it is too bitter, add a small sprinkling of sugar to the mixture.

The mixture can now be left to cool and refrigerated (it will keep for a few days). If you want to cook it straight away, while still warm, fill the pastry case(s) and bake in the oven until set. For the individual pies this will take only 8–10 minutes; for a larger flan allow 15–20 minutes. If the mixture has been left to cool and then refrigerated, the individuals will take 15 minutes and the larger one 25–30.

Once the tarts have set, they are ready to serve.

The dressing is quite simple and quick and holds lots of flavours that go very well with the bittersweet onion taste. If using mushrooms, quarter them and pan-fry in 2 tablespoons of olive oil for a few minutes until tender and golden. Remove them from the pan and add a tablespoon more olive oil. Fry the leeks until tender; add the cooked mushrooms and tomatoes. Season with salt and pepper, adding the last tablespoon of olive oil and finishing with the lemon juice.

This chunky dressing can now be spooned over and around the tarts. A few lettuce leaves or watercress can be used to finish the dish, sitting them on top of the tartlets.

Note: The pastry case(s) can be removed from the tin(s) before cooking with the filling; however, the rings are a good security and can simply be removed once finished.

Fresh herbs such as basil, tarragon, parsley, chervil and so on also go very well in the dressing. A little finely chopped fresh red chilli will add extra fire to the flavour!

More or less all the flavours used in the dressing, that is, the mushrooms, tomatoes and leeks, can be added to the bittersweet onion mixture to give the tarts even more texture.

The tart also goes well with the Pan-fried or Grilled Liver (page 98). You can serve it with the sherry-vinegar-based sauce from the Pan-fried Liver recipe and for the ultimate combination pan-fry a slice of *foie gras* and sit it on top of the tart!

Potato Gnocchi and Gnocchi Tartare

The word gnocchi means 'small dumpling'. There are several varieties of gnocchi: gnocchi parisienne, which is choux-paste-based; gnocchi romaine, which is semolina-based; gnocchi piedmontaise, which is potato-based.

This recipe is for piedmontaise gnocchi. Gnocchi are very easy to make and lend themselves to any course and any meal, whether accompanying a main course or as a complete vegetarian dish on its own. The potato variety goes very well with a good tomato sauce and lots of Parmesan; or simply roll the gnocchi in pesto sauce or good olive oil with chopped herbs, tomatoes and fresh olives. This is a basic recipe for potato-based gnocchi. I also give the ingredients for turning them into Gnocchi Tartare, using flavours from the classic mayonnaise-based tartare sauce: shallots, capers and tarragon.

Serves 6

1.2 kg (2½ lb) large potatoes
100–175 g (4–6 oz) plain flour
25 g (1 oz) butter or 2 teaspoons
   olive oil
1 egg
1 egg yolk
Salt and pepper
Grated nutmeg

For Gnocchi Tartare:

2 heaped tablespoons finely
   chopped shallots or onions
2 tablespoons olive oil
2 tablespoons chopped capers
1 tablespoon chopped fresh
   tarragon
1 tablespoon chopped fresh parsley
A knob of butter
Grated Parmesan

Cook the potatoes whole in salted, boiling water until tender. Peel the warm cooked potatoes and mash to a smooth texture (the potato can simply be pushed through a sieve). Add and mix in the flour, butter or olive oil, egg and egg yolk. Season with salt and pepper and a touch of nutmeg. Roll the mix on a floured surface into 1–2 cm (½–¾ in) balls.

The gnocchi are now ready to poach in simmering salted water for 3–4 minutes; 5 minutes is the maximum they will need. If using immediately, lift from the water and serve with a sauce of your choice and grated Parmesan. If cooking ahead, either refresh in cold water or leave to stand and cool on a cloth. They can be re-heated, perhaps by pan-frying, when needed.

To make gnocchi tartare, first cook the shallots or onions without letting them colour in the olive oil until softened. Allow to cool.

When adding the flour and eggs to the mashed potatoes to make the gnocchi, also add the tartare sauce ingredients. Prepare and cook as for the standard gnocchi. They are best then pan-fried to golden brown in butter to give a slightly crisp edge, and then rolled or sprinkled with Parmesan.

Pasta with 'Pork Stuffing' Sauce

I was going to call this a British pasta dish, but I'm not quite sure that pasta can really be called British! This is a vegetarian 'pork stuffing'. I've taken the traditional onion and sage combination and a couple of additions and turned them into a sauce topped with crisp, crunchy white breadcrumbs.

Serves 4

450 g (1 lb) fresh or dried noodles

A knob of butter

2 onions, finely chopped

1 garlic clove, crushed

150 ml (5 fl oz) apple juice or white wine

150 ml (5 fl oz) Vegetable Stock (page 240; good-quality stock cubes can be used)

150 ml (5 fl oz) double cream

A squeeze of lemon juice

12 fresh sage leaves, chopped

50 g (2 oz) pinenuts, toasted and chopped

50–75 g (2–3 oz) fresh white breadcrumbs, toasted to golden brown

Olive oil

Salt and pepper

Grated Parmesan (optional)

Melt the butter with the onions and garlic. Cook for 6–7 minutes until softened. Add the apple juice or white wine and reduce by three-quarters. Add the vegetable stock and reduce by half. Now it is time to add the double cream and simmer for a few minutes. Season with salt and pepper and add a squeeze of lemon juice to lift all the flavours. Keep warm while you cook the pasta.

Now it's time to cook the pasta. Fresh noodles take approximately 3–5 minutes, dried ones 10–12 minutes.

Mix the noodles with the sauce, adding the chopped sage, and check for seasoning. Spoon the noodles into bowls and sprinkle with the toasted pinenuts and breadcrumbs. Trickle with some olive oil and serve. The grated Parmesan can also be sprinkled on top or offered separately.

Note: If you prefer non-vegetarian pasta dishes, add strips of ham or bacon to the sauce.

Barbecued Vegetables

Most Summer barbecues are filled with steaks, burgers, chicken wings and sausages, all of which we enjoy, but how about a nice change? The variations of colours, textures and flavours with vegetables are almost unlimited! So here are some which I've chosen that will give you not only a great vegetarian dish but make a change for everybody's tastebuds this summer.

Serves 4

8 asparagus spears

6 baby leeks

4 baby fennel, or 1 large, quartered

2 small red onions, sliced in
   1 cm (½ in) rings

½ red pepper, seeded and cut in
   thick strips

½ yellow pepper, seeded and cut in
   thick strips

2 plum tomatoes, halved lengthways

1 courgette, sliced diagonally

8 tablespoons olive oil

1 lemon

Mustard Dressing
   (page 244, optional)

Salt and pepper

A few fresh basil and tarragon leaves

The asparagus, leeks and large fennel will all need to be blanched in salted, boiling water and refreshed before grilling.

The asparagus should be lightly peeled before blanching for 1–2 minutes. Trim the leeks, removing the tougher green ends, and blanch them for 2 minutes. Small fennels can be grilled from raw, but the large should first be quartered and then blanched for 2–3 minutes. To grill the vegetables, make sure the barbecue is very hot. Toss the vegetables in 2 tablespoons of oil.

Next, place the vegetables on the barbecue and then cook and turn them until they become slightly soft to touch and with golden brown tinges. This will only take a few minutes for each vegetable. If you do not have room to cook all the vegetables at the same time, it's best to cook the fennel, onions, peppers and tomatoes first, keeping them warm while the rest are cooking.

Once all the vegetables have been barbecued, season with salt and pepper and arrange on plates. Mix together the remaining olive oil and lemon juice and season with salt and pepper. This dressing can now be drizzled over the vegetables. I also like to repeat the same process with the mustard dressing. Simply sprinkle over the basil and tarragon leaves before serving. You now have a colourful selection of textures and flavours to enjoy.

Note: The vegetables go very well with a lemon mayonnaise dip or a classic tartare sauce. Good-quality crusty bread or barbecued garlic bread also go very well with this dish. Olive bread brushed with olive oil and cooked on the open grill is also sensational to eat with this dish. And here's just one more suggestion: grilled salmon, arranged on top of the vegetables – the flavours are immense. Enjoy your Summer and barbecuing!

Roast Potatoes

This is one of Britain's favourite potato dishes, along with good creamy mash! Roast potatoes are a weekly institution in every family. It is our standard procedure: Sunday lunch means roast potatoes! And quite right too. Good roasts are just irresistible, hot or cold.

The first question normally asked is which is the best potato to use? Almost any potato will roast, but for the perfect, crispy finish, I use Désirée, King Edward or Maris Piper – all are easily available.

If you want a good, crisp, roast finish, potatoes will take longer than you think in the oven – up to 1½ hours. One more tip: if you are serving them with your roast of the day – pour off some of the fat from the roast and cook the potatoes in that to get tastier and crispier potatoes.

Serves 4–6
900 g (2 lb) potatoes, left in skins

Olive oil, cooking oil or lard
Salt

Pre-heat the oven to 200°C/400°F/Gas Mark 6. The potatoes can be first boiled for up to 10 minutes in their skins before being drained, peeled, and shaken in the dry pan to roughen the surface (which helps them to become crisp). Heat enough cooking oil or fat to cover the base of a good roasting tray. Add the potatoes and turn them in the fat until coated all over. Season, place in the oven and roast for 30 minutes before turning and continuing to roast for a further 30 minutes. The potatoes should now be crisp and golden.

To give burnt tinges, turn the oven up to 240°C/475°F/Gas Mark 9. Leave the potatoes in the oven on their own for a further 10–15 minutes.

The potatoes can also be peeled before par-boiling. Boil for 8–10 minutes, drain well and then roll lightly in seasoned plain flour to give them a new edge. They will need to be roasted in a little extra oil for the same time. If not par-boiled, the potatoes will need up to 1½ hours in the oven.

'Banana' Roasts

To make these, you need large potatoes. Peel them and cut lengthways with a sharp knife. Shape them, cutting away the edges from top to tail, leaving sharp points. Create a curved edge in the 'centre' with the sharp knife or peeler to give a banana shape. Four 'bananas' make one portion.

To roast the bananas, par-boil for 3–4 minutes before draining and allowing them to cool for 10 minutes. Heat olive or cooking oil in a roasting tray or frying-pan and colour the potatoes to a golden brown. Before placing in the oven, add a knob or two of butter. These will now take 20–30 minutes to become rich in colour and texture with the points almost burnt. Season with coarse or table salt and serve.

Note: Any roast potatoes will taste better if you add a good knob of butter during cooking.

VEGETARIAN AND VEGETABLES

Mashed Potatoes

There are two varieties of potato that work particularly well for mashing. This first is a real old favourite, Maris Piper, and the second is Désirée. You will find that they have a good, crumbly texture that 'creams' well without becoming too starchy.

The mashed potato sauce is made with single cream and milk, just enough to give the potatoes a spreading consistency.

Serves 4–6
900 g (2 lb) potatoes, peeled and
  quartered
100 g (4 oz) unsalted butter

120 ml (4 fl oz) double cream or
  milk
Salt and freshly ground white
  pepper
Grated nutmeg

Boil the potatoes in salted water until tender, about 20–25 minutes, depending on size. Drain off all the water and replace the lid. Shake the pan vigorously, which will start to break up the potatoes. Add the butter and cream or milk, a little at a time, while mashing the potatoes. Season with salt, pepper and nutmeg. The potatoes will be light, fluffy and creamy.

Mashed Potato Sauce

For this potato dish, you will only need 450 g (1 lb) of cooked, mashed potato with nothing added. The 'sauce' literally just melts in the mouth and will go with so many dishes. I recommend serving it with Slow-honey-roast Duck (see page 82).

Serves 4–6
450 g (1 lb) Mashed Potatoes
  (above)
150 ml (¼ pint) single cream

50 g (2 oz) butter
Salt, pepper, and grated nutmeg
Milk or extra single cream, if needed

Warm the cream.

Season the potato with salt, pepper and nutmeg. Work the butter into the potato to give it a richer consistency.

Pour the warmed single cream a little at a time and work until you have a good, soft, dropping and spreading consistency. Check the seasoning and the 'sauce' is ready. If the 'sauce' is made in advance, when re-heating it, you may well find it will have thickened and will need more warm milk or cream to loosen it.

Potato and Vegetable Hot-pot Cake

This dish can be served as a complete vegetarian main course or as a vegetable accompaniment to a meat main course. I am making a Lancashire hot-pot without the lamb: lots of vegetables layered in the pot with vegetable stock and baked in the oven. The result is succulent flavours, topped with crisp potatoes. The dish can be made in a deep baking tray, but I prefer to use a flameproof baking pot.

Serves 4–6

750 g (1½ lb) potatoes, thinly sliced
3 onions, sliced 5 mm (¼ in) thick
75 g (3 oz) butter
4 carrots, sliced 5 mm (¼ in) thick
4 parsnips, peeled and quartered
 lengthways

1 small swede, peeled, halved and
 sliced 5 mm (¼ in) thick
350 g (12 oz) turnips, peeled and
 sliced 5 mm (¼ in) thick
900 ml (1½ pints) Vegetable Stock
 (page 240; good-quality stock
 cubes can be used)
Salt and pepper

Pre-heat the oven to 220°C/425°F/Gas Mark 7.

Fry the onions for a few minutes in a knob of the butter until softened. Leave to cool. Butter the baking pot or tray, lay half of the potatoes in the base and season with salt and pepper. Spoon a third of the onions on top and then lay the carrots on top. Season and brush with butter and then cover with the parsnip quarters. Season again and spoon another third of the onions on top. Lay the swede on top, season and brush with butter. Lay the turnips over, season and lay the remaining onions on top. Overlap the potatoes neatly to make the top layer, brush with the remaining butter and season with a sprinkle of salt. Add 600 ml (1 pint) of the vegetable stock and bring to the simmer.

Place in the hot oven for 30 minutes. During this time, the potatoes will start to colour. Cover with a lid or foil and continue to cook for a further 50 minutes. During this time, press the potatoes down into the vegetables to help form a cake. If the vegetables are absorbing the stock too quickly and turning dry, add the remaining 300 ml (10 fl oz) of vegetable stock. For the last 10 minutes of cooking, remove the lid or foil to crispen the potatoes.

Note: The potato finish can be crispened even more under the grill. To give a Lancashire feel to the dish, serve the hot-pot with roast lamb.

1 Break the stalk from the base of the artichokes. Cut 2–3 mm (⅛ in) from the base, revealing the artichoke bottoms.

2 Cut around the artichokes, removing the outside leaves. Cut the tops away, leaving 2.5 cm (1 in) deep chokes.

3 Trim off any excess green on the bottoms. Scoop out the furry 'chokes' from the centre.

  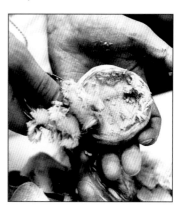

Cooking Globe Artichokes

Globe artichokes can have so many uses. The outside leaves can be cooked and used as garnishes or in salads. There is a small bite of flesh to be eaten at the base of them. The small, younger leaves attached to the artichoke bottoms in the centre can be cooked still attached and then used in salads, or as complete vegetarian dishes. I'm really after the artichoke bottom itself, which for me is the best and most succulent part.

To cook them, I like to make a tomato and lemon stock. The acidity from the lemon and sweetness of the tomato give the artichoke even more flavour without masking its own.

Serves 6

For the Stock:
6 over-ripe tomatoes, roughly
    chopped
Juice of 1 lemon
300 ml (10 fl oz) water
Salt

1 teaspoon coriander seeds
    (optional)
1 bay leaf (optional)

For the Artichokes:
6 globe artichokes
Juice of 1 lemon
1 sharp knife!

To make the stock, place all of the ingredients together in a pan and bring to the simmer. The stock is now ready to use.

Break the stalk from the base of the artichokes. Cut 2–3 mm (⅛ in) from the base with a sharp knife, revealing the artichoke bottom. Cut around the artichoke, removing the outside leaves; this will leave you with a cylinder shape. Cut the top of the cylinder away, leaving you with about a 2.5 cm (1 in) deep choke. Tidy and trim off any excess green left on the bottoms and scoop out the furry 'choke' from the centre.

Once each artichoke is prepared, roll in the lemon juice to prevent any discolouring. The artichokes can now be placed in the simmering cooking liquor. Cover with greaseproof paper.

The artichokes will take 20–25 minutes to become completely tender. Remove from the heat and leave to cool. Once cooled, lift the artichokes from the stock and strain the stock through a sieve. Pour the stock over the chokes and keep refrigerated until needed.

Garlic Mushrooms and Spinach *with* *Melting Gruyère*

Garlic mushrooms are a very popular favourite as starters or side dishes. This dish can be either of these. You can leave out the spinach and cheese and just make the garlic mushrooms. But having the spinach to balance the strong garlic flavour, along with the grated melting cheese, is quite special.

Serves 4
450 g (1 lb) button, cup or
    chestnut mushrooms
350 g (12 oz) spinach,
    picked and washed
3 tablespoons olive oil
50 g (2 oz) butter

3 garlic cloves, crushed
1 shallot, finely chopped (optional)
A squeeze of lemon juice (optional)
100 g (4 oz) Gruyère, grated
Salt and pepper

Wipe the mushrooms clean and then if using cups or chestnuts, cut into quarters. Heat the olive oil in a large frying-pan until very hot. Add the mushrooms and fry quickly to give an immediate colour. Add the butter and continue to fry for a further minute. Add the garlic and season with salt and pepper. The mushrooms will have been cooking now for 3–4 minutes. Add the chopped shallot, if using, and the spinach. Continue to fry for 2–3 minutes more and check for seasoning. Add a squeeze of lemon, if using, and divide between four serving dishes or plates. Sprinkle the cheese on top and finish by melting under the grill.

Note: Cheddar can also be used.

Glazed Lemon Broad Beans *on Spinach Toast with Tomato Sauce*

The cheese is being used to make cheese on toast as a base for the dish. Parmesan is my first choice, or a slice of Gruyère; Cheddar can also be used.

Serves 2

175 g (6 oz) shelled fresh
   broad beans
225 g (8 oz) picked and
   washed spinach
2 large slices of crusty bread,
   1 cm (½ in) thick
3 tablespoons olive oil
6 tomatoes, blanched in boiling
   water for 10 seconds and skinned

1 small garlic clove, crushed
A knob of butter
2 tablespoons grated Parmesan,
   Cheddar or Gruyère
2 egg yolks
Juice of ½ lemon
Salt and pepper

Brush the bread with olive oil and toast until golden brown; keep warm.

Cook the broad beans in salted, boiling water for 6–8 minutes. If they are particularly big, they may need an extra few minutes. Once cooked, drain off, keeping two tablespoons of the cooking liquor. Slip the beans out of their skins and season.

Seed the tomatoes and chop the tomato flesh into a 5 mm (¼ in) dice. Heat a tablespoon of olive oil with the clove of garlic and add the tomatoes. Cook them until tender and almost reduced to a pulp, allowing the natural waters to reduce. Once reduced, season with salt and pepper and add the remaining olive oil.

In another pan, melt the butter and add the spinach. Cook for a few minutes until tender and season with salt and pepper.

Melt the cheese on the toast under the grill.

Quickly whisk the egg yolks with the reserved broad bean cooking liquor and lemon juice in a bowl over simmering water to a thick *sabayon* consistency (like soft-peak whipped cream). Season with salt and pepper and use 1 tablespoon to bind the warm broad beans. Squeeze any excess liquor from the spinach and sit it on top of the cheese toasts. Spoon the broad beans onto the spinach. Coat the broad beans with the remaining lemon *sabayon* and glaze to a golden brown under the grill. Spoon the tomato sauce around and serve.

Note: Chopped fresh basil, tarragon or parsley can be added to the tomato sauce.

Parsleyed Crispy Carrots

For this dish, I like the carrots to be slightly overcooked. This makes them softer and more succulent to eat, once you've crunched through the crispy crumbs!

Serves 6

450 g (1 lb) baby carrots with tops
Finely grated zest of ½ orange
225 g (8 oz) fresh white
  breadcrumbs

1 heaped teaspoon chopped fresh
  parsley
6 tablespoons plain flour, seasoned
1–2 eggs, beaten
Oil, for deep-frying
Salt and pepper

Peel the carrots and trim the stalk tops to a 1–2 cm (½–¾ in) stem. Cook them in salted, boiling water until completely tender. This will take 15–20 minutes, depending on the thickness of the carrots.

Once cooked, drain off all the excess water and leave the carrots to cool. Rub the orange zest into the breadcrumbs, season with salt and pepper and add the parsley. The carrots can now be rolled in the seasoned plain flour, dipped in the beaten egg and then rolled in the breadcrumbs. Roll the crumbs reasonably firmly around the carrots, leaving the green tops uncovered. The carrots are now ready to be carefully fried in the hot oil. They will take just a few minutes to become golden and crisp. Lift them from the oil and put them to drain on kitchen paper. Season with a pinch of salt.

The parsleyed crispy carrots are now ready to serve.

Note: For an even crispier finish, the carrots can be passed through the egg and crumbs again for a second coating.

The parsley can be left out and the orange zest doubled to give you crisp, crunchy, orange carrots.

The orange zest can be replaced with lemon zest for another flavour.

Cooking Curly Kale

Curly kale is a green, cabbage-like vegetable, grown in the Winter and early Spring. It is similar to Spring greens in flavour but with a thicker and firmer texture. When raw, it has a 'curly' parsley look about it.

Although similar to Spring greens, curly kale holds its own texture and flavour and keeps an amazing deep green colour when cooked. I like to eat it just boiled and then tossed in butter and seasoned. It can also be used in stir-fries (once blanched) and mixed with spices, pasta or potatoes.

In this book, I have recommended serving curly kale with the Parsleyed Cod on page 62, where it is just lightly bound with a mustard butter sauce. Or how about glazing kale with the soft Gorgonzola Rarebit (page 233)?

Serves 4
750–900 g (1½–2 lb) curly kale

Salt and pepper
A knob of butter

Remove the stalks from the kale and wash the leaves. The kale can now be cooked in salted, boiling water for 3–4 minutes. Drain in a colander, removing excess water. Season with salt and pepper and stir through the butter.

The kale can also be cooked ahead and refreshed in iced water. Then season and butter it while cold and refrigerate until needed. Now all you need to do is microwave and serve.

Lemon-buttered Broccoli *with*
Crisp Anchovies

This is a vegetable dish that is packed with flavour. It goes best with fish, chicken or pork. A simple grilled sole with a portion of the broccoli creates a totally different dish. As with most of my recipes using anchovies, I am using the marinated rather than the tinned ones.

Serves 4

900 g (2 lb) broccoli

10–12 marinated anchovy fillets

2–3 tablespoons milk

1 tablespoon self-raising flour, mixed
   with ¼ teaspoon cayenne pepper

Oil, for deep-frying

Salt

For the Lemon Butter:

50–75 g (2–3 oz) butter, softened

Juice of 1 lemon

3 tablespoons Vegetable Stock (page
   240; good-quality stock cubes can
   be used), water or single cream

Salt and pepper

Split the anchovies down the centre, separating the two fillets and then cut at an angle into 1 cm (½ in) pieces. Drop the anchovies into the milk and then into the cayenne flour, shaking off any excess. Deep-fry the anchovies until golden and crisp. A deep-fat fryer is not necessary – 2.5 cm (1 in) of hot oil in a saucepan will also do the trick.

Bring the lemon juice and stock, water or single cream to the simmer. Whisk in the butter to emulsify. Once all is whisked in, it is important that it doesn't boil or the butter will separate. Season with salt and pepper. If you have an electric hand-whisk, a quick blitz will totally emulsify the sauce and lighten the flavour.

Trim excess stalk and leaves from the broccoli, leaving nice, small florets. Cook them in salted, boiling water until just tender. The cooking time will range between 2 and 6 minutes, depending on the size of the florets.

To serve the broccoli, season the florets and place them in a vegetable dish. Spoon the lemon sauce over and finish with a good sprinkling of crisp anchovies.

Note: This dish can be turned into a vegetarian one by replacing the anchovies with roasted or toasted pinenuts. The pinenuts can also be added to the anchovy version for an extra nutty finish.

Roast Pumpkin

Pumpkin has quite a large family – English, American, squash and butternut squash all being part of it. Marrows, courgettes and cucumber are also relatives.

Pumpkin and butternut squash make good purées and soups and roast very well too. It is best to buy small pumpkins, which can easily be cut into wedges and roasted.

Serves 6
A 900 g (2 lb) pumpkin
3 tablespoons cooking oil

25 g (1 oz) butter
Salt and pepper
Grated nutmeg

Pre-heat the oven to 200°C/400°F/Gas Mark 6. Cut the pumpkin into 12–16 wedges and remove the seeds. The skin can be left or cut off. It will not become tender and edible; however, it does guarantee that the pumpkin wedges don't break up, so they keep the nice half-moon shape. The cooking time will be the same.

Heat a frying pan with a drop of the oil. Season the pumpkin with salt and pepper and fry to a golden brown on both sides (5–6 minutes). When ready, transfer to a roasting tray. Repeat this process until all the wedges are coloured. Add the butter and roast in the oven for 20 minutes, turning them half-way through. If the pumpkin still feels a little too firm, return it to the oven for a further 5–10 minutes.

Once cooked, transfer to a serving plate or bowl, pouring any buttery juices over, and finish with a little grated nutmeg.

Note: Chopped pinenuts, lightly roasted and sprinkled over, go very well with the pumpkin.

Turnip Purée

A classic British vegetable, which can be used with almost as much variety as potatoes, turnips seem to have an overcooked, boiled and bitter image, so that none of us really wants to know or try them.

This recipe does away with all that. Cooking the turnips in milk gives them a totally different flavour and they retain a brilliant white finish. So now there's no excuse – this dish has got to be tried.

Serves 4–6
900 g (2 lb) turnips
450 ml (15 fl oz) milk
150 ml (5 fl oz) water

1 small garlic clove (optional)
50–85 ml (2–3 fl oz) double cream
  (optional)
Salt and pepper

Peel the turnips and cut them into a rough dice. Cover with the milk and water in a saucepan and add a pinch of salt and the garlic clove, if using. Bring to the simmer and cook for 5–10 minutes until tender. Lift the turnips (and garlic) from the cooking liquor and push through a sieve or purée in a food processor. If the purée is too wet and loose, return to a saucepan and cook on a low heat. This will slowly evaporate the liquid content, giving a firmer consistency.

Add the cream, if using, to enrich the flavour and create a creamy texture. Season with salt and pepper and serve.

Note: In place of the double cream, some of the cooking milk can be used.

Sautéed New Potatoes *with Onions, Garlic and Orange*

The flavour of orange is an old-fashioned favourite with duck. This potato dish goes perfectly with duck or game dishes, whether they are feathered or furred.

Serves 4

750 g (1½ lb) new potatoes, slightly overcooked in their skins

50 g (2 oz) butter, with a splash of cooking oil

1 large onion, sliced (or 2 small onions)

1 garlic clove, crushed

Zest of 1 large orange, finely grated

Salt and pepper

1 teaspoon chopped fresh parsley or tarragon (optional)

Peel the cooked new potatoes and halve. Because they have been overcooked, they will break up a bit. This is exactly the texture we are looking for, to give an almost creamy, sautéed flavour. Heat a frying-pan with a splash of oil. Add half the butter and, once bubbling, add the potatoes. Season with salt and pepper and sauté on a high heat to give a good golden colour and texture (4–5 minutes).

While the potatoes are sautéing, heat another pan with the remaining butter and fry the onion with the garlic and orange until softened and golden brown. Season with salt and pepper. When the potatoes are sautéed, add the onions and toss together. Finish by sprinkling with the chopped parsley or tarragon, if using.

Sautéed, Vinegared Peppers

This sounds like quite an acidic dish with the sharp flavour of vinegar finishing it off. In fact, the vinegar just lifts and adds lots of flavour to the peppers. I serve these with barbecued dishes (fish or meat) and also with roast chicken or lamb.

Serves 3–4

1 large red pepper

1 large green pepper

1 large yellow pepper

2 tablespoons olive or groundnut oil

A knob of butter

1–2 tablespoons white-wine or other vinegar e.g. red-wine, tarragon or sherry vinegar

Salt and pepper

You can leave the skin of the peppers on or blanch them and remove their skins. Blanching and skinning will leave the peppers with a more tender finish. To blanch, place in salted, boiling water for 3–4 minutes. Remove from the water and peel off the skins. Split the peppers lengthways and remove all seeds and core. If you're not blanching and skinning the peppers, just seed them.

Cut the peppers into strips or 2.5 cm (1 in) dice. Heat the oil in a frying-pan and once hot add the peppers. Cook for a few minutes, adding a knob of butter to give a nutty taste. Once the peppers have started to colour and soften, season with salt and pepper and add the vinegar. This will evaporate very quickly as the peppers absorb the flavour.

Note: Fresh herbs can be added at the end of cooking – parsley, tarragon or basil all work well and garlic can also be used.

A sprinkling of sugar will give the peppers a sweet and sour finish.

The peppers can also be skinned by grilling until almost burnt and then placing in a plastic bag. This creates a steam and helps loosen the skin.

Spicy Fried Cauliflower

This recipe is a vegetarian version of the spicy fried chicken in Open Rhodes. *I was cooking for some friends and had decided to keep it simple with spicy fried chicken, rice, salad and naan bread. One friend was a vegetarian, so I made this with florets of cauliflower and finely chopped sweet peppers to finish. It turned out a winner, so here's the recipe.*

Serves 2

- 1 small cooked cauliflower, cut into small florets
- 2 tablespoons natural yoghurt
- Juice of 1 lime
- ½ teaspoon ground turmeric
- ½ teaspoon paprika
- 2 cardamom pods, finely crushed
- ¼ teaspoon salt
- 1 garlic clove, crushed
- 1 tablespoon vegetable oil
- A knob of butter
- 1 tablespoon sesame oil (or more vegetable oil)
- ⅓ red pepper, seeded and cut in small dice
- ⅓ green pepper, seeded and cut in small dice
- Salt and pepper
- 1 teaspoon chopped fresh coriander (optional)

Mix together the yoghurt, lime juice, turmeric, paprika, cardamom, salt and garlic. Heat a tablespoon of vegetable oil and butter in a wok or frying-pan to a medium heat. Add the cauliflower and fry to a light golden colour. Add the yoghurt marinade and increase the heat. Continue to fry for 1–2 minutes until the marinade has thickened and coated the cauliflowers.

While the cauliflower is frying, heat another small pan and heat the sesame or vegetable oil. Quickly fry the peppers for a few minutes, season with salt and pepper. Spoon the cauliflower into a bowl and sprinkle with the peppers and chopped coriander, if using.

Note: This recipe will work with other vegetables; perhaps you could make a spicy fried ratatouille.

French Bean Purée

I have always said that good-quality green vegetables should never be puréed but now I'm changing my mind. Spinach purée has always been good, along with broccoli and asparagus, so why not French beans? This purée is very good, with the flavour of bubbling butter giving the beans a lovely nutty finish.

Serves 4

450 g (1 lb) French beans, topped and tailed

1 tablespoon butter

2 tablespoons double cream

Salt and pepper

Cook the beans in salted, boiling water until completely tender but still with their brilliant green colour. Drain off the water and place the beans in a food processor. Season with salt and pepper and blitz to a smooth purée. While blitzing, heat a small frying-pan and add the butter. Once bubbling and at a nutty brown stage, add to the purée. Finish by adding the double cream. The French bean purée is now ready to serve.

Note: This recipe will work very well using almost any green vegetable.

Curried Fried Potatoes

These potatoes are 'parmentier', as featured in Open Rhodes*: a shallow-fried, diced potato cooked until golden and crisp and soft in the centre. The difference with these is that I'm rolling the potatoes in Madras curry powder before frying. As the potato cooks, so does the curry flavour. The potatoes are very, very tasty and moreish!*

A soured cream dip can easily be made to go with them by mixing 150 ml (5 fl oz) of soured cream with the juice of 1–2 limes or lemons, seasoned with salt and pepper. (Natural yoghurt can also be used.) Another finishing touch is garam masala. This is often sprinkled on top of finished curries to spice them up even more. It is simply a mix of roasted spices (see my recipe on page 76 or it can be bought in small jars and keeps almost indefinitely in an air-tight container).

Serves 4

750 g (1½ lb) potatoes, cut in
   1 cm (½ in) dice
1 teaspoon Madras curry powder
4 tablespoons cooking oil
   (preferably groundnut)

A knob of butter
Salt
A pinch of garam masala (optional)
1 teaspoon chopped fresh coriander
   (optional)

Heat the oil in a large frying-pan. Make sure the diced potatoes are dry and then roll them in the curry powder, making sure they are all well covered. Season with salt. Once the oil is up to a medium–high temperature, add the potatoes. Allow the potatoes to fry and turn a light golden colour, which takes 3–4 minutes, before turning the heat down. This will prevent them from overcolouring before being cooked. Continue to fry, adding the butter and turning the potatoes from time to time, for 8–10 minutes. Towards the end of the cooking, increase the heat to give a richer golden colour. To finish, sprinkle with garam masala and chopped coriander, if you like.

Note: Any remaining cooking oil will have taken on the curry flavour, so you can use this as a dressing to drizzle over the finished crispy potatoes.

These potatoes go very well with chicken and fish dishes.

PUDDINGS

puddings

*t*he pudding chapter always seems to be the busiest. I start off with just a few ideas and then tend to get totally carried away, tasting and testing as many as possible. The puddings have taken one or two new directions – one of which is a sort of 'afternoon-tea cake' theme. Home-made Eccles Cakes (page 218), which are lovely to serve as a complete pudding with custard and extra-thick cream, Home-made Crumpets (page 221), Golden Ginger 'Flapjack' Cake (page 220), Black Treacle Loaf (page 217) and Mini Madeira Prune Cakes (page 205) are all well suited for puddings or to accompany a good pot of English tea.

There are also some interesting combinations; Potato and Mascarpone Cheesecake Flan (page 180) is certainly one, with the everyday vegetable becoming a pudding, enlivened with a squeeze of lemon.

Pumpernickel Bread and Butter Pudding (page 193), I promise you, is not just an excuse to feature 'B & B' again, although I have to admit I just can't leave the whole concept of that dish alone! The pumpernickel pudding is a proper loaf, but with custard and black treacle in place of sugar to give you a toffee-like dream.

The sorbets have moved on to sherbets, which are a slightly different concept. The basic syrup mixture is made with milk and has egg white added towards the end. The finished result gives you a very lively 'sorbet' that sparkles on the palate. There are also parfaits, fritters, tarts, pies, different-flavoured pastry recipes, creams, brûlées and two puddings that I promised from *Open Rhodes* – Bourbon Biscuits (page 210) and Wagon Wheel® Pudding (page 190)! The biscuit pudding revival lives on in these with two very tasty results: a chocolate biscuit, which cuts through to a slice of brownie and then some chocolate ganache, or shortbread biscuits sandwiched with jam, through to marshmallow in the centre, all totally covered in chocolate. You know it's so true what they say – 'the proof is in the pudding'!

Soft Fruit Ice-creams

This has to be one of the easiest ice-cream recipes you will ever find. It is made simply with soft fruit, stock syrup, a squeeze of lemon and crème fraîche.

This recipe is for fresh fruits but tinned ones can be used – just purée almost any fruit in its own syrup, sweeten further, if necessary, with icing sugar and add a few tablespoons of crème fraîche and the ice-cream is made.

Here's the fresh-fruit version.

Serves 4
225 g (8 oz) soft fruit, raspberries,
   blackberries, strawberries, etc.
50 g (2 oz) caster sugar

120 ml (4 fl oz) water
A squeeze of lemon juice
3 heaped tablespoons crème fraîche
Icing sugar, to taste (if needed)

To make the fruit purée, boil together the sugar and water. Leave to cool. Add the soft fruits and lemon juice and blitz to a purée in a food processor. Push through a sieve. Add the crème fraîche and taste for sweetness. If it's too tart, add icing sugar to taste. The ice-cream mix is now ready to churn for 15–20 minutes. If you don't have an ice-cream machine, freeze it in a bowl and stir every 5–10 minutes. When almost set, whisk to a smooth creamy finish and then leave to freeze completely.

Note: An extra 50 g (2 oz) of soft fruits can be chopped and added just before setting point for a different texture.

You can also serve a trickle of fruit syrup (page 229) with this soft-fruit ice-cream.

Iced Pear Parfait *with Caramelized Pears in a Hazelnut Tart*

This recipe is quite full, with tarts, parfaits, sauces and caramelizing all to be done. But most parts, if not all, can be made well in advance. Also, as with all of my recipes, all the parts don't have to stay together. The pear parfait can become a dessert on its own.

For this particular recipe, I'm using quite an unusual mould. To freeze the parfait in a cylinder shape, which can then be sliced and put in the tart case, I'm using drain pipes! I buy 7.5 cm (3 in) diameter plastic drain pipes, about 15–20 cm (6–8 in) long, from a local DIY store. Wash them well and you have cylinder parfait moulds!

Serves 4

For the Pear Purée:
4 fresh or tinned pears, peeled,
    cored and cut in rough dice
A knob of butter
25 g (1 oz) caster sugar

For the Parfait:
4 egg yolks
50 g (2 oz) caster sugar

A splash of Poire William liqueur
    (optional)
300 ml (10 fl oz) double cream,
    lightly whipped to soft peaks
4 Hazelnut 'Marzipan' Tart cases
    (page 164)
4 Caramelized Pears (page 164)
1 quantity of Red-wine Caramel
    Sauce with Hazelnuts (page 165)
8–12 tablespoons Anglaise Sauce
    (page 223)

For the purée, cook the fresh pears in the butter and caster sugar until completely tender; blitz to a smooth purée in a food processor or liquidizer. If using tinned pears, just blitz with some of their own syrup. For the parfait, whisk the egg yolks and caster sugar together over a pan of simmering water until it holds a thick ribbon trail (*sabayon* stage). Remove from the heat and continue to whisk until cold. Fold in the pear purée and the Poire William liqueur, if using. Now fold in the whipped cream. Cover one end of the 'pipe' with cling film and stand upright on a tray or plate. Pour the parfait in and leave to set in the freezer. It will take 3–4 hours to freeze totally.

Prepare the Hazelnut 'Marzipan' Tart cases, the Caramelized Pears, the Red-wine Caramel Sauce with Hazelnuts and the Anglaise Sauce.

To assemble the dessert: spoon a line of the red wine and hazelnut caramel sauce around the plate. Spoon 2–3 tablespoons of the anglaise sauce in the centre. Remove the parfait 'pipe' from the freezer and run the pipe very briefly under warm water. The parfait will now push out quite easily. Cut a 1–2 cm (½–¾ in) slice per portion and sit one in each hazelnut tart. Put two or four halves of caramelized pear (depending on the size) on top of the parfait, spooning or brushing some of the excess caramel syrup over to glaze. Put the tarts on top of the anglaise sauce. The complete dessert is ready to serve.

For the Hazelnut 'Marzipan' Tart Cases

The tart cases are very similar to a marzipan, but using hazelnuts. They become very, very crisp, with a biscuit texture. The individual tartlet tins I use are 8 x 1 cm (3½ x ½ in) deep.

Makes 4

100 g (4 oz) ground hazelnuts
50 g (2 oz) caster sugar
50 g (2 oz) icing sugar, plus extra for
   rolling out paste

1 egg yolk
1 teaspoon lemon juice

Sieve together the hazelnuts and sugars. Add the egg yolk and lemon juice and combine to a marzipan paste. Roll it out very thinly on a surface covered with more icing sugar and use to line the loose-bottomed tartlet tins, trimming off any excess paste. These can now be left out to dry at room temperature for 24 hours. This will allow the marzipan to set and leave very crisp tart cases.

For the Caramelized Pears

The recipe I am giving you here actually cooks the pears in a caramel syrup. The pears can also be cooked in a basic stock syrup and, once cool, caramelized with icing or caster sugar under the grill or with a gas gun.

Serves 4

4 large, firm or 8 small, firm pears,
   peeled, halved and cored

225 g (8 oz) caster sugar
300 ml (10 fl oz) water

Bring the sugar and water to the boil and continue to boil fast until it turns into a light golden caramel. Add the pears along with another 6 tablespoons of water and continue to cook for 15 minutes until the syrup turns into a darker, richer coloured caramel. Remove from the stove and leave to cool. Once cooled, remove the pears. They will have a good full caramel flavour and colour. The remaining caramel can be kept to glaze them just before serving.

Note: Instead of caramel poached pears, you can use tinned halves, glazed under the grill with icing or caster sugar.

For the Red-wine Caramel Sauce with Hazelnuts

Another caramel sauce made with wine and hazelnuts gives the dish a totally different taste and finish. The finished consistency is very thick.

Serves 4

200 ml (7 fl oz) red wine, preferably
   burgundy
I tablespoon red-wine vinegar
200 g (7 oz) caster sugar

50 g (2 oz) butter
I vanilla pod, split and scraped or
   I teaspoon vanilla essence
50 g (2 oz) chopped hazelnuts

Bring the wine and vinegar together to the boil and then boil rapidly until it has reduced by half. Set aside. Gently melt the sugar in a separate pan over a medium heat until it has turned into a golden caramel. Add the butter and the scraped vanilla pod or essence and cook for a further 2 minutes. Add the reduced wine mixture, remove from the heat and add the chopped hazelnuts. Leave the sauce to cool to room temperature. It is best served at this temperature.

sherbets

These are essentially recipes for sorbets with a sharp, zingy finish. Sorbets are made from a fruit purée, mixed with stock syrup and usually a twist of lemon. Sherbets have milk and whisked egg whites added to them. If you want to make sorbets instead, simply omit the egg whites and milk.

Lemon Sherbet

This recipe can be made into lime, orange or grapefruit sherbet by replacing the lemon with the citrus fruit of your choice.

Serves 6–8
Finely grated zest and juice of
5 lemons

375 ml (13 fl oz) Basic Stock Syrup
(page 227)
120 ml (4 fl oz) milk
2 egg whites

Boil the lemon juice, zest and stock syrup. Remove from the heat, add the milk and leave to infuse and cool. Once cooled, churn the mixture in an ice-cream or sorbet machine. It will take 20–25 minutes to churn to a creamy texture.

Five minutes before the sherbet is ready, whisk the egg whites to the soft peak stage and add to the sherbet while mixing. Continue to churn until ready. The sherbet is now ready and can be left in the freezer to firm.

Note: If preferred, the zest can be strained from the mixture before churning. This sherbet is featured with the Char-grilled Glazed Pumpkin Slices on page 200.

Bellini Champagne Sherbet

Bellini is a famous cocktail made from puréed white peach juice and Prosecco, which is the Italian alternative to champagne. These aren't white peaches I am using but the flavour is fantastic and tastes like an iced cocktail!

Serves 6–8

500 g (1 lb 2 oz) fresh peaches, chopped

350 ml (12 fl oz) Basic Stock Syrup (page 227)

350 ml (12 fl oz) champagne or sparkling wine

A squeeze of lemon juice

120 ml (4 fl oz) milk

2 egg whites, whisked to soft peaks

Bring the chopped peaches and stock syrup to the simmer. Cook for a few minutes or until the peaches have softened. Add the champagne or sparkling wine and lemon juice and return to the simmer. Remove from the stove and blitz to a fine purée in a food processor or liquidizer. Push the purée through a sieve and leave to cool. Add the milk and churn in an ice-cream machine for 20–25 minutes. When almost ready, add the whisked egg whites and continue to churn. When the sherbet is thick and creamy, remove from the machine and finish setting in the freezer.

Note: Apricots, plums, and other soft fruits will also work with the champagne. Justify the Bellini name by presenting it in a cocktail glass with a trickle of champagne poured over and fresh peach slices to garnish.

Tinned peaches can also be used. Purée the peaches in their own syrup and omit the basic stock syrup from the recipe.

Raspberry Sherbet

This is a favourite with everyone. The fresh, fruity flavour whisked to a creamy ice is so good. Adding the red-wine vinegar lifts it even more. The raspberry flavour just tastes stronger. This sherbet would go very well with the Roast Peaches or Nectarines on page 198 or with 'Burnt' Peach and Mascarpone Cheesecake Tart (page 181) with thick cream (almost a peach melba tart!).

Serves 6–8

400 ml (14 fl oz) Raspberry Purée (page 161) (tinned or frozen raspberries can also be puréed)

4 tablespoons caster sugar

2 tablespoons strong red-wine vinegar, preferably Cabernet Sauvignon

200 ml (7 fl oz) milk

2 egg whites, whisked to soft peaks

Warm the purée with the sugar. Add the vinegar and milk and leave to cool. Churn for 20–25 minutes to the sorbet stage. A few minutes before it is ready, add the whisked egg whites. Once ready, remove from the machine and finish in the freezer.

Note: Sherbets can be turned into sorbets by omitting the egg whites and milk.
Add another tablespoon of vinegar if the one you are using isn't very strong.

Madeira Sherbet

This Madeira sherbet has a totally different flavour. I like to serve this with Mini Madeira Prune Cakes (page 205) and Madeira Syrup (page 228) to give a complete Madeira experience. Other fortified wines can also be used, such as sherry or port.

Serves 4–6

450 ml (15 fl oz) Madeira
200 ml (7 fl oz) water
150 g (5 oz) caster sugar
120 ml (4 fl oz) milk
2 egg whites, whisked to soft peaks

Boil the Madeira to reduce the quantity by half. Add the water and sugar and return to the boil. Remove from the heat, add the milk and leave to cool. Once cool, churn in the machine for 20 minutes. After 20 minutes, add the beaten soft-peak egg whites and continue to churn for a further 5–10 minutes. Remove from the machine and leave to set in the freezer.

Cinnamon Ice-cream

Baked apples, apple crumbles, apple pies and tarts would all benefit from being served with this ice-cream. In this book, I recommend serving it with the Date and Orange Mascarpone Fritters (page 208). Hot fritters and cold ice-cream always sounds tasty to me!

Serves 4–6

250 ml (8 fl oz) double cream
250 ml (8 fl oz) milk
2 cinnamon sticks, broken
100 g (4 oz) caster sugar
6 egg yolks
50 ml (2 fl oz) rum

Bring the cream, milk and broken cinnamon sticks to the boil. Cream together the sugar and egg yolks. Pour the boiling cream mixture onto the creamed yolks, stirring from time to time until cooled. Pour through a sieve and then churn in the ice-cream machine for 15–20 minutes until very thick. Freeze. The ice-cream will be nice and rich and packed with cinnamon flavour.

Blood Orange Sorbet

Rich, zesty and tasty!

Serves 4–6

The juice and finely grated zest of
   10 blood oranges

150 g (5 oz) caster sugar
150 ml (5 fl oz) water
The juice from 2 lemons

Place the sugar, water and orange zest in a saucepan and bring to the simmer. Cook for 10–15 minutes. Strain the juice of the oranges and lemons together. Add to the syrup and leave to cool. The sorbet syrup is now ready to be finished in the ice-cream maker and churned for 20–25 minutes to a smooth consistency. Freeze until firm. If you do not have an ice-cream machine, freeze the mix, whisking occasionally to help create the same consistency.

Note: Diced blood orange segments can be stirred into the finished mix for a more fruity, coarser texture.

Blood oranges are not essential for this recipe. Any fresh, ripe orange will also work to give you a rich orange sorbet.

Chocolate Banana Bread Pudding *with Chocolate Sorbet*

This pudding will fulfil all chocolate lovers' fantasies! Imagine a rich chocolate and banana cake filled with melting chocolate ganache. And then imagine a chocolate sauce and chocolate sorbet to go with it. Just thinking about eating this dessert makes me melt! The beauty of this recipe is that it can be made well in advance and then just microwaved. This process obviously warms the cake and starts the chocolate melting inside.

I'm giving you the recipe for banana loaf, but a bought variety will also work. In fact, you needn't stick to banana bread – a golden syrup or Jamaican gingerbread loaf will also work very well and, if you're the ultimate chocolate freak, use a chocolate cake!

Serves 6

For the Banana Bread:
120 g (4½ oz) butter
100 g (4 oz) soft light-brown sugar
100 g (4 oz) granulated sugar
2 medium eggs
250 g (9 oz) very ripe bananas, mashed
325 g (11½ oz) plain flour
1 teaspoon baking powder
A good pinch of salt

For the Chocolate Custard:
175 ml (6 fl oz) double cream
575 ml (19 fl oz) milk
65 g (2½ oz) butter, diced
250 g (9 oz) dark plain chocolate, broken in small pieces
3 eggs
2 egg yolks
150 g (5 oz) soft brown sugar

For the Chocolate Ganache:
190 ml (6½ fl oz) double cream
2 tablespoons granulated sugar
120 g (4½ oz) plain chocolate, broken in small pieces
1 tablespoon butter, diced

For the Chocolate Tuile Biscuits (Makes about 10–12):
15 g (½ oz) cocoa powder
50 g (2 oz) icing sugar
50 g (2 oz) plain flour
1 egg white
50 g (2 oz) butter, melted

Pre-heat the oven to 180°C/350°F/Gas Mark 4. Butter a 900 g (2 lb) loaf tin and line it with greaseproof paper. Cream the butter with the soft light-brown and granulated sugars. Beat the eggs together and add slowly to the butter mix. Mix the mashed ripe banana into the butter mixture. Sieve together the flour and baking powder with the salt and fold into the banana-butter mix. Spoon the mixture into the lined tin and cook for 50–60 minutes. Leave to cool for 10–15 minutes before turning out of the tin. Once cold, remove all the crust from the loaf. The banana bread can now be cut into 1 cm (½ in) dice. This is now ready to be soaked with the chocolate custard.

To make the chocolate custard, bring the cream and milk to the boil in a saucepan. Put the butter and chocolate in a bowl, pour on the cream mixture and stir, melting the two together. Whisk together the eggs, egg yolks and sugar. Pour on the chocolate cream and strain through a sieve. Pour the chocolate custard onto the diced banana bread; mix in well to help the banana bread soak up the chocolate flavour. Leave to soak for 30 minutes.

For the chocolate ganache, bring the double cream to the boil with the granulated sugar, and pour over the chocolate and butter in a bowl and mix well. Leave to chill and set.

Once set and firm, roll the ganache into balls approximately 2.5 cm (1 in) in diameter and refrigerate until needed. These ganache balls will be placed in the centre of the cakes, creating the melted chocolate filling.

Now make the chocolate tuiles. You will need a large sheet of baking parchment to spread the biscuits on and a stencil to shape them, which could be a triangle, leaf shape, circle, etc. I prefer to cut a circle 7.5–10 cm (3–4 in) in diameter from a plastic carton or lid. This gives you a permanent stencil to wash and use time and time again. Pre-heat the oven to 160°C/325°F/Gas Mark 3.

Sieve together the cocoa powder, icing sugar and flour. Slowly mix in the egg white, then the melted butter. Place the stencil on the baking parchment. Spread over enough of the mixture to give a thin shape. Lift and repeat the stencil shapes. Bake for 5–6 minutes. Once they are cooked and while still warm, lift the biscuits off the paper with a palette knife and drape them over upturned cups or small bowls to give you a biscuit-cup shape to sit the sorbet in. You could also cut a cardboard cylinder from the centre of a roll of foil or cling film in half lengthways. Push a tuile into it, which will give you a curved biscuit once it has cooled. The cooked tuile biscuits will keep for 48 hours if kept in an air-tight container.

Prepare the Chocolate Sorbet and the Ultimate Chocolate Sauce.

To finish the dish, pre-heat the oven to 160°C/325°F/Gas Mark 3, or a little higher. Butter six 7.5 cm (3 in) diameter, 5 cm (2 in) deep pastry rings. Put them on greased baking parchment or greaseproof paper on a baking sheet. Spoon a layer of the soaked cake into the moulds and put a ball of ganache in the centre. Continue to fill the moulds with care until the ganache ball is covered. Bake the puddings for 10–15 minutes.

During the baking, the chocolate custard and banana cake mixture will set and give a baked-cake finish with melting ganache inside. Leave the puddings to cool or serve immediately. The advantage of this dessert is that these puddings can be left to cool and then refrigerated. To serve, they then simply need to be microwaved.

To finish the presentation, thread some of the chocolate sauce across each plate and sit the warm pudding on top. Next to the pudding, put a tuile biscuit and using a dessertspoon or ice-cream scoop fill with the chocolate sorbet.

The pudding is now complete and ready to eat!

Note: Clotted cream, placed on top of the cake, eats very well with this dish.

For the Chocolate Sorbet

Serves 6

150 g (5 oz) good-quality plain
chocolate, broken in pieces

500 ml (17 fl oz) water
150 g (5 oz) caster sugar
25 g (1 oz) glucose syrup

Put the chocolate pieces in a bowl. Bring the water, sugar and glucose to the boil and pour onto the chocolate pieces. Stir until the chocolate has melted, and allow to cool and then chill in the fridge. The sorbet mix is now ready to churn in an ice-cream maker which should take approximately 20-25 minutes. Transfer the sorbet to a box, cover and slide into the freezer. If you do not have an ice-cream machine, simply freeze this mix, whisking it occasionally as it hardens to help create a smooth consistency.

For the Ultimate Chocolate Sauce:

**Makes about 300 ml
(10 fl oz)**

225 g (8 oz) good-quality plain
chocolate

250 ml (8 fl oz) double cream
25 g (1 oz) unsalted butter

To make the ultimate chocolate sauce, melt the chocolate with the cream in a bowl over a pan of hot water and once warm add the butter. You now have a thick, rich chocolate sauce. This is best eaten cold or just warm. Trying to serve this as a hot sauce will simply cause the butter to separate.

Lemon Yoghurt Ice-cream

This ice-cream is packed with lemony flavour and the consistency is helped along by the yoghurt and cream. It is totally different from the Lemon Sherbet on page 166 and, if you can't choose between them, make both! If you want to test this recipe for maximum flavour, the best way is to eat lots of it!

Makes enough for the whole family!

The juice and finely grated zest
  of 2 lemons

100 g (4 oz) granulated sugar
425 g (15 oz) natural yoghurt
150 ml (5 fl oz) double cream

Liquidize the lemon juice and granulated sugar together until fine.

Mix the yoghurt with the double cream. Stir the sugared lemon juice into the yoghurt and churn in the ice-cream machine.

As with most ice-creams, this will take 15–20 minutes to churn, which still keeps it creamy before finishing in the freezer.

If you do not have an ice-cream machine, freeze until almost set and then whisk and refreeze until completely frozen.

fruit tarts

Fruit tarts and flans can be made to suit almost any fruit. The simplest are often the best: a crisp pastry case filled with pastry cream and with lots of baked fruits on top. Raw fruits will also make very good flans. To appreciate all the wonderful fresh flavours from the fruit, cream and crisp, crumbly pastry, never serve flans straight from the fridge. Eating them at room temperature or slightly warm will keep every taste alive. A selection of fruit tarts – such as rhubarb, gooseberry and raspberry meringue – is featured here with suggestions and recipes for different flavours of pastry bases to go with them. Here's a list of pastries you can find in this book with suggestions of the fruits to go with them:

Sweet Shortcrust Pastry (page 224): raspberries, strawberries, gooseberries, plums, damsons, cherries and greengages

Sweet Lemon and Raisin Shortcrust Pastry (page 224): raspberries, strawberries, gooseberries, plums, damsons, cherries and greengages

Sweet Black Pepper and Crunchy Sugar Pastry (page 225): strawberries, raspberries and most other Summer fruits

Shortbread Pastry (page 226): rhubarb, strawberries and raspberries

Hazelnut Pastry (page 226): Summer fruits, plums, damsons, peaches, nectarines and apricots

Quick Puff Pastry (page 225): apples, figs, peaches and nectarines

Rhubarb Tart

This rhubarb tart can take on two or three different cooking and serving combinations. The pastry base is a basic sweet shortcrust pastry. This can either be blind-baked or the pastry and filling can be baked together from raw. There is a choice of two bases to place in the pastry case: the first is Pastry Cream (page 231) and the second is a slice of Lemon Genoise Sponge (page 222). The pastry cream will give a creamy base, while the sponge absorbs all of the fruit juices.

Serves 6

225 g (8 oz) Sweet Shortcrust Pastry or Shortcrust Pastry case (page 224)

750–900 g (1½–2 lb) fresh rhubarb

1 cm (½ in) thick, round slice (20–25 cm/8–10 in diameter) of plain or Lemon Genoise Sponge

(page 222) or 12 tablespoons of Pastry Cream (page 231)

25 g (1 oz) butter

4–6 tablespoons water

100–175 g (4–6 oz) caster sugar

2–3 tablespoons apricot jam glaze (optional) plus 2 tablespoons water, or icing sugar, sifted (optional)

PUDDINGS

176

Pre-heat the oven to 220°C/425°F/Gas Mark 7. Put the sponge or spoon the pastry cream in the base of a 20–25 cm (8–10 in) unbaked pastry case. Peel the rhubarb (if stringy) and cut into 2 cm (¾ in) slices. Melt the butter in a large saucepan and add the rhubarb, water and sugar. Carefully turn the rhubarb in the syrup for 1–2 minutes. Remove from the stove and allow to cool. Drain off any liquor and keep separate. Spoon all the rhubarb into the tart cases and bake for 35–40 minutes.

The rhubarb will have cooked and broken down slightly in texture. Remove the tart from the oven and place on a wire rack to cool for 10–15 minutes. Remove the tart from the ring and leave it to cool at room temperature. If using apricot jam as a glaze, mix any rhubarb liquor and the 2 tablespoons of water with the jam and warm. Strain through a sieve and brush the rhubarb for a glazed finish. If you're not using the jam, trickle any excess liquor over and dust with icing sugar.

Here is an alternative method: line the pastry case with foil or greaseproof paper, fill with baking beans or rice and bake blind for 20–30 minutes until golden and crisp. Leave to cool. Remove the foil or greaseproof paper and beans or rice. Trim off any excess pastry to give you a neat edge. Spread with pastry cream or line with the genoise sponge. Melt the butter and add the sliced rhubarb with the caster sugar. Cook and stir carefully until completely tender. This will only take 5–6 minutes. If the pastry case is sponge-based, spoon the hot rhubarb on top; the sponge will then soak up any juices. If using pastry cream, allow the rhubarb to cool before spooning it on top. Make apricot glaze, warming the jam with just the water, sieving and then brushing or spooning it over. An alternative to the jam for both versions of the tart is to dust liberally with icing sugar.

Note: This recipe can be used to make fresh gooseberry tarts. The fruit to sugar quantities are the same but very sharp gooseberries may well need 50 g (2 oz) of extra caster sugar.

The gooseberry tart will also go well with either a pastry cream or a sponge base and will become even tastier if the Sweet Lemon and Raisin Shortcrust Pastry (page 224) is used. For a neater finish with the gooseberry tart, arrange the fruits standing up in the tart case. With this method, it is best to cook them almost from raw in the pastry. For an absolutely fool-proof method of cooking fruits e.g. gooseberries, greengages, damsons, cherries or plums for tarts, use 100 g (4 oz) of caster sugar for every 450 g (1 lb) of fruit with 4 tablespoons of water. Bring to the boil and then remove from the stove and leave to cool in the liquor. The liquor can be used to loosen the apricot jam for the glaze.

Baked Fig Tart or Tartlets

This recipe can be used to make four individual tartlets or one large one. If making just one large tart, you will need a 20–25 cm (8–10 in) ovenproof frying-pan and for individual tartlets, four 10 cm (4 in) diameter tartlet tins. The advantage of making these into individual tartlets is that their size is perfect for the shape of the fruit. For each tart, three figs are needed to cover the base. The quantities and method are identical for either size and only the cooking time varies slightly.

Makes a 20–25 cm (8–10 in) Tart or four 10 cm (4 in) Tartlets

12 fresh figs, halved lengthways
100–175 g (4–6 oz) Quick Puff Pastry (page 225)
100 g (4 oz) soft light-brown sugar
75 g (3 oz) butter

Pre-heat the oven to 200°C/400°F/Gas Mark 6. Butter the ovenproof frying-pan or the individual tartlet tins very well. It is very important that the mould(s) are very well buttered. This will prevent the figs from sticking and also help the sugar to caramelize. Sprinkle 15 g (½ oz) of the sugar in each tin or 50 g (2 oz) in the frying-pan. Heat the frying-pan and melt 15 g (½ oz) of butter. Shallow-fry half the figs, cut-side down, very quickly on a high heat to a golden brown. Remove from the pan and set aside or arrange in two of the tartlet tins, facing the points towards the centre. Melt another 15 g (½ oz) of butter and shallow-fry the remaining figs. Fill the remaining tartlet tins. If making one large tart, return the first batch of cooked figs to the pan.

Roll out the puff pastry thinly and cut it into four 10 cm (4 in) circles or a 20 cm (8 in) circle. Sit a circle of puff pastry on top of the fruit and bake for 20 minutes (small) or 25–30 minutes (large).

Once baked, remove from the oven and leave to rest for 5–6 minutes. This relaxes the figs and when turned out they will have a neater finish. Warm the base of the frying-pan or tins on the hob and turn the tarts out. They will sit caramelized on a crisp puff pastry base and look very appetizing.

For extra butter caramel to spoon over, melt the remaining 50 g (2 oz) of butter with the 50 g (2 oz) of soft, light-brown sugar to a silky, golden syrup and trickle over and around. The tarts are ready to serve and will eat very well with vanilla or Cinnamon Ice-cream (page 169) or just thick cream.

Note: A shallow cake tin can be used in place of the frying-pan for the large tart.

Potato and Mascarpone Cheesecake Flan

Potato cheesecake is a great British dessert that always eats well, but I have decided to give it an Italian touch with the addition of mascarpone. I find this gives the pudding a richer and creamier finish, almost like a baked custard tart. I am using lemon zest in this recipe to lift all the other flavours, but orange zest can also be used.

Makes a 23 cm (9 in) Flan

225 g (8 oz) Sweet Shortcrust
   Pastry (page 224)
100 g (4 oz) plain mashed potatoes
100 g (4 oz) mascarpone

The finely grated zest of 3 lemons
100 g (4 oz) icing sugar
50 g (2 oz) butter, softened
4 egg yolks and 2 egg whites,
   beaten together

Pre-heat the oven to 200°C/400°F/Gas Mark 6. Butter a 23 cm (9 in) loose-based flan tin. Roll the pastry out thinly. Line the flan ring with pastry, leaving any excess pastry hanging over the edge of the ring. Line with foil or greaseproof paper and fill with baking beans or rice. Bake blind for 20–25 minutes. Once cooked, leave to cool. Remove the greaseproof paper or foil, beans or rice and trim off any excess pastry. Turn the oven down to 180°C/350°F/Gas Mark 4.

Place the finely grated lemon zest in a small saucepan of cold water, bring to the simmer and simmer for a few minutes. Drain through a fine sieve, refresh under cold water and squeeze out any excess liquor. Mix with the icing sugar.

Whisk the mashed potato and then whisk in the mascarpone and butter. Add the beaten 4 egg yolks and 2 egg whites and pour into the pre-baked pastry case.

The flan will take 35–40 minutes to become baked, golden and set. Once cooked, remove from the oven and leave to rest. This dessert is best eaten just warm with lots of pouring cream!

Note: Before placing the flan in the oven, it can be topped with finely grated nutmeg. This dessert also goes very well with raspberries and most other Summer fruits. Put the raspberries on top, completely covering the warm flan, and leave them natural or brush with a raspberry-jam glaze.

'Burnt' Peach and Mascarpone Cheesecake Tart

The base for this recipe is a sweet shortcrust pastry tartlet. Puff pastry can also be used. If using a biscuit base, the home-made ginger shortcake (see Rhubarb and Ginger Shortcake Pudding, page 189) can be rolled out and cooked in the cake ring. Or just make a mixture of half crushed ginger snaps and half digestive biscuits for a quick and easy base (see Note below).

Makes a 20 cm (8 in) deep Tart

6 small–medium fresh peaches (tinned can be used)
The juice of ½ lemon
250 g (9 oz) caster sugar
600 ml (1 pint) water
225 g (8 oz) Sweet Shortcrust Pastry (page 224) or Quick Puff Pastry (page 225)
The juice of 1 lemon or lime
100 g (4 oz) mascarpone
150 ml (5 fl oz) double cream
Icing sugar, sifted, for dusting

Pre-heat the oven to 200°C/400°F/Gas Mark 6. Butter a 20 cm (8 in) diameter, 2.5 cm (1 in) deep, loose-based tart tin. Roll out the pastry thinly and use it to line the tart tin. Bake blind for 20–30 minutes until golden and crisp. Once cooked, leave to cool. Remove the greaseproof paper or foil, beans or rice and trim off any excess pastry.

Put the peaches in a saucepan with the lemon juice, 225 g (8 oz) caster sugar and water. Add more water, if needed, just to cover. Cover with greaseproof paper to allow the tops of the peaches also to cook, and bring to the boil. Simmer the peaches for 5 minutes and then leave to cool in the sweet liquor. Do not poach the peaches if using tinned.

To make the cheesecake, beat the remaining 25 g (1 oz) caster sugar and lemon or lime juice into the mascarpone cheese. Whisk the double cream to soft peaks and fold into the mascarpone. Spread or pipe the mixture into the pastry case. Refrigerate for 30 minutes to set. Take the peaches from the syrup and peel them. Carefully cut into halves and remove the stones. The peaches can now be packed on top of the tart.

To finish, dust the peaches heavily with icing sugar and glaze under the grill or with a gas gun. Dust and grill again; this will give an almost crème-brûlée-like crunchy topping and also a 'burnt' edge to the sweet peaches. Before glazing, the pastry edge can be covered with foil to prevent it from burning.

Note: For a basic biscuit base, take 100 g (4 oz) of ginger snaps and 100 g (4 oz) digestive biscuits and crush with a rolling pin or in a plastic bag. Melt 25 g (1 oz) of butter and mix into the crumbs. Press the mixture into a 20–25 cm (8–10 in) greased, loose-based flan ring and refrigerate to set before spreading the cream on top. To spice the pastry case, take 50 g (2 oz) of stem ginger, chop it and add it to the pastry recipe; or add a teaspoon of ground ginger.

Raspberry Meringue Pie

I call this dish 'upside-down meringue pudding'. This is because the fresh raspberries sit on top of the meringue, which is directly on the pastry case, rather than the meringue being the topping, as is usual. I have used Italian meringue as the filling. This is a meringue that is made with boiled sugar and then continuously whipped until cold, which gives it a fuller flavour and texture. In this recipe, I add some grated zest of lemon, a citrus fruit that goes very well with raspberries, although the basic meringue recipe is the same with or without the lemon. The hazelnut pastry goes very well with the meringue; the crumbly, nutty flavour with the meringue and raspberry topping is delicious.

You will need a sugar thermometer for this recipe.

Makes a 25 cm (10 in) Pie
350 g (12 oz) fresh raspberries,
  washed
225 g (8 oz) Hazelnut Pastry
  (page 226)
Icing sugar, sifted, for dusting
  (optional)

For the Meringue:
175 g (6 oz) caster sugar
85 ml (3 fl oz) water
The finely grated zest of 2 lemons
4 egg whites

Pre-heat the oven to 180°C/350°F/Gas Mark 4. Butter a 20 cm (8 in) loose-based tart tin. Roll the pastry out thinly and line the tin. Line with foil or greaseproof paper, fill with baking beans or rice and bake blind for 25–30 minutes until set and golden. Remove the foil or greaseproof paper and beans or rice. Trim off any excess pastry to give you a neat finish.

For the meringue, boil the sugar and water with the lemon juice to 121°C. While the sugar is boiling, whisk the egg whites to soft peaks. When the sugar has reached the right temperature, pour it slowly onto the egg whites, whisking all the time. Once all has been added, continue to whisk until cooled. Spread the meringue in the baked pastry case almost to the top and bake for 10 minutes. During the cooking time, the meringue will rise. Once baked, it will cool and relax back into the case.

Once the pie has cooled to room temperature, spoon the raspberries all over or arrange them upright side by side, covering the whole tart. Dust with icing sugar, if using, just before serving.

Note: The raspberries can be tossed in a knob of butter, water and sugar to give them a glaze before you spoon them over the tart.

Pumpkin and Raisin Crumble Tart

Pumpkin is a vegetable that is reported to have been used at least 400 years ago. The members of the pumpkin family run into literally hundreds — squash being one of them with marrows and courgettes joining along the way. It is best to select smaller pumpkins for this tart for a richer colour and flavour. Serve with custard, cream or clotted cream.

Makes a 25 cm (10 in) deep Tart

225 g (8 oz) Sweet Shortcrust Pastry (page 224)
750 g (1½ lb) fresh pumpkin flesh, cut in 1 cm (½ in) dice
75 g (3 oz) raisins
25 g (1 oz) candied mixed peel
75 g (3 oz) soft light-brown sugar
25 g (1 oz) butter, melted
1 teaspoon ground mixed spice

For the Crumble Topping:

350 g (12 oz) plain flour
225 g (8 oz) butter, diced
100 g (4 oz) caster sugar
100 g (4 oz) chopped mixed nuts e.g. pecan, walnut, almond and hazelnut

Pre-heat the oven to 200°C/400°F/Gas Mark 6. Butter a 25 cm (10 in), loose-based tart tin that is at least 2.5–3 cm (1–1½ in) deep. Roll and line the tin with the pastry, leaving any excess pastry hanging over the edge. Line with greaseproof paper or foil and fill with baking beans or rice. Bake blind for 20–25 minutes until golden.

Once cooked, remove the paper and beans and trim the excess pastry, leaving a neat finish to the tart.

Mix the pumpkin with the raisins, mixed peel, sugar, butter and mixed spice. Pack the mixture into the pastry case.

For the crumble topping, put all the ingredients into an electric mixer, using the beater attachment, or a food processor. It should be slightly over mixed if anything to give a lumpy, textured crumble mixture. Spoon on top of the pumpkin and bake for 40–45 minutes. The 'lumpy' crumble topping will cook to a crunchy finish with the pumpkin underneath very tender. It is now ready to serve.

Glazed Lemon and Apple Rice Pies

I'm basically making a lemon-flavoured baked rice pudding, which is going to be served cold in a pastry case, finished with a crème-brûlée-style crisp topping. The apples are the dominant feature, adding a coarser texture to the finished dish.

Makes a 20 cm (8 in) shallow Pie

225 g (8 oz) Sweet Shortcrust Pastry (page 224)
300 ml (10 fl oz) milk
The finely grated zest of 2 lemons
25 g (1 oz) long-grain rice
3 tablespoons double cream
450 g (1 lb) green apples, peeled, cored and diced

25 g (1 oz) candied mixed peel
A pinch of ground cinnamon and nutmeg
50 ml (2 fl oz) white wine
A knob of butter
15 g (½ oz) caster sugar
2 eggs, separated
Icing sugar, sifted, to glaze

Pre-heat the oven to 200°C/400°F/Gas Mark 6. Butter a shallow 20 cm (8 in), loose-based tart tin. Roll out the pastry thinly and line the tin with it, leaving any excess pastry hanging over the edge. Line with greaseproof paper or foil and fill with rice or baking beans. Bake blind for 20 minutes. Remove the greaseproof paper or foil and beans or rice. Trim the excess pastry and you will have a neat finish.

Reduce the temperature of the oven to 180°C/350°F/Gas Mark 4. Boil the milk in a pan with the lemon zest, add the rice and slowly simmer for 30–35 minutes.

Remove from the heat. Add the double cream, apples, candied peel, cinnamon, nutmeg, white wine, butter, sugar and egg yolks. Whisk the egg whites to soft peaks and gently fold them in.

Spoon the mixture into the pastry case and bake for 30–35 minutes. Once cooked, remove from the oven and leave to cool. Dust with icing sugar and glaze under the grill or with a gas gun. Repeat the same process with extra icing sugar to give a thicker, caramelized topping.

Note: When glazing, it is best to cover the pastry edge with the foil to prevent it from burning.

Apricot Pies or Pie

All apricots used in this recipe can be replaced with tinned, so there's no excuse for not trying this dessert when fresh apricots are not in season.

Makes 6–8 Individual Pies or one 23 cm (9 in) Pie

350 g (12 oz) Sweet Shortcrust Pastry (page 224)

For the Frangipane (Almond Paste):

250 g (9 oz) butter, softened

250 g (9 oz) caster sugar

4 eggs

175 g (6 oz) ground almonds

50 g (2 oz) plain flour

100 g (4 oz) dried, ready-to-eat apricots, chopped

For the Chunky Apricots:

450 g (1 lb) apricots, cut in rough 1 cm (½ in) dice or a 420 g (14¾ oz) tin of apricot halves

About 50 g (2 oz) caster sugar, if using fresh apricots

For the Topping:

1 apricot half (tinned or fresh) per individual tart or 8 for 1 large tart

150 ml (5 fl oz) water

50 g (2 oz) caster sugar

For the Apricot Syrup Glaze:

4 tablespoons apricot jam

To Serve:

300 ml (10 fl oz) Anglaise Sauce (page 223)

Pre-heat the oven to 140°C/275°F/Gas Mark 1 if you're making one large pie and 160°C/325°F/Gas Mark 3 if you're making individual ones. Butter six or eight 7.5 cm (3 in) diameter, 5 cm (2 in) deep tartlet tins or a 23 cm (9 in) loose-based tart tin. Roll out the pastry and use to line the tin(s).

The frangipane (almond paste) can be made in an electric mixer. Cream together the butter and sugar. Add the eggs one at a time until all are incorporated. Mix together the ground almonds and flour and fold into the creamed butter mixture. Add the chopped, dried apricots. Spead a little of this mixture over the base of each pastry-lined tin.

Now make the 'chunky' apricots. If using canned, simply take 8–10 halves and cut into 1 cm (½ in) dice. Divide between the tin(s). If using fresh, mix the chopped apricots with the sugar and cook on a low heat to a chunky purée. Taste and add more sugar if too sharp. Place a heaped tablespoon of the mixture into the tin(s), leaving at least 5 mm (¼ in) space from the top. Any remaining chunky apricot mixture can be used to serve separately or added to the apricot glaze.

Bake the individual pies for 25–30 minutes and the large one for 1–1¼ hours. During cooking, the frangipane mixture will rise, leaving a domed finish. Remove from the oven and leave to rest for 10 minutes. Lift the pie(s) out of the tin(s).

Prepare the apricots for the topping. If using canned, just drain and cut carefully into thin slices and overlap around the top of the pies. If using fresh, bring the water to the boil with the sugar and simmer for 3–4 minutes. Reserve the syrup. Halve the apricots and remove the stones. Slice very thinly and drop straight into the hot syrup. Remove the pan from the heat and leave the syrup to cool. Lift the slices out of the syrup (reserve the syrup) and arrange, overlapping, around the top of the pie(s). Dust with icing sugar and glaze under the grill or with a gas gun to give a 'burnt' edge to each slice.

For the apricot syrup glaze, bring the jam to a simmer with 4–6 tablespoons of the reserved syrup from the can or that used for cooking the fresh apricot slices. Simmer for 2–3 minutes to a coating consistency. The glaze is now ready. If you're using tinned apricots, simply add water to the jam.

To present the dish, spoon some anglaise sauce in the middle of the plates, sit an individual pie or a wedge from the larger pie on top and pour some apricot syrup over. The flavours are just immense.

Note: For a richer and thicker glaze, add any remaining chunky apricot mixture to the jam and syrup. Once tender, simply push through a sieve for a deeper glaze.

You can also use pears or peaches for this recipe.

A 5 mm–1 cm (¼–½ in) thick slice of Lemon Genoise Sponge (page 222) can be placed in the base of each pie for an even richer texture and taste.

Rhubarb and Ginger Shortcake Pudding

This classic pudding is built up like mille-feuilles: *extra-thin ginger shortcakes are layered with rhubarb pieces and pastry cream. The pastry cream does work very well with this dish, but simple whipped cream, or a couple of spoons of clotted cream will also do the trick.*

Serves 4

750 g (1½ lb) rhubarb
25 g (1 oz) butter
150 g (5 oz) caster sugar
4 tablespoons ginger ale
Icing sugar (optional)
150 ml (5 fl oz) Pastry Cream
　(page 231), or whipped or
　clotted cream

For the Biscuits

150 g (5 oz) plain flour
1 teaspoon ground ginger
100 g (4 oz) butter
50 g (2 oz) icing sugar
50 g (2 oz) stem ginger, finely
　chopped
2 egg yolks

Pre-heat the oven to 200°C/400°F/Gas Mark 6.

To make the biscuits, sieve the flour with the ground ginger. Rub the butter into the flour. Add the sugar and the stem ginger. Mix in the egg yolks and work to a smooth dough. Leave to rest for 20 minutes. Roll the dough very thinly. Using a pastry cutter of 7.5 cm (3 in) diameter, cut into about 12 discs, allowing three per portion. Sit the discs on a greaseproof-paper-lined baking sheet and rest for 10 minutes. Bake for 15–18 minutes. They will be golden brown and crisp. Remove from the oven and leave to cool.

Take 650 g (1¼ lb) of the rhubarb and, if it's young and tender, just wash and cut into 2 cm (¾ in) thick rounds. If it feels stringy, lightly peel it and then cut into rounds. Melt the butter in a large saucepan and add the rhubarb rounds. Stir for 2–3 minutes before adding the sugar and ginger ale. The rhubarb will cook and become tender within 3–5 minutes. Once cooked, remove four-fifths from the pan and set aside to cool. This is the rhubarb filling. Continue to cook the remaining one-fifth rhubarb to a purée and then push through a sieve to give you a rhubarb syrup. Finely dice the remaining 100 g (4 oz) raw rhubarb, add to the syrup to give it some texture and bring to the simmer for 2–3 minutes. Remove from the stove and leave to cool. If the syrup now tastes too sharp, add a sprinkling of icing sugar.

To serve per portion: put the rhubarb filling around the edge of two of the biscuits, leaving a narrow border. Spoon some pastry cream or cream in the centre of the rhubarb. Stack the rhubarb-covered biscuits one on top of the other (so you have two layers of rhubarb and cream) and finish by topping with one last biscuit. Dust the top biscuit with icing sugar. Spoon around the rhubarb syrup and serve.

Note: The biscuits can be made without ginger. Fresh raspberries or strawberrries can also be used.

Wagon Wheel® Pudding

This recipe came from memories of tuck-shop days at school. The Wagon Wheel® had just come out then and it was a revelation: a chocolate topping encasing two biscuits, filled with marshmallow. They are still available and seeing them again gave me the inspiration to turn them into a dessert. Offer this pudding to your friends and family and, I guarantee, the conversation will turn to schoolday treats.

If you want a perfect finishing touch to your dessert, I suggest you double the topping quantities and apply the chocolate in stages. The chocolate keeps the biscuits fresh for days, so this pudding can be made in advance.

Serves 6

Raspberry or strawberry jam,
    for spreading

For the Marshmallow:

225 g (8 oz) icing sugar

85 ml (3 fl oz) water

25 g (1 oz) liquid glucose

15 g (½ oz) leaf gelatine, soaked in
    water, or 1½ x 11.7 g sachets of
    powdered gelatine, dissolved in
    4 tablespoons of water and then
    gently heated until clear

1 egg white

Cornflour, for dusting

**For the Biscuits
  (Makes 12–15):**

225 g (8 oz) butter

75 g (3 oz) caster sugar

1 egg yolk

1 tablespoon maple or golden syrup

250 g (9 oz) plain flour

For the Chocolate Topping:

100 g (4 oz) good-quality plain or
    milk chocolate

150 ml (5 fl oz) double cream

50 g (2 oz) butter

Pre-heat the oven to 180°C/350°F/Gas Mark 4. First make the marshmallow. Mix the icing sugar, water and glucose together and bring to the boil. Simmer for 2–3 minutes. Add the gelatine and as soon as it has fully dissolved pour onto the egg white in a mixing bowl. Whisk immediately (preferably with an electric mixer) to a thick, creamy consistency.

Dust well a large, shallow baking tray or dish (it must be at least 1 cm/½ in deep and big enough to allow you to cut six 8 cm/3½ in discs) with the cornflour and pour in the marshmallow mix. Refrigerate and leave to set for 1–1½ hours. Once set, cut out six 8 cm (3½ in) discs with a plain biscuit cutter and keep ready for the finished dessert.

Next, make the biscuits. Cream together the butter and sugar and then add the egg yolk and syrup. Fold in the flour and mix to a smooth dough. Refrigerate for 15–20 minutes.

Roll out to 2–3 mm (⅛ in) thick. Cut out twelve 8 cm (3½ in) discs, allowing two per portion, and bake for 10–15 minutes until golden. Remove from the oven and allow to cool.

To make the chocolate topping, melt the chocolate with the cream in a bowl over simmering water. Once melted, add the butter and stir in. Remove from the heat to prevent the butter from becoming too liquid. The butter should have melted and emulsified into the chocolate mixture. If the mixture is a little too thin, leave to cool to thicken slightly.

Spread some of the jam fairly generously onto four biscuits. Sit a marshmallow disc on each and then spread some more jam on top. Finish with another biscuit on top to create a 'sandwich'.

For a perfect chocolate finish, spoon on the chocolate mixture in stages. First, sit the biscuits on a wire rack and set over a baking tray or plate and spoon some of the chocolate topping over to cover completely. Refrigerate for 15–20 minutes until set. Remove and turn the biscuits upside-down on the rack. Spoon some more of the chocolate over the biscuits to cover. Refrigerate again until set. Remove and spoon over any remaining chocolate again (you might need to reuse some of the topping from the tray) for a smoother, thicker finish. Refrigerate and leave to set.

For an even more luscious ending, serve with a trickle of pouring cream.

Note: This pudding can be made more fruity and even richer by placing fresh raspberries or strawberries on top of the marshmallow and finishing as above.

Pumpernickel Bread and Butter Pudding

Pumpernickel is a dark rye bread that tastes of sweet molasses with a slight black-treacle-like flavour. It is best to find a pumpernickel bread that has a light texture and one that's not too close and heavy. As for the dessert, I couldn't resist adding yet another bread and butter pudding recipe! This one is very rich, fudgy, treacly and good.

Serves 6

10 slices of soft pumpernickel bread
  (crusts can be left on)
50 g (2 oz) unsalted butter
50 g (2 oz) chopped prunes
8 egg yolks
2 tablespoons soft light-brown sugar
2 tablespoons black treacle
300 ml (10 fl oz) double cream
300 ml (10 fl oz) milk
4 tablespoons caster sugar

Pre-heat the oven to 180°C/350°F/Gas Mark 4. Butter the bread and lay five slices, overlapping, in a pudding dish. Sprinkle with the prunes and top with the remaining overlapping slices. Whisk the egg yolks with the brown sugar and black treacle for 1–2 minutes until paler in colour. Bring the double cream and milk to the boil and pour onto the egg yolk mixture. Pour the custard over the bread and leave to stand for 20 minutes. During this time, the bread will soak up and absorb some of the custard.

Put the pudding dish in a baking tray, half-filled with warm water. Bake for 20–30 minutes. The custard will have thickened and almost have reached setting point but will still be liquid in the centre. Remove from the oven and baking tray. Dust with caster sugar and glaze under the grill or with a gas gun.

Note: The chopped prunes can be substituted with raisins.

Steamed Lemon Dumpling Puddings

These are more than just simple steamed puddings. The rich moistness and flavour of the lemon and suet dough bites into your taste buds. The puddings eat very well when just calmed with a spoonful of cream. If you're a real lemon-lover, then serve with a rich lemon custard (Lemon Anglaise Sauce, page 223), or simply with a trickle of golden syrup.

Serves 6

175 g (6 oz) white breadcrumbs
175 g (6 oz) suet
175 g (6 oz) caster sugar
175 g (6 oz) self-raising flour
The finely grated zest of 4 lemons
The juice of 2 lemons
2 eggs, beaten

Butter and lightly flour six 150 ml (5 fl oz) individual pudding basins. Mix together the breadcrumbs, suet, sugar, flour and grated lemon zest. Bind the dough together with the lemon juice and beaten eggs. Fill each basin three-quarters full and top with buttered foil, leaving enough space for the puddings to rise.

Steam on a trivet in a large pan of boiling water (keeping a check on the water level) covered with a lid for 40-45 minutes. The puddings can now be turned out and served.

Note: You can of course use the juice and zest of oranges or limes to give you a different flavoured pudding.

Lemon and Sultana Savarin *served with*
Lemon Yoghurt Ice-cream

You can't find a moister sponge to eat than a savarin dipped in a syrup. The lemony flavour can be changed to orange or lime or left plain (without the fruit juices) and garnished with fruit.

Serves 6

Lemon Yoghurt Ice-cream
  (page 175), to serve

For the Savarin:
10 g (¼ oz) caster sugar
20 g (¾ oz) fresh yeast or 7 g (¼ oz)
  dried easy-blend yeast
50 ml (2 fl oz) tepid milk
3 eggs
250 g (9 oz) plain flour
100 g (4 oz) sultanas

135 g (4¾ oz) butter, diced and
  softened

For the Syrup:
150 ml (5 fl oz) lemon juice
Very thinly sliced julienne strips of
  lemon zest (optional)
300 ml (10 fl oz) water
100 g (4 oz) caster sugar
2 cinnamon sticks (optional)
1 vanilla pod or 1 teaspoon of
  vanilla essence

Pre-heat the oven to 190°C/375°F/Gas Mark 5. Butter six 7.5 cm (3 in) savarin rings or one 23 cm (9 in) ring. Work the sugar and fresh yeast together until liquid and then add to the tepid milk. Beat the eggs and add to the milk mix. Sieve the flour and mix with the sultanas. If using easy-blend yeast, just add it to the flour and sultanas. Pour the yeast or egg mix into the flour and work to a dough. Spoon the diced butter onto the dough and cover. Keep in a warm place, allowing to prove for 20–30 minutes. Once proved, knock back, incorporating the butter. Scrape the mixture into a large nylon piping bag, pipe into the prepared ring(s) and bake for 20–25 minutes. Once cooked, remove from the oven and leave to cool.

The next stage is to make a syrup for soaking. It is from this syrup that the savarin will pick up the rich lemon flavour. The lemon julienne strips, if using, must first be blanched in fresh boiling water three times. This will take out any bitterness. Mix all of the other ingredients together and bring to the boil with the addition of the lemon zest. Simmer for 5 minutes. Remove the cinnamon and vanilla pod. The lemon zest can also be removed and kept separate in some syrup. Spoon some of the warm syrup over the savarins and leave to soak in for a few minutes before turning out onto serving plates. Any remaining lemon syrup can be reduced by half. This will result in a thick, very rich, lemony syrup to decorate the savarin(s).

To present the dish, spoon some lemon yoghurt ice-cream in the centre of the savarins, drizzle the reduced lemon syrup over and sit the lemon zest julienne on top.

Note: For an even better finish you can spoon Sultana Syrup Sauce (page 228) around. or add chopped fresh mint to the lemon syrup.

Baked Apple and Lime Syrup Pudding

This is a classic Sunday-lunch pudding. It is nice and easy to make and will suit the whole family. The lime flavour can be swapped with lemon or orange (add a spoonful or two of marmalade to the sponge mixture, if using orange) and other fruits can be added to the apples – raspberries, blackberries, blackcurrants and so on. I like to serve this pudding with custard, cream or crème fraîche.

Serves 6

6 green dessert apples, peeled and
   quartered
100 g (4 oz) butter, melted
A generous pinch of ground
   cinnamon
25 g (1 oz) caster sugar

2 eggs
50 g (2 oz) soft light-brown sugar
2 tablespoons golden syrup
6 tablespoons milk
225 g (8 oz) self-raising flour
The finely grated zest and juice
   of 2 limes

Pre-heat the oven to 180°C/350°F/Gas Mark 4. Butter a 20–25 cm (8–10 in) ovenproof pudding dish. Remove all cores from the apple quarters and halve each quarter, giving you eight pieces per apple. Using a tablespoon or two of the melted butter, pan-fry the apples with the cinnamon and caster sugar for 2–3 minutes. Remove from the heat and allow to cool. This will have helped just to soften the apples. Place the apples in the dish.

Beat the eggs with the soft light-brown sugar and golden syrup. Stir in the remaining melted butter and the milk. Sift the flour into the egg mixture and whisk it in with the lime juice and zest.

Pour the batter over the apples and bake for 25–30 minutes. Once golden brown and baked, glaze the pudding with a mixture of icing sugar and lemon or lime juice. Simply mix the sugar with the juice until a thin icing consistency is achieved. Spread over the pudding and serve. Apricot jam or a dusting of icing sugar can also be used.

Roast Peaches or Nectarines *with*
Blackberry Ice-cream

Apples or bananas are probably the most common fruits that are 'roasted' to give baked apples and barbecued bananas. Both are excellent, but I thought I would introduce another two. Roasting whole peaches or nectarines keeps all of the fruit texture and the flavour gets even better. The blackberry ice-cream finishes the dish off beautifully.

Serves 4
4 whole peaches or nectarines, skin left on
50 g (2 oz) butter

25 g (1 oz) soft light-brown sugar
4 tablespoons of water
Blackberry Ice-cream (page 161) or bought vanilla ice-cream, to serve

Pre-heat the oven to 200°C/400°F/Gas Mark 6.

Heat an ovenproof frying-pan with 25 g (1 oz) of the butter. Add the fruits and shallow-fry for 4–5 minutes until they start to become golden brown. Turn occasionally. Arrange the fruits stalk-side down and bake for 15–20 minutes (20–25 if under-ripe). Remove from the oven and lift the fruits from the pan. Pour off any excess butter and wipe the pan clean. Add the remaining butter with the sugar and water. Bring to the simmer and return the fruits to the pan. Simmer and reduce the syrup while rolling the fruits to coat them with the glaze. Once the syrup has reached a coating consistency, put the peaches or nectarines on serving plates and trickle any remaining syrup over. Serve a large scoop of blackberry ice-cream next to the fruit.

Note: Extra syrup can be made by doubling the sugar, water and remaining butter quantities.

You don't have to serve home-made ice-cream: a good-quality, shop-bought variety will also go very well.

The fruits can be glazed with warm honey or golden syrup.

The peaches or nectarines will also go very well with custard and/or cream.

A scoop of vanilla ice-cream with Raspberry Syrup (page 229) will give you 'roast peach Melba'!

Char-grilled Glazed Pumpkin Slices
with Lemon Sherbet and Cream

This dish works wonders on a barbecue grill. The real charred flavour is good and strong and is nicely balanced with the sweetness from the glaze, giving a bittersweet finish. All of these tastes are sharpened with a spoonful of the lemon sherbet, balanced by the fresh cream. I think I've said enough!

This recipe doesn't have to rely on a barbecue. A small ridged, cast-iron grill pan can also be used. If you don't have either, simply pan-fry and glaze and you'll still be very happy with the results.

Serves 4
450–750 g (1–1½ lb) small pumpkin
25 g (1 oz) butter, melted
Icing sugar, sifted

To Serve:
4 portions of Lemon Sherbet
  (page 166)
150–300 ml (5–10 fl oz) extra-thick
  double cream

Cut the pumpkin into 8–12 wedges. Remove the seeds and with a sharp knife cut away the skin. Brush each slice with butter and sit them on the hot barbecue or grill pan. The pumpkin will only need 7–8 minutes before being turned; repeat with the same cooking time for the other side. The pumpkin will now be tender without being overcooked.

Lay the slices on a buttered baking tray and dust heavily with icing sugar. Put the tray under a very hot grill and the sugar will begin to caramelize. Once the sugar has totally melted and begins to bubble, remove the tray, dust heavily again with icing sugar and slide back under the grill. This time, the icing sugar will colour and begin to form a sweet crust. Once totally golden and crisp, the pumpkin wedges are ready. Arrange them on plates with a large scoop of the lemon sherbet and a good spoonful of extra-thick cream.

Note: A third dusting of icing sugar and glazing will give an even crispier topping. Another form of glaze is to omit the sugar and simply trickle golden syrup or honey over the grilled pumpkin.

Lime sherbet also goes very well with the pumpkin slices.

Clotted Cream Brûlée

Crème brûlée – thick vanilla custard topped with a caramel glaze – is a dessert I cannot resist. Imagine eating a crème brûlée that has clotted cream in the middle: you can taste it mingling with the custard in every bite. There's no need to imagine any more – the recipe is here!

Serves 6

10 egg yolks
100 g (4 oz) caster sugar
450 ml (15 fl oz) double cream
150 ml (5 fl oz) milk

2 vanilla pods, split lengthways, or
  2–3 drops of vanilla essence
6 heaped tablespoons clotted cream
Icing sugar, sifted

Cream together the egg yolks and sugar. Boil the cream, milk and vanilla pods or essence. Pour the vanilla cream onto the egg yolks and sugar and then pour this mixture into a bowl. Cook over a pan of simmering water, stirring occasionally, until thickened. This will take 20–25 minutes.

Once thickened, remove from the stove and use to half-fill all six 150 ml (5 fl oz) ramekins. Refrigerate until set. The remaining crème brûlée mix can be left to cool. Once the first half of the brûlée has set, spoon the clotted cream on top into the centre. Pour over the remaining brûlée mix. Return the ramekins to the fridge to set completely.

Dust heavily with icing sugar and glaze under the grill or with a gas gun. Dust with more icing sugar and finish glazing. The clotted cream brûlées are now crispy on top and ready to eat.

Crème Chiboust *with Fresh Fruit Salad*

Crème chiboust is the cream used to finish a Gâteau St Honoré. Chiboust was the name of the chef who first put together the St Honoré and the cream to go with it. It is a pastry cream, finished with Italian meringue. In this dessert, it is flavoured with lemon, frozen, cut into shapes and caramelized very quickly under a hot grill and then served with a delicious fresh fruit salad.

Serves 6–8
150 ml (5 fl oz) lemon juice, plus the
   grated zest of 2 lemons
150 ml (5 fl oz) double cream
4 tablespoons caster sugar
25 g (1 oz) cornflour
6 egg yolks
1 × 11.7 g sachet powdered
   gelatine, dissolved in
3 tablespoons of cold water for
5 minutes

For the Italian Meringue:
200 g (7 oz) caster sugar
50 ml (2 fl oz) water
6 egg whites

For the Fruit Salad:
Selection of soft fruit e.g.
   raspberries, strawberries, peaches,
   bananas, kiwi fruit, oranges, melon,
   blackberries and/or blackcurrants,
   prepared as necessary
150 ml (5 fl oz) Raspberry or
   Strawberry Syrup (page 229)

Boil together the lemon juice, zest and cream. Mix the sugar, cornflour and egg yolks together in a bowl and pour on the boiled juice and cream, whisking constantly. Return the mixture to the pan and cook on a low heat for 8–10 minutes until thickened (do not allow to boil). Dissolve the gelatine over a gentle heat until clear and add to the thickened lemon custard.

For the meringue, boil together the caster sugar and water to 121–130°C, which takes 2–3 minutes. While the sugar is boiling, whisk the egg whites to firm peaks. Gradually pour the boiled sugar onto the egg whites, whisking all the time; slowly continue to whisk the egg whites until just warm. Fold the meringue into the custard. Line a large baking tray with cling film and spoon in the chiboust cream (you need it to be about 2.5–3 cm/1–1½ in deep). Freeze until firm.

Once frozen, remove and cut into shapes as required. I like to serve these cut in rectangles 8–10 × 5 cm (3½–4 × 2 in). Re-freeze for 2–3 hours.

Prepare the fruits for the salad. Arrange on serving plates and pour 2–3 tablespoons of syrup over each portion.

Glaze the tops of crème chiboust shapes with a gas gun or under the grill. Put the shapes on top of the fruit. After a few moments, the chiboust will soften. It's now ready to serve.

Warm Cherry Chocolate Cakes

You can use fresh or tinned cherries in this recipe. If using fresh, cook them in a small knob of butter with a sprinkling of sugar, just enough to soften them lightly. You can leave out the cherries and just add extra grated chocolate to create a melting consistency.

Serves 4

100 g (4 oz) fresh stoned or tinned cherries, quartered

100 g (4 oz) butter, plus a small knob

120 g (4½ oz) caster sugar

A drop of kirsch (optional)

100 g (4 oz) dark bitter chocolate, chopped, plus 25–50 g (1–2 oz) dark bitter chocolate, grated (optional)

50 g (2 oz) plain flour

3 eggs, separated

To Serve:

Extra-thick or clotted cream (optional)

Icing sugar, sifted (optional)

Extra finely grated chocolate (optional)

Pre-heat the oven to 180°C/350°F/Gas Mark 4. Butter four 7.5 cm (3 in) diameter tartlet tins or one 15–18 cm (6–7 in) diameter tart tin. Line the base(s) with greaseproof paper.

Melt the small knob of butter, add the cherries, 15 g (½ oz) caster sugar and kirsch, if using. Cook on a high heat for 1–2 minutes and then leave to cool. Melt the chocolate in a bowl over simmering water or in the microwave. Once melted, add the butter and stir until emulsified. Stir in the flour, the remaining caster sugar and cherries. Beat the egg yolks until pale and slightly thickened and add to the chocolate mixture.

Whisk the egg whites to soft peaks and carefully fold them in. If using extra grated chocolate, add it now. Spoon into the prepared cake tins so they are just over half full. Individual cakes will now take 15–20 minutes to cook; a large cake will take 30–35 minutes.

Once cooked, remove from the oven and leave to cool to just warm. Remove from the tins and peel off the paper. Carefully cut off the crusty tops. Spoon extra-thick or clotted cream on top of the cake while still warm and place the crusty tops back on. The cake has a fudgy texture and is sensational to eat when served warm with the cream melting in. I like to decorate the plates with a dusting of icing sugar and a sprinkling of finely grated chocolate.

Note: The cherries can be also left in halves; double the quantity to 225 g (8 oz) and sauté with the butter and sugar. Flambé with brandy or kirsch and spoon over the cakes with the cream on top.

The Fruit Jam Sauce on page 230 can also be used: warm blackcurrant-jam sauce works wonderfully.

Mini Madeira Prune Cakes *with Madeira Sherbet and Syrup*

This is a basic Madeira cake recipe, but with the addition of chopped prunes. The prunes give another flavour and also add moistness to the texture. This recipe doesn't have to be for mini cakes; an 15 cm (6 in) cake tin can be used and the prunes can be left in or out.

Serves 6

175 g (6 oz) butter
175 g (6 oz) caster sugar
3 eggs, beaten
175 g (6 oz) plain flour
The finely grated zest of 2 lemons
175 g (6 oz) chopped prunes

To Serve:

6 portions of Madeira Sherbet
  (page 169)
12 tablespoons Madeira Syrup
  (page 228)

Pre-heat the oven to 180°C/350°F/Gas Mark 4. Butter six pastry rings, 7.5 cm (3 in) in diameter and 5 cm (2 in) deep. Alternatively, use six shallower 10 cm (4 in) diameter, 1 cm (½ in) deep tartlet tins or an 18 cm (6 in) sandwich tin. Put the pastry rings on a greaseproof-paper-lined baking sheet or base-line the individual tins or larger tin with greaseproof paper.

Beat the butter and sugar together until very light and creamy. Whisk the eggs in a bowl over a pan of simmering water until thick and pale in colour to a *sabayon*-like consistency. Fold the eggs into the butter mix and then sift in the flour. Stir in the lemon zest and chopped prunes. Divide between the rings or tins and bake for 20–25 minutes. Leave the cake(s) to cool for 10 minutes. Lift them from their mould(s) and peel off the paper if necessary.

Sit the warm Madeira cakes on plates and garnish with a scoop of Madeira sherbet and trickles of Madeira syrup.

Note: Cinnamon Ice-cream (page 169) also goes very well with the Madeira cake.

The cakes don't have to be eaten as a dessert; they are very nice to offer with afternoon tea.

Creamy Fried Slice *with Blackberry-jam Sauce and Extra-thick Cream*

The fried slice is a 2 cm (¾ in) piece of brioche, soaked in a cream, egg and sugar mixture and then shallow-fried in butter. It's served with a loose, fresh blackberry-jam sauce spooned on top with melting extra-thick cream. Yum!!

Serves 4

4 x 2 cm (¾ in) slices of home-made
    or bought brioche (a good plain,
    soft loaf will also work)

4 eggs

4 tablespoons caster sugar

4 tablespoons double cream

50 g (2 oz) butter

8 heaped tablespoons warm
    blackberry (or other fruit) Fruit
    Jam Sauce (page 230), warmed

Extra-thick cream, to serve

Whisk together the eggs, sugar and cream. Soak both sides of the brioche in the cream for a few minutes. Melt the butter in a large frying-pan on a medium heat. Shallow-fry the slices for 2–3 minutes on both sides. This will give a golden brown, slightly crisp texture, leaving an almost warm "doughnut" consistency inside. Put the slices on plates and spoon the warm jam sauce on top. Finish with extra-thick cream and serve.

Note: Add grated nutmeg to the cream for a spicier finish.

Date and Orange Mascarpone Fritters

These are best made by using the sweet, thick, fleshy medjool dates which grow in Egypt and California. Although they are on the expensive side, they are worth it. The fritters are made by stoning the medjool dates and filling them with orange-zest-flavoured mascarpone. Once battered and deep-fried, the mascarpone just melts in the mouth as you bite through the batter. I normally serve these with Cinnamon Ice-cream (page 169), along with either Orange and Rum or Sultana Syrup (pages 227 and 228).

Serves 4

20 medjool dates

The finely grated zest of 2 oranges

8 tablespoons mascarpone

Plain flour, for dusting

Oil, for deep-frying

Vanilla or Cinnamon Ice-cream
   (page 169), or cream, to serve

For the Batter:

300 ml (10 fl oz) sweet cider

100 g (4 oz) plain flour

25 g (1 oz) caster sugar

Heat the oil for deep-frying to 190°C/375°F or until a cube of day-old bread browns in 30 seconds.

Split the dates along one side and remove the stones. Mix the orange zest with the mascarpone. Make the batter by whisking all the ingredients together. Stuff the dates with the mascarpone mixture and push back into shape. Dust the dates with plain flour and then coat with the batter. Carefully place the dates in the hot oil. Cook for 5–6 minutes until completely crisp and golden. Lift from the fat onto kitchen paper to absorb any excess oil.

Serve the fritters with the cinnamon ice-cream and syrup, or just with vanilla ice-cream.

Chocolate Brownies

This is the recipe I use for the Bourbon Biscuit dessert (page 210) to add another texture to the biscuits. But to eat them as actual brownies, I've added toasted, chopped nuts and I've offered a recipe for a chocolate spread to finish them off. The ingredients may look like a lot but that's what gives you the extra flavours.

Makes 12 Slices

225 g (8 oz) butter

150 g (5 oz) cocoa powder

4 eggs

450 g (1 lb) caster sugar

150 g (5 oz) plain flour

2 teaspoons vanilla essence

2 tablespoons strong coffee

100 g (4 oz) mixed chopped nuts
   e.g. hazelnuts, pecans, walnuts
   and/or almonds, toasted

For the Chocolate Spread:

100 g (4 oz) good-quality plain
   chocolate, chopped

2 tablespoons strong coffee

100 g (4 oz) unsalted butter,
   softened

Pre-heat the oven to 180°C/350°F/Gas Mark 4. Butter a 25 cm (10 in) square or round cake tin and line the base with greaseproof paper.

Melt the butter and mix with the cocoa powder. Whisk together the eggs and caster sugar and add to the cocoa mixture. Add all the remaining ingredients and pour into the cake tin. Bake for 15–20 minutes. Leave to cool before turning out of the tin and peeling off the paper. Dust with cocoa powder, leave as it is or top with the chocolate spread.

For the spread, melt the chocolate with the coffee in a bowl over warm simmering water. Once it has a smooth, creamy consistency, remove from the heat and beat in the butter, a tablespoon at a time. Leave to cool. Once at a spreading consistency, cover the brownies. These can now be cut into wedges or squares.

Bourbon Biscuits

Another biscuit idea turned into a pudding recipe, Bourbon biscuits are definitely a dessert for chocoholics. The brownie sponge between the chocolate ganache and biscuit gives you more texture, more flavour and lots more chocolate. The biscuit eats very well with Coffee Anglaise Sauce (page 223) and/or a trickling of Coffee Syrup (page 230).

Serves 8

1 quantity Chocolate Brownies (page 209), omitting the nuts and chocolate spread

For the Biscuits (Makes 16):

150 g (5 oz) butter

150g (5 oz) caster sugar, plus extra for sprinkling

300 g (11 oz) self-raising flour

A pinch of salt

8 tablespoons cocoa powder

1 egg, beaten

8–10 teaspoons milk

For the Ganache:

225 g (8 oz) good-quality plain chocolate, chopped

250 ml (8 fl oz) double cream

2 egg yolks

25 g (1 oz) caster sugar

Pre-heat the oven to 180°C/350°F/Gas Mark 4. Make the brownies and spread into a large, shallow baking tray to give a layer 5 mm–1 cm (¼–½ in) thick. Bake for 7 minutes to leave the brownies very moist.

1 Make the biscuit mix, roll out, cut into 16 biscuits and make 15–18 holes in the top. Bake for 10 minutes.

2 For the ganache, melt the chocolate with half the cream. Whisk the egg yolks and sugar together and add to the chocolate mix. Lightly whisk and add the remaining cream.

3 Cut the brownies into rectangles slightly smaller than the biscuits.

4 Layer the biscuit with ganache, brownie, ganache, another brownie, more ganache and top with a biscuit.

For the biscuits, cream together the butter and caster sugar. Sieve together the flour, salt and cocoa powder. Add the egg to the creamed butter and then beat in the flour and cocoa mixture. Soften with the milk. Wrap the dough in cling film and refrigerate for 20-30 minutes.

Roll out the biscuit paste on a lightly floured surface to 2–3 mm (⅛ in) thick. Cut into 16 biscuits, 10 cm (4 in) long by 5 cm (2 in) wide. Transfer to a greaseproof-paper-lined baking tray. Make 15–18 small holes in the top (a cocktail stick will do the job) and bake for 10 minutes. Once cooked and while still warm, sprinkle with caster sugar. Leave to cool.

For the ganache, melt the chocolate with half the cream. Whisk the egg yolks and sugar together until they hold a thick ribbon trail. Lightly whip the remaining cream. Mix the egg yolk and sugar mix with the melted chocolate cream. Fold in the whipped cream and leave to cool to a piping consistency.

Turn half the baked biscuits over and spread very thinly with some ganache (to hold it to the brownie cake). Cut the brownies into rectangles just 2 mm (⅛ in) smaller than the biscuits and put them on the ganache-covered biscuits. Pipe a 5 mm–1 cm (¼–½ in) layer of ganache on top. Put another rectangle of brownie on the ganache. Lightly spread with ganache and finish with the top biscuit. Now put them on plates and dust with sugar.

Note: Finely grated orange zest can be added to the ganache and brownie-cake recipes (1 orange for each), plus a splash of Grand Marnier, to give you a chocolate-orange Bourbon Biscuit.

Banana Fool *with Warm Chocolate Sauce*

This is a quick dessert to make and can be made with the fruit of your choice – peaches, mangoes, Summer berries, etc. The fool can be served in glasses or ramekins. If ramekins, the chocolate sauce can be replaced with grated plain or milk chocolate on top.

Serves 6

For the Fool:
8 over-ripe bananas
1 tablespoon lemon juice
1 egg white (optional)
50 g (2 oz) caster sugar
300 ml (10 fl oz) double cream

For the Chocolate Sauce:
100 g (4 oz) good-quality plain
  chocolate, chopped
150 ml (5 fl oz) double cream
15 g (½ oz) butter

To make the fool, purée the bananas in a food processor with the lemon juice. Whisk the egg white if using to soft peaks and then add the caster sugar and continue to whisk to a meringue stage. Whip the double cream to soft peaks and fold with the meringue into the puréed bananas. Pipe or spoon into glasses, leaving at least 1 cm (½ in) of space from the top for the sauce. Refrigerate to set.

For the chocolate sauce, melt the chocolate with the double cream in a bowl over warm water. Once melted, add the butter, remove from the heat and stir in. Once at a warm temperature, pour into the glasses and serve.

Hot Chocolate 'Cappuccino'

This isn't a dessert but an absolutely fabulous drink. It was made for me a little while ago. The flavour and smooth, silky consistency were so good I had to have the recipe! I've made a couple of changes and topped it with soft whipped cream. You can either dust with cocoa or scatter over lots of finely grated dark chocolate.

Serves 4
100 g (4 oz) plain chocolate,
    broken into pieces
25 g (1 oz) milk chocolate,
    broken into pieces
600 ml (1 pint) milk
6 tablespoons double cream
A splash of Camp coffee essence
    (optional)
4 mugs!

For the Topping:
150 ml (5 fl oz) double cream,
    lightly whipped
Cocoa powder or 25–50 g (1–2 oz)
    finely grated plain or milk
    chocolate

Melt the chocolates in a bowl over a pan of simmering water. While melting, bring the milk to the boil. Add the 6 tablespoons of double cream to the chocolate and take it off the heat. Mix the hot milk and melted chocolate cream together, adding the Camp coffee, if using. Pour into the mugs and spoon the whipped cream carefully on top. Dust with cocoa or grated chocolate and serve.

Note: This can become a strong liqueur chocolate by adding a few measures of Baileys, whisky, brandy, rum, Cointreau, Grand Marnier, Drambuie, or any other liqueur you like.

The recipe can be made entirely with plain chocolate for a really rich chocolate flavour. However, this does make it quite bitter, so if you are going to use just plain chocolate, add 25 g (1oz) of soft, light-brown sugar to the milk.

Home-made Brioche

Brioche is a buttery loaf that can be used in or to accompany many courses: a toasted slice with pâté, stuffed with cheese, fried and topped with sweet peppers and olives, or made into brioche bread and butter pudding. This recipe makes quite a large amount – three loaves – but I think it is very practical because you can freeze two loaves for later. Perhaps you could make them go even further by cutting all three loaves in half and freezing five halves.

Makes 3 x 1 kg (2 lb) loaves

500 ml (17 fl oz) milk, warmed
120 g (4½ oz) fresh yeast
500 g (1¼ lb) strong white flour
12 eggs

1.9 kg (4¼ lb) plain flour
120 g (4½ oz) sugar
30 g (1¼ oz) salt
1.7 kg (4 lb) butter, melted

Pre-heat the oven to 180°C/350°F/Gas Mark 4. Butter three 1 kg (2 lb) loaf tins and line the bases with greaseproof paper.

Dissolve the yeast in the warm milk and leave it somewhere warm until it goes frothy. Add to the 500 g (1¼ lb) strong white flour, cover with a cloth and leave to prove in a warm place until doubled in size.

Once doubled in volume, add the eggs, plain flour, sugar and salt and mix well. Beat the butter into the dough, mix and then divide the mixture between the three tins. Leave to prove in a warm place for 20 minutes.

Bake until golden for 30–40 minutes. Remove the loaves from the oven and leave to cool for 10 minutes before lifting from the tins to cool completely.

Note: For a glossier finish, brush the loaves with beaten egg 5 minutes before the end of baking.

For a Prune and Walnut Brioche, add 225 g (8 oz) chopped prunes and 175 g (6 oz) chopped walnuts per loaf. Add the prunes with the eggs. This enables them to be broken into the mixture and the prune flavour to spread throughout. Add the walnuts with the butter and the job is done.

If you wish to make only one of the loaves into a prune and walnut one, add both ingredients to a third of the dough once it's made and knead them in. The prune and walnut brioche eats very well creamy-fried with fruit sauce, as on page 206. It is also a perfect accompaniment to cheese. The quantity of prunes and walnuts used for one loaf will give you a very rich prune and nutty taste. For a slightly less rich finish, simply halve the quantity of both these ingredients.

The number of loaves can be changed in various ways:
1. Make 6 x 450 g (1 lb) loaves
2. Cut the recipe in half for 3 x 450 g (1 lb) loaves
3. Make a third of the recipe for 1 x 1 kg (2 lb) or 2 x 450 g (1 lb) loaves.

Fruity Ravioli

It's pudding time for pasta! These home-made ravioli, filled with fresh or tinned fruits, can also be topped with Crisp 'Parmesan' Lemon Crumbs (page 231), or trickled with a fruity syrup and served with custard, ice-cream or cream: a fun pudding with fun flavours.

Serves 4

150 ml (5 fl oz) Basic Stock Syrup
(page 227)
Cream, soured cream or Anglaise
Sauce (page 223), to serve

For the Ravioli Paste:

350 g (12 oz) fine semolina
2 eggs
1 scraped vanilla pod or 1 teaspoon
of strong vanilla essence

The finely grated zest of 1 lemon, lime
or orange (optional)
Icing sugar, sifted, for rolling

For the Filling:

750–900 g (1½–2 lb) soft fruits e.g.
apricots, peaches, mangoes or Summer
fruits (tinned fruits can be used)
A knob of butter
25–50 g (1–2 oz) caster sugar
Soft fruits, mint leaves and lemon or
orange zest, to garnish

Work the egg into the semolina with the vanilla and zest. Once worked into a dough, cover and leave to rest for 15–20 minutes.

Meanwhile, to cook the filling, halve or chop any of the soft fruits that need it (berries can be left whole). Melt the butter, add the fruits and 25 g (1 oz) of sugar. Cook until pulpy but still with some texture left in the fruit. Taste for sweetness – if it's too sharp, add the remaining sugar. Leave to cool. If using tinned fruits, just drain and chop them.

The paste can now be rolled out very thinly (about 3 mm/⅛ in thick) with a pasta machine, if you have one, or by hand on plenty of icing sugar. Cut the paste into 10 cm (4 in) discs with a plain biscuit cutter, allowing 2–3 ravioli (4–6 discs) per portion. Put a tablespoon or two of fruit in the centre. Brush water around the outside rim and press a lid on top. Add any remaining fruits to the stock syrup and warm to make a purée. Push through a sieve to give a rich, thick, fruity syrup.

Cook the ravioli in boiling water for 3–4 minutes. This will cook the ravioli paste and warm the fruits through. Remove from the water with a draining spoon.

Trickle some cream, soured cream or Anglaise sauce across the base of the serving bowls with some fruit syrup. Sit the ravioli on top, dust with icing sugar and spoon more fruity syrup on top. Garnish with some of the fruits used in the filling and mint leaves or shreds of citrus zest.

Note: Liqueurs such as Cointreau, Grand Marnier, cognac and rum can be added to the syrup.

Water can be used in place of the stock syrup to purée any remaining fruits. Simply add water and simmer until a good, thick consistency is reached and push through a sieve.

Black Treacle Loaf

I am sure we all do the same thing – find a recipe and then play with it, making adjustments to improve (we hope!) the results. Well, here's an example of this. I love the rich flavour of black treacle but I did find the original recipe a little too dry. This loaf has a texture very similar to malt loaf, with a moist finish. With these changes, the result is rich and moreish!

Makes a 500 g (1 lb) Loaf

75 g (3 oz) black treacle
50 g (2 oz) soft brown sugar
1 egg
225 g (8 oz) plain flour

1 teaspoon ground mixed spice
50 g (2 oz) currants
50 g (2 oz) sultanas
50 g (2 oz) butter
65 ml (2½ fl oz) milk

Pre-heat the oven to 180°C/350°F/Gas Mark 4. Butter a 500 g (1 lb) loaf tin and line the base with greaseproof paper.

Cream the treacle with the sugar and egg. Sieve together the flour and spice and mix into the black treacle mixture. Add the currants and sultanas. Melt the butter with the milk and add to the mixture. Mix well. Spoon the mix into the tin and bake for 30–40 minutes.

After 30 minutes, check the loaf by piercing with a skewer or small knife. The skewer should come out clean but moist. Once it's cooked, remove the loaf from the oven and leave to stand for 10 minutes. Turn out the loaf, peel off the paper and slice once cool.

Note: This black treacle loaf mix does not really rise like bread in the tin, but becomes quite dense in texture, giving a richer, almost chewy taste.

Home-made Eccles Cakes

Eccles cakes are a classic for our corner-shop bakers and for us to eat! So, why not have a go at making your own? They really are very simple and easy to make and even more delicious to eat.

To lift the basic flavours of currants, sugar and butter, I have added some grated orange zest and a dusting of cinnamon.

Makes 4 Cakes

225 g (8 oz) Quick Puff Pastry
   (page 225) or frozen bought
   puff pastry, thawed
50 g (2 oz) currants
25 g (1 oz) soft light-brown sugar

25 g (1 oz) butter, softened
A pinch of ground cinnamon
The finely grated zest of 1 orange
1 egg white
Granulated sugar

Pre-heat the oven to 200°C/400°F/Gas Mark 6.

Roll out the pastry to about 2 mm (⅛ in) thick. Mix together the currants, soft brown sugar, butter, cinnamon and grated zest of orange.

Cut four 15 cm (6 in) discs of pastry. Divide the filling between each of the discs, placing a dome of mix in the centre of each one. Brush the edges of the pastry with water and gather all together, creating a 'bag' effect. Press the pastry together, cutting off any excess. The 'bag' can now be turned over onto a lightly floured board and softly rolled so that the pastry thins a little to reveal the currants, keeping a good circular shape. Repeat this simple process for the remaining three.

Brush each cake with egg white and sprinkle with granulated sugar. Score the tops with a sharp knife, making three or four lines. Rest in the fridge for 15–20 minutes. Bake on buttered greaseproof paper for 25 minutes until rich, golden and crispy.

The eccles cakes can be eaten as a pastry cake, warm or cold. However, they can also be served as a dessert with custard, clotted cream, vanilla ice-cream, or the lot!

Golden Ginger 'Flapjack' Cake

This is a rich afternoon-tea cake, flavoured with a lot of golden syrup and ginger to spice it up.

Makes about 12 Slices

175 g (6 oz) butter
100 g (4 oz) plain flour
450 g (1 lb) oatmeal
100 g (4 oz) soft light-brown sugar

15 g (½ oz) ground ginger
25 g (1 oz) bicarbonate of soda
450 g (1 lb) golden syrup
50 ml (2 fl oz) milk

Pre-heat the oven to 180°C/350°F/Gas Mark 4. Butter a 20 cm (8 in) round cake tin and line the base with greaseproof paper.

Rub the butter into the plain flour and then add the oatmeal, sugar, ginger and bicarbonate of soda.

Warm the syrup with the milk and pour into the dry ingredients, mixing well, to give quite a thick consistency. Spoon into the cake tin and bake for 45–50 minutes. The mix will rise slightly, giving a 3–5 cm (1½–2 in) deep cake.

Once cooked, leave to stand for 10–15 minutes to cool a little and turn out while still warm and peel off the paper. Slice into wedges and serve as a pudding with pouring or clotted cream, or leave to serve cold as an afternoon-tea cake.

Home-made Crumpets

I love having a go at the afternoon-tea cakes, hot-cross buns and scones. They are treats we all enjoy and they are so easy to get hold of, as almost every shop sells them. Crumpets warmed, and served toasted with lots of butter and jam are also a favourite. So, when a friend of mine passed on this recipe to me, I just had to have a go. They do work and, with lots of butter, are delicious.

Makes about 20
450 g (1 lb) plain flour
15 g (½ oz) salt

15 g (½ oz) fresh yeast
600 ml (1 pint) warm water

Sieve together the flour and salt. Mix the yeast with a few tablespoons of the warm water. Whisk three-quarters of the remaining warm water into the flour and then add the yeasty liquid. Cover and leave in a warm place until the mixture has risen. Once risen, check the consistency. If the batter is very thick, loosen with the remaining water. The batter should now be left to stand for 8–10 minutes.

Warm a non-stick frying-pan on a low heat. Grease some crumpet rings or small tartlet rings and rub the pan with butter.

Place the rings into the frying-pan and pour in some of the batter until half-full (5 mm–1 cm/¼–½ in deep). Cook on a low heat until small holes appear and the top has started to dry. The base of the crumpet will now be golden and it can be turned over and cooked for a further minute. The crumpets are now ready for lots of melting butter!

Note: The crumpets can be cooked without turning: simply cook until the tops are completely dry.

The finely grated zest of 1 lemon can also be added to the batter to give a lemon bite.

Lemon Genoise Sponge

This sponge can be used for many things: cakes, gâteaux, trifles or puddings. If you keep a couple of vanilla pods in an air-tight jar with your caster sugar, you will have vanilla sugar ready whenever you need it.

**Makes 1 x 15–20 cm
(6–8 in) Sponge**
3 eggs
75 g (3 oz) caster sugar flavoured
  with a vanilla pod

75 g (3 oz) plain flour
25 g (1 oz) unsalted butter, melted
Juice and zest of 1 lemon

Pre-heat the oven to 200°C/400°F/Gas Mark 6. Grease a 15–20 cm (6–8 in) round cake tin and dust with flour.

Whisk the eggs and sugar together in a bowl over a pan of hot water. Continue to whisk until the mixture has doubled in volume and is light and creamy. Remove from the heat and continue to whisk until cold and thick. This is called the ribbon stage, as the mixture will trail off the whisk in ribbons when you lift it out of the mixture. Lightly fold in the flour, melted butter, the juice and lemon zest. Gently pour the mix into the prepared tin and bake in the pre-heated oven for about 30 minutes. The easiest way to test is with a skewer, which will come out clean when the sponge is ready.

Allow to cool for 10 minutes in the tin, then turn out onto a wire rack and leave to go cold.

Note: To make a Chocolate Lemon Genoise Sponge, replace 25 g (1 oz) of the flour with 2 tablespoons of cocoa.

Anglaise (Fresh Custard) Sauce

This recipe is for a fresh custard or anglaise sauce which can act as a base for so many different flavours. You must only ever serve it warm, not boiled, or you will scramble the egg yolks in the cream mix. The fresh vanilla is optional and can be omitted when using other flavours.

Makes 750 ml (1¼ pints)

8 egg yolks
75 g (3 oz) caster sugar
1 vanilla pod (optional)
300 ml (10 fl oz) milk
300 ml (10 fl oz) double cream

Beat the egg yolks and sugar together in a bowl until well blended. Split and scrape the insides of the vanilla pod, if using, into the milk and cream and bring to the boil. Sit the bowl over a pan of hot water and whisk the cream into the egg mixture. As the egg yolks warm, the cream will thicken to create a custard. Keep stirring until it coats the back of a spoon. Remove the bowl from the heat. The custard can now be served warm or stirred occasionally until it cools. Serve warm or cold.

Variations: For Lemon Custard Sauce, add the pared rind, not the pith, of two lemons to the milk and cream when heating, then leave it in the mix throughout the cooking process. Once the custard has thickened, add the juice of one lemon and taste. If the lemon flavour is not strong enough, simply add more lemon juice to taste. Strain the custard through a sieve to serve.

For Orange Custard Sauce, add the pared rind of two oranges to the milk and cream when heating, then cook as for the basic recipe. Orange juice will not be used in this recipe. To lift the flavour of the sauce, try adding a few drops of Cointreau or Grand Marnier.

For Rum Custard Sauce, add some rum to taste at the end of cooking the vanilla custard. Desiccated coconut could also be added to this recipe during the cooking process and/or coconut milk added at the end.

Coffee Custard Sauce can be made by replacing the vanilla pod with 2 teaspoons of freshly ground coffee and made as for the vanilla recipe. Once the coffee custard has completely cooled, just strain through a sieve to remove any excess granules.

Shortcrust and Sweet Shortcrust Pastry

Both of these pastries have the same method; the difference is the sugar. Other recipes ideas giving the pastry different flavours follow (below and page 225), appropriate to use with the different fillings given on page 176.

Makes 350 g (12 oz)
225 g (8 oz) plain flour
150 g (5 oz) butter, chopped
1 egg (an extra egg yolk can be
    added for a stronger flavour)

For Sweet Shortcrust Pastry
1 quantity Shortcrust Pastry
50 g (2 oz) caster or icing sugar,

For the basic shortcrust pastry, rub the flour and butter together to a crumble texture. Add the egg and mix briefly to a smooth dough. Wrap in cling film and refrigerate for 20 minutes before rolling and using.

To make the sweet pastry, add the sugar to the flour and butter mixture.

Note: When blind-baking any pastry-lined flan case or ring, line with greaseproof paper or foil and fill with baking beans or rice. This applies to all the pastry recipes.

For a Sweet Lemon and Raisin Shortcrust Pastry, add the finely grated zest of 2 lemons and 50 g (2 oz) chopped raisins to the sweet shortcrust pastry mix. These flavours give the pastry a completely different finish. The pastry works well with fruit, especially with the Gooseberry Tart (see Note on page 177).

Rich Shortcrust Pepper Pastry

The only pepper that really works in this pastry is the black variety. Once it has been milled, I strain it through a sieve, taking out any over-coarse lumps. I use this recipe for savoury flans and quiches.

Makes 400 g (14 oz)
250 g (9 oz) plain flour
150 g (5 oz) salted butter
1 egg, beaten

1 teaspoon freshly ground black
    pepper (heaped, if you are a real
    pepper fan!)

Rub the butter into the flour with the black pepper until it resembles breadcrumbs. Add the egg and 1–2 tablespoons of very cold water to give a good pastry texture. Wrap in cling film and leave to rest in the fridge before rolling.

Sweet Black Pepper and Crunchy Sugar Pastry

Black pepper can be added to unsweetened shortcrust pastry for savoury flans and quiches to give an extra bite (see page 224). The pepper flavour also works well in the sweet pastry: it spices up the tart without being overpowering. The crunchy texture of demerara sugar helps balance the 'hot' flavour.

Makes 400 g (14 oz)

1 quantity of Sweet Shortcrust Pastry (page 224)

1 teaspoon cracked black peppercorns (not too coarse)
50–75 g (2–3 oz) demerara sugar

Cracked black pepper can be found in most supermarkets. This guarantees that the coarse pepper is totally even in size. Add the pepper to the flour and then complete the sweet shortcrust pastry recipe. Once rested, roll out and sprinkle half with demerara sugar. Fold the other half over and re-roll. The demerara sugar will keep its crunchy texture inside the pastry.

Note: This pastry works very well with strawberries, especially peppered strawberries and with the crunchy sugar they will eat even better! Some Pastry Cream (page 231) can be spooned into the cooked pastry case before covering with strawberries. These can now be heavily dusted with icing sugar and glazed (and burnt slightly) under the grill or with a gas gun.

Quick Puff Pastry

Making puff pastry the traditional way cannot really be matched. But here's a recipe that gets you very close to it. Of course the quickest puff pastry is bought frozen!

Makes about 750 g (1½ lb)

450 g (1 lb) plain flour
275 g (10 oz) butter, chilled

1 teaspoon salt
300 ml (10 fl oz) water

Cut the butter into small pieces. Sieve the flour with the salt. Mix together all of the ingredients without totally breaking down the butter. This will enable the butter to work its way into the pastry while it's being rolled. Once the dough is made, roll as for classic puff pastry, into a rectangle (approximately 45 × 15 cm/18 × 6 in). Fold in the right-hand one-third and then fold in the left-hand side on top. Leave to rest for 20 minutes. The pastry needs to be rolled three times in the same way, resting it for 20 minutes between each turn.

Shortbread Pastry

This recipe is for a basic shortbread dough. Shortbreads normally finish up as biscuits or cakes. With this recipe, I am using the dough to line flan or tart cases. A good fresh raspberry flan, or strawberries, peaches or Summer fruits on a shortbread pastry case is delicious. Put the raw fruits directly on the shortbread or spread clotted or extra-thick cream on the base and arrange all the fruits on top.

Makes 350 g (12 oz)
100 g (4 oz) butter
50 g (2 oz) caster sugar

The grated zest of 1 lemon
175 g (6 oz) plain flour

Cream the butter and sugar together. Add the zest and flour and work to a dough. Once completely mixed, wrap in cling film and rest for 20 minutes before re-rolling and baking.

Hazelnut Pastry

This pastry is virtually impossible to roll! Don't be put off, though, because this mixture can be just pressed by hand into a flan or tart case. It is important to work the ground hazelnuts and flour into the sugar and butter mixture for some time, preferably using a food processor or electric mixer. This technique will release the natural hazelnut oils which in turn will help bind the pastry.

Makes 500 g (1 lb 2 oz)
100 g (4 oz) butter
50 g (2 oz) caster sugar

150 g (5 oz) ground hazelnuts
200 g (7 oz) plain flour
1 egg yolk

Pre-heat the oven to 200°C/400°F/Gas Mark 6.

Cream the butter and sugar together. Add the ground hazelnuts and flour and leave to work well in the processor or mixer. Add the egg yolk and bind together. This will have a very dry texture. Press the mixture evenly into a greased flan ring. Line with greaseproof paper or foil and fill with baking beans or rice. Leave to rest in the fridge for 20 minutes.

Bake blind for approximately 30 minutes. The pastry case will now be crisp and, when eaten, quite crumbly and packed with hazelnut taste.

Note: This is the perfect base for the Raspberry Meringue Pie (page 182).

Basic Stock Syrup

Stock syrups are used mostly for poaching fresh fruits and as sorbet bases. This recipe gives you the quantities needed.

The basic recipe is usually 450 g (1 lb) sugar to 600 ml (1 pint) of water. This quantity will give you at least 900 ml (1½ pints) of finished, very thick syrup. For a less sweet and thick syrup, use 350 g (12 oz) of sugar to 600 ml (1 pint) of water. Here are the quantities to give you approximately 450 ml (15 fl oz) of sweet, thick syrup.

**Makes about 450 ml
(15 fl oz)**

225 g (8 oz) sugar
300 ml (10 fl oz) water

Bring both ingredients to the boil and simmer for 8–10 minutes. The syrup will now have thickened and is ready to use.

Note: Other flavours can be added, such as grated fruit zests or liqueurs.

Blood Orange Syrup

The rich, red colour from blood oranges makes this syrup even more exciting but if blood oranges are unavailable, just use another variety.

Makes 300 ml (10 fl oz)
600 ml (1 pint) blood-orange juice
225 g (8 oz) caster sugar

The juice of 2 lemons
50–75 ml (2–3 fl oz) Cointreau
(optional)

Bring all the ingredients to the boil and reduce to 300 ml (10 fl oz). Strain through a sieve and the syrup is ready.

Note: This recipe can also be made into an orange and rum syrup with the addition of 2-3 tablespoons – or more! – of good rum.

Madeira Syrup

Madeira was traditionally always served with Madeira cake. This syrup can be served warm over Mini Madeira Prune Cakes (page 205), and it will keep the cake, taste and tradition very much alive.

Makes about 250 ml
(8 fl oz)
½ bottle Madeira

175 g (6 oz) sugar
150 ml (5 fl oz) pint water

Simply boil all the ingredients together and simmer to a thick, syrupy consistency.

Note: This syrup will also liven up ice-creams, meringues and sponges.

Sultana Syrup Sauce

I made this syrup originally to serve around the Lemon and Sultana Savarin on page 196. I have used it since with many other desserts, ranging from hot steamed puddings to ice-creams.

Makes 250–300 ml
(8–10 fl oz)
100 g (4 oz) sultanas

150 ml (5 fl oz) water
50 g (2 oz) sugar
The juice of 1 lemon

Mix all the ingredients together and bring to the simmer. Cook for 10 minutes and then blitz to a purée in a food processor. Push through a sieve and the sauce is ready.

Note: The lemon juice can be replaced with rum, Madeira, cognac and more!

Mint Syrup

Here's another syrup to finish many dishes. It's a great alternative to use with a simple fruit salad, giving the dish a completely different taste. It can also be used as a garnish for almost any chocolate pudding. The flavour is immense and the colour just as strong. The quantity of mint seems high, but is needed to achieve the right strength of flavour.

Makes about 250 ml (8 fl oz)
225 g (8 oz) fresh mint leaves

175 g (6 oz) caster sugar
120 ml (4 fl oz) water

Blanch the mint leaves in boiling water and then refresh in iced water. Once cold, drain off all the water and chop the mint.

Bring the sugar and water to the simmer and cook for 10 minutes until it has reached a thick syrup. Remove from the heat and leave to cool.

Add the mint to the cold syrup and blitz to a smooth paste in the food processor. Leave to infuse for at least 8 hours and preferably overnight. Once infused, pass through a sieve. The syrup is ready and is best kept refrigerated before using.

Strawberry (or Raspberry) Syrup

This syrup will also work with other red or black berries. The strawberry version is featured in the Crème Chiboust on page 202 and the raspberry with the Roast Peach Melba (see Note on page 198).

Makes 300 ml (10 fl oz)
225 g (8 oz) red, ripe strawberries, chopped

85–120 ml (3–4 fl oz) water
50 g (2 oz) caster sugar

Simmer all the ingredients together until the strawberries are tender. Remove from the heat, cover the saucepan with cling film and leave to cool. Once cooled, push the strawberries and syrup through a sieve. Return to the heat and reduce to a thick syrup.

Coffee Syrup

This coffee syrup can be made with fresh or instant coffee. The fresh coffee will obviously give you a fuller taste, but the instant a quicker result. All you'll need is coffee and sugar.

Makes 150 ml (5 fl oz)

300 ml (10 fl oz) strong fresh or instant coffee

150 g (5 oz) caster sugar

Boil the coffee and sugar together and reduce by half. You now have a rich coffee syrup that is best served at room temperature or cold.

Note: For a liqueur coffee syrup, simply add a splash of Tia Maria.

Fruit Jam Sauce

This is really a recipe for home-made, loose jam, using preserving sugar. This means it has a double use; once you've made it for a pudding, use it the next morning to spread on your toast! The sauce goes very well with the Creamy Fried Slice on page 206 or spooned into pudding basins for your next steamed sponge. Various fruits can be used, for example, blackberries, blackcurrants, rhubarb, raspberries, loganberries, apricots, strawberries, gooseberries or peaches.

Makes 450–750 g (1–1½ lb)

450 g (1 lb) blackberries, washed

4 tablespoons water

225 g (8 oz) preserving sugar

Place all the ingredients in a saucepan and bring to the simmer. Increase the heat to boiling, skimming off any impurities. Return to simmer and cook for 4–5 minutes. Remove the pan from the boil and leave to cool. You now have the rich fruit jam sauce. You can keep it refrigerated in sterilized jam jars for several weeks. This sauce is best served warm, rather than hot, due to the high sugar content.

Note: For jam increase the sugar to the same quantity as the fruit.

When making jams, the longer the cooking time the smoother the jam becomes; simmering it for 4–5 minutes will give you a chunky finish, and increasing the time to 10–15 minutes or longer will leave you with a fruit jelly consistency.

Crisp 'Parmesan' Lemon Crumbs

Whenever pasta is made, I always think about freshly grated 'Parmesan'. It seems to be a natural companion. Here's a recipe for crispy 'Parmesan' for any pasta puddings, especially the fruity Raviolis on page 216.

Serves 4

4 slices of white bread, crusts
  removed, quartered
The finely grated zest of 1 large
  lemon or orange

A knob of butter
1 teaspoon chopped fresh mint
  (optional)
A good pinch of icing sugar
  (optional)

Blitz the bread to crumbs in a food processor with the grated zest. Melt the butter, and shallow-fry the crumbs until golden and crisp. The crumbs are now ready to sprinkle over the pasta. Chopped fresh mint can be added to the food processor at the last minute along with a good pinch of icing sugar to balance the acidity with sweetness.

Pastry Cream

This is a wonderful base for fruit tarts and flans. It is spooned into baked tart cases and then covered with fresh fruits. Quickly cooked rhubarb and gooseberries or raspberries and strawberries, topping a good pastry cream, in crisp pastry – how does that sound?

**Makes about 600 ml
  (1 pint)**
4 egg yolks
50 g (2 oz) caster sugar
1½ tablespoons cornflour

450 ml (15 fl oz) milk
1 vanilla pod, split and scraped, or
  2 teaspoons vanilla essence
2 tablespoons double cream
1 tablespoon butter

Cream together the egg yolks and sugar in a bowl. Add the cornflour. Bring the milk to the boil with the vanilla and pour onto the egg yolk mixture. Return the mixture to the pan, bring back to the simmer and cook for a few minutes, making sure it doesn't boil. Add the cream and butter and then pass through a sieve. Press a piece of greaseproof paper or cling film onto the surface to prevent a skin from forming. Leave to cool. The fresh, vanilla-tasting pastry cream is ready to use.

Note: Grated fruit zests can be added to the milk for a different flavour.

stocks, sauces and basics

*t*his is a chapter for basics and extras. The stocks and recipes haven't really changed from the previous books. One or two have been tweaked here and there, but basics are basic and shouldn't really need a change.

However, making stocks and sauces doesn't have to become a chore. Good-quality stock cubes or packet bases can be found quite easily and will give very good results. The rarebit recipe has reappeared but this time it is flavoured with Gorgonzola. The flavour is immense and goes well with green vegetables. The Gorgonzola can be replaced with almost any other blue cheese; Stilton, Roquefort and so on, or just make it the classic way with Cheddar.

There are combinations of the Butter Sauce recipe (page 236), some flavoured oils, chutneys and relishes. The flavour of the Macerated Grapes (page 239) is quite sensational, working equally well hot or cold with *foie gras*, pâtés and salads.

A basic chapter that finishes the rest of the book – in every sense!

Gorgonzola Rarebit

Here's another rarebit alternative, others having been featured in the Rhodes Around Britain *trilogy. I find this goes very well melted over green vegetables such as cabbage, greens, broccoli and leeks. It also tastes lovely with cauliflower or as a topping for the vegetarian Roast Mushroom and Leek Shepherd's Pie (page 125).*

Gorgonzola is an Italian cow's-milk blue cheese with a mild creamy texture and not too overpowering in flavour. The Cheddar is still needed to balance the strength of the Gorgonzola; half and half seems to be the right proportion.

Makes 400 g (14 oz)
175 g (6 oz) Cheddar, grated
85 ml (3 fl oz) milk
175 g (6 oz) Gorgonzola, chopped
25 g (1 oz) plain flour
25 g (1 oz) white breadcrumbs

½ tablespoon English mustard
  powder
1–2 shakes of Worcestershire sauce
1 egg
1 egg yolk
Salt and pepper

Melt the Cheddar with the milk over a low heat. Once melted, add the Gorgonzola and stir it in until it melts. Bring the mixture to a soft bubble on the stove and add the flour, crumbs, mustard and season with salt and pepper. Cook for a few minutes until the mixture comes away from the sides of the pan and begins to form a ball shape. Add the Worcestershire sauce and leave to cool.

When cold, beat in the egg and egg yolk (this can be done easily in a food processor). Once totally mixed, chill for a few hours before using. The rarebit mix is ready to use.

Home-made Pasta

This pasta recipe can be used for so many different pasta dishes: lasagne, ravioli, fettucine, spaghetti and others. It is simple to make and can be put together in an electric mixer, food processor or, best of all, by hand. When working the dough by hand, you will be able to feel the texture you are looking for – it should have a slightly elastic finish. The pasta dough can be rolled either by hand or, if you have one, with a pasta machine.

Makes about 250 g (9 oz)
250 g (9 oz) fine semolina
   or plain flour
A pinch of salt

½ teaspoon olive oil
2 eggs, beaten
3 egg yolks, beaten

Add the semolina or flour to the salt and olive oil and mix well. Add the eggs and egg yolks and work to a dough. On a clean, lightly floured board, work the dough for 10 minutes until you have a good, slightly elastic, smooth dough. Wrap the dough in cling film and leave to rest for 30 minutes.

For whatever pasta you are making, it will first need to be rolled by hand to approximately 3 mm (⅛ in) thick.

The choice of pasta shapes is yours!

Note: For a better taste, use Italian or French 00 flour if you can get it.

Quick Hollandaise Sauce

This is a quick way of making a Hollandaise sauce, without having to make a flavoured reduction. I use this as a base for the Confit of Sea Trout on page 70 with the addition of a tablespoon or two of Dijon mustard to fire up the flavour. I originally included the recipe in More Rhodes Around Britain, *but I'm repeating it here for convenience.*

Makes about 300 ml (10 fl oz)

225 g (8 oz) unsalted butter
2 egg yolks

1 tablespoon warm water
The juice of ½ lemon
Salt and cayenne pepper or freshly
    ground white pepper

Melt the butter in a pan and then leave it to cool slightly, so that it is just warm when added to the sauce; if it is too hot, the sauce will curdle. The butter should have separated, so you will only be adding the butter oil to the sauce, not the buttermilk that will have collected at the bottom of the pan. This is clarified butter.

Add the egg yolks to the water in a bowl and whisk over a pan of hot water until lighter in colour and thickened. Remove from the heat and slowly add the clarified butter, whisking until the sauce is thick. Add the lemon juice and season with salt and cayenne or pepper.

Maltaise Sauce

This is also a fairly quick recipe, following the Hollandaise method above but replacing the lemon juice and water with a reduction of white-wine vinegar and blood-orange juice. The chopped blood-orange segments give the sauce a lot more texture.

Makes about 300 ml (10 fl oz)

85–120 ml (3–4 fl oz) white-wine
    vinegar
4 blood oranges, juiced

1 blood orange, segmented
    and diced
Ingredients for 1 quantity of Quick
    Hollandaise Sauce (above)

Boil the vinegar and orange juice and reduce by three-quarters. Allow to cool slightly and then mix with the egg yolks and follow the method for Hollandaise sauce. Season with salt and pepper and add the diced blood-orange segments to finish.

butter sauces

The sauce is better known amongst chefs as beurre blanc. It is a very simple and very buttery sauce that works with many dishes, whether they're fish, meat or vegetarian. The basic ingredients are, normally, white-wine vinegar, water, chopped shallots and butter. I have added a few more ingredients to this recipe to add a lot more flavour.

I have also given four 'stocks' as alternatives, starting with water and running through fish, chicken and vegetarian. It will really depend on which dish you are serving the sauce with. Three alternative ideas for flavourings follow the basic recipe.

Basic Butter Sauce

Makes about 300 ml (10 fl oz)

250 g (9 oz) butter, chilled and cubed

2 shallots or 1 small onion, finely chopped

½ star-anise (optional)

2–3 cardamom pods (optional)

1 bay leaf (optional)

Freshly ground black pepper

85 ml (3 fl oz) white-wine vinegar

175 ml (6 fl oz) white wine

150 ml (5 fl oz) water or Fish, Chicken or Vegetable Stock (page 240/1) or alternative (page 243)

2 tablespoons double cream (optional)

Salt and pepper

Melt a small knob of the butter and add the shallots or onion, star-anise, cardamom pods, bay leaf, if using, and a twist of black pepper. Cook for a few minutes, without letting the vegetables colour, until softened. Add the vinegar and reduce by three-quarters. Add the wine and reduce by three-quarters. Pour in the water or stock of your choice and reduce again by three-quarters. If using the double cream to help emulsify the butter, pour it in at this stage.

Bring the reduction to a simmer and whisk in all of the butter, a few pieces at a time. Season with salt and pepper and strain through a sieve. If the sauce is too thick, loosen it with a few drops of water or lemon juice. The basic butter sauce is now ready to use.

Coriander Butter Sauce

**Makes about 300 ml
(10 fl oz)**
1 quantity Basic Butter Sauce
(opposite)

1 bunch of fresh coriander
1 teaspoon lightly crushed coriander
seeds

Reserve a quarter of the coriander leaves for chopping and adding to the finished sauce. Roughly chop the remaining leaves and stalks and add to the basic butter-sauce reduction with the crushed coriander seeds. Once the sauce has been cooked and strained, add the chopped coriander just before serving.

Carrot Butter Sauce

**Makes about 300 ml
(10 fl oz)**
1 quantity Basic Butter Sauce
(opposite)

3 carrots, peeled
The juice of 1 orange

Grate 2 of the carrots and add to the chopped shallots at the start of the cooking period. This will release a lot of sweet carrot flavour and colour. Cut the remaining carrot into very small dice and then cook in salted water for a few minutes until tender. The carrot dice will be used to garnish the sauce before serving. Add the orange juice to the sauce once the white wine has reduced. Finish as for the basic recipe and the carrot butter sauce is made.

Mustard Butter Sauce

**Makes about 300 ml
(10 fl oz)**

1 quantity Basic Butter Sauce
(opposite)
2 tablespoons whole-grain mustard

Push the butter sauce through a sieve and then add the mustard. I like the sauce to have a fairly strong flavour and 2 tablespoons of whole-grain mustard will give you just that. Add more if you like it stronger.

Orange Oil

This flavoured oil works well as a dressing for many dishes. A tasty duck à l'orange Summer salad would go very well with this dressing. I use it to help flavour the Seared Scallops with Home-made Pasta on page 66.

Makes 600 ml (1 pint)

300 ml (10 fl oz) olive oil, preferably extra virgin
300 ml (10 fl oz) groundnut oil
2 garlic cloves, sliced
3–4 cardamom pods, lightly crushed
1 bay leaf
1 star-anise
The finely grated zest and juice of 4 oranges (blood oranges can also be used)
Salt and pepper

Place all the ingredients, bar the orange juice, in a saucepan and bring to the simmer. Remove the pan from the heat and leave to stand for a few hours to help all the flavours infuse.

Boil the orange juice and reduce by three-quarters, giving you a very strongly orange-flavoured reduction.

Once the oil has infused, season with salt and pepper and strain through a sieve, squeezing out all of the oil. Add the orange juice and store in a bottle or jar. The oil, without the juice, will keep almost indefinitely. With the juice, it is best to keep it refrigerated for up to 10 days.

Macerated Grapes

These grapes can be used to help flavour so many dishes. In this book they are featured with Roast Foie Gras on Potato Pancakes (page 42), but I also like to use them as a warm salad dressing. They keep very well, refrigerated and in an air-tight jar, for a few weeks; although the grapes become softer and start to break down, the flavour just keeps getting better.

Makes about 300 ml (10 fl oz)

450 g (1 lb) seedless white grapes, washed
1 tablespoon groundnut oil
A knob of butter
1 heaped teaspoon soft light-brown sugar
1 tablespoon brandy
2 tablespoons sherry vinegar
1 teaspoon strong balsamic vinegar
150 ml (5 fl oz) sweet white wine or white wine with ½ teaspoon soft light-brown sugar
Salt and pepper

Heat a frying-pan with the groundnut oil. Add the grapes and pan-fry for 2–3 minutes until coloured and golden. Add a knob of butter and continue to fry for a further minute. Add the soft brown sugar, which will start to caramelize, with the butter. Add the brandy, which can be flambéed and reduced. Add the sherry vinegar and reduce by half and then follow with the balsamic vinegar and sweet white wine. Reduce by half and lightly season with salt and a twist of pepper.

Remove the grapes from the heat and leave to cool. They are now ready to use and will improve in flavour after a few days of marinating. The grapes are best kept in a jar or other air-tight container.

Chicken Stock

**Makes 2.25 litres
(4 pints)**

2 onions, chopped
2 celery sticks, chopped
2 leeks, chopped
25 g (1 oz) unsalted butter
1 garlic clove, crushed

1 bay leaf
1 fresh thyme sprig
A few black peppercorns
1.75 kg (4 lb) chicken carcasses,
 chopped
3.4 litres (6 pints) water
Salt

In a large stock pot, lightly soften the vegetables in the butter, without letting them colour. Add the garlic, bay leaf, thyme, peppercorns and chopped carcasses. Cover with the cold water, season with salt and bring to the simmer, skimming off the impurities all the time. Allow the stock to simmer for 2–3 hours.

Drain through a sieve. The stock is now ready to use and will keep well, chilled or frozen.

Vegetable Stock

**Makes about 1.2 litres
(2 pints)**

225 g (8 oz) carrots (optional)
2 onions
4 celery sticks
2 leeks, white part only
1 fennel bulb
1–2 courgettes

1 bay leaf
1 sprig fresh thyme
1 teaspoon coriander seeds
1 teaspoon pink peppercorns
½ lemon, sliced
1.5 litres (2½ pints) water
A pinch of salt
Vegetable oil

Cut all the vegetables roughly into 1 cm (½ in) dice. Warm the vegetable oil in a pan, then add all the diced vegetables, the herbs, coriander, peppercorns and lemon. Cook without colour for 8–10 minutes, allowing them to soften slightly. Add the water with a good pinch of salt and bring to a simmer. Once at simmering point, cook for 30 minutes without a lid. During this time the stock should have reduced, increasing the flavour and depth.

The stock can now be strained through a sieve, leaving you with about 1.2 litres (2 pints). If you find there is more than this quantity, simply boil rapidly to reduce. You can also reduce it if you find that the flavour is not full enough.

Fish Stock

Makes about 2 litres (3½ pints)

1 large onion, sliced
1 leek, sliced
2 celery sticks, sliced
50 g (2 oz) unsalted butter
A few fresh parsley stalks
1 bay leaf
6 black peppercorns
1 kg (2 lb) turbot or sole bones, washed
300 ml (10 fl oz) dry white wine
2.25 litres (4 pints) water
Salt

Sweat the sliced vegetables in the butter, without letting them colour. Add the parsley stalks, bay leaf and peppercorns. Chop the fish bones, making sure there are no blood clots left on them. Add to the vegetables and continue to cook for a few minutes. Add the wine and boil to reduce until almost dry. Add the water, season with salt and bring to the simmer. Allow to simmer for 20 minutes, then drain through a sieve. The stock is now ready to use, or you can store it in the fridge for a few days.

Veal or Beef Stock and *Jus*/Gravy

**Makes 4.5–6 litres
(8–10 pints) stock
or 600 ml–1.2 litres
(1–2 pints) *jus*/gravy**
3 onions, halved
2–3 tablespoons water
2.25 kg (5 lb) veal or beef bones
225 g (8 oz) veal or beef trimmings
 from the butcher
225 g (8 oz) carrots, coarsely
 chopped
3 celery sticks, coarsely chopped
1 leek, chopped
3–4 tomatoes, chopped
1 garlic clove, halved
1 bay leaf
1 fresh thyme sprig
Salt

Pre-heat the oven to 120°C/250°F/Gas Mark ½. Lay the onion halves flat in a roasting tray with the water. Place the onions in the oven and allow to caramelize slowly until they have totally softened and coloured. This process will take 1–2 hours. The sugars in the onions will cook slowly and give a wonderful taste.

Pop the onions into a large stock pot and leave on one side. Increase the oven temperature to 200°C/400°F/Gas Mark 6. Place all the bones and trimmings in a roasting tray and roast for about 30 minutes until well coloured. Roast the chopped carrots and celery in another roasting tray for about 20 minutes until lightly coloured.

When ready, add the roasted bones, trimmings and vegetables to the onions in the pot, along with the leek, tomatoes, garlic, bay leaf and thyme. Fill the pot with cold water – you'll need about 6–7.2 litres (10–12 pints). Bring the stock to the simmer, season with salt and skim off any impurities. Allow to cook for 6–8 hours for the maximum flavour. If it seems to be reducing too quickly, top up with cold water.

When ready, drain and discard the bones and vegetables. This is now your veal stock, and you can cool it and freeze it in convenient quantitites.

Alternatively, make a veal *jus*/gravy with the stock. Allow the liquid to boil and reduce to 600 ml–1.2 litres (1–2 pints), skimming all the time. The stock should be thick and of a sauce-like consistency. Make sure that you taste all the time during reduction. If the sauce tastes right but is not thick enough, thicken it slightly with cornflour. (Of course, I do hope that won't be necessary!) You now have a veal *jus*/gravy, a classic sauce.

Alternative Stocks and Sauces

Fish and Chicken Stocks

Alternatives to these can be found in the chill cabinet of most quality supermarkets. They are sold in plastic tubs, each containing about 284ml (9–10 fl oz). The beauty of these is they taste great, they have a good colour and jelly texture and they are sold as stocks ready to use. They really are the best I've found but, if you can't get hold of them, there are also some good-quality stock cubes.

Beef and Veal *Jus*/Gravy

In the basic recipe, the beef and veal *jus* start out as stocks and are then reduced to a sauce consistency for other recipes. I've found a sauce which will cut out all of this and is an instant *jus* to use as a base sauce in many of the recipes that need veal or beef *jus*. Madeira Wine Gravy or White Wine Gravy are both made by Crosse & Blackwell in their Bonne Cuisine range, and should be available in just about every supermarket or grocery shop. The Madeira flavour gives good body and, when made, has a lovely, glossy finish. My only advice is to mix them with 450 ml (¾ pint) of water instead of 300 ml (10 fl oz). This way, when slow-braising or stewing, there's room for reducing without them becoming too thick.

Other Sauces and Ingredients

Another sauce I found, also in the Bonne Cuisine range, is Hollandaise Sauce. If you are unsure about making Hollandaise, give this version a try: it's so easy.

As for dried pastas and ready-made pastry, all varieties can be found in local shops. If you're lucky enough to have a good delicatessen nearby, then buy your pasta there; it's often made on the premises.

Mustard Dressing

This is a basic recipe for a simple dressing that I have used in many recipes. It's so versatile and has a creamy texture. If you have a favourite mustard – such as English, French or grain – then simply use the one of your choice.

Makes 300 ml (10 fl oz)

4 teaspoons Dijon mustard

2 tablespoons white-wine vinegar

8 tablespoons walnut oil

8 tablespoons groundnut oil

Salt and freshly ground black pepper

Whisk the mustard with the vinegar. Mix together the two oils and gradually add to the mustard, whisking all the time as you would if making mayonnaise. Once everything is thoroughly mixed, season with salt and pepper.

Note: This can also be made into a herb dressing by adding a choice of chopped mixed fresh herbs, or perhaps just chopped fresh tarragon to give you a mustard and tarragon dressing that will go well with fish or poultry.

The addition of 1–2 egg yolks, mixed with the mustard and white wine vinegar, will guarantee a creamy texture, almost like mayonnaise.

Mustard Seed Butter

This isn't so much a recipe as a flavouring. Melting this butter over fish or roasted pork or chicken dishes gives the finished result a much fuller flavour, with the crunch from the mustard seeds adding a new texture.

Makes 100 g (4 oz)

50 g (2 oz) unsalted butter, softened

50 g (2 oz) whole-grain mustard

Simply mix the two ingredients together. This can now be kept chilled or used immediately.

STOCKS, SAUCES AND BASICS

Onion Gravy (1)

Making this onion gravy with chopped onions gives you a completely different result in terms of consistency from the recipe below. This onion gravy can be cooked and reduced to an almost hot onion chutney/relish stage. Thick, rich and tasty!

Makes 450–600 ml (15–20 fl oz)

4 large onions, finely chopped
2 tablespoons water

300–450 ml (10–15 fl oz) Veal or Beef Jus/Gravy (page 242) or alternative (page 243)

To make the onion gravy, place the chopped onions in a pan with the water. They must now be cooked on a very low heat, which will slowly draw the natural sugar content from the onions; together with its juices, the two will caramelize. This is a slow process, possibly taking up to 2 hours. It is very important that the onions do not burn as this will create a bitter taste. Once a golden caramel flavour has been achieved, add the gravy. By adding just 300 ml (10 fl oz) you will have a thick onion marmalade. This goes very well just spooned into cooked Yorkshire puddings. For a thinner sauce consistency, use 450 ml (15 fl oz) of *jus*.

For a quicker caramelizing method, cook the onions to a golden brown in a knob of butter. Add a teaspoon of demerara sugar and cook for 1–2 minutes. Taste the onions for sweetness. If you feel they need more, add more sugar until the flavour you are after is achieved. Now just add the gravy and cook for 6–8 minutes before serving.

Onion Gravy (2)

Makes 600 ml (1 pint)

8 onions, thinly sliced
2 tablespoons water

600ml (1 pint) Veal or Beef Jus/Gravy (page 242) or alternative (page 243)

Place the onions in a pan with the water and cook very slowly, stirring all the time. The sugar from the onions will slowly caramelize and become brown and sweet-tasting. The process will take 1½–2 hours.

Add the *jus*/gravy and simmer for a further 30 minutes. The gravy will now be even richer in taste and colour with a lovely shiny finish.

Hot Mustard Shallot Sauce

This sauce is, in fact, a French classic called sauce diable – 'devilled sauce'. *It is traditionally served with grilled or fried fish or meats. I've taken the sauce and played with the basic flavours. It is sweet, sharp and has a good bite. I also like to use it as a dip for cocktail sausages, chicken or grilled prawns on sticks.*

The shallots can be replaced with onions but they don't quite give you the same result.

Makes about ½ pint

300 ml (10 fl oz) finely diced shallots
   or onions
A small knob of butter
A good twist of freshly ground
   pepper
50 ml (2 fl oz) red-wine vinegar,
   preferably a thick, strong Cabernet
   Sauvignon variety

1 glass white wine
150 ml (5 fl oz) Jus/Gravy
   (page 242) or alternative
   (page 243) (it must have a good
   coating consistency)
1 teaspoon (or more) of English
   mustard (not powder)
Salt and pepper

Melt the butter in a small pan and add the chopped shallots or onions. Cook on a medium heat until they have started to take on a good golden brown colour for about 4–5 minutes. Season with a twist of pepper and add the vinegar. Reduce the vinegar until almost dry, about 2–3 minutes. Add the wine and continue to reduce, again until almost dry. Add the *jus*/gravy and bring to the simmer. Lightly simmer for 5–10 minutes and then add the mustard. Season with salt and pepper, if needed, and taste. The sauce will now have a sharp, sweet flavour with a bite from the pepper and mustard. The taste can be strengthened with a little more mustard.

Note: The shallots have to be measured by volume to take into account the various sizes of shallot. The 300 ml (10 fl oz) listed in the ingredients guarantees the right quantity.

A small pinch of cayenne pepper can be added to the shallots while they are cooking in the butter to lift the 'bite'. Also, 1 tablespoon of brandy can be added before the red-wine vinegar to give a fuller flavour.

STOCKS, SAUCES AND BASICS

Home-made Redcurrant Jelly

Redcurrant jelly and mint sauce are two flavours and accompaniments usually offered with lamb. A good roast joint of lamb helped along with either (or both) is delicious to eat. So, I thought I would feature a recipe for the red one. The green one – the mint sauce – has already been featured in one of my previous books and I didn't want the redcurrants to feel left out.

Makes 750–900 g (1½–2 lb)

1.5 kg (3 lb) freshly picked redcurrants
Preserving sugar

Place the picked redcurrants in a saucepan and barely cover with water. Bring to the boil and then reduce the heat and simmer for 25–30 minutes until the currants have become overcooked and mushy.

Leave to strain through a fine sieve or muslin bag and allow to drain naturally. This will take all of the flavour and colour from the fruit. After several hours, when the dripping has stopped, measure the quantity of juice. For every 600 ml (1 pint) of juice, add 350 g (12 oz) of preserving sugar. (Normally, the quantity is 450 g/1 lb sugar to 600 ml/1 pint of juice but I find this too sweet and sickly. Redcurrants have a high pectin level, and with preserving sugar, 350 g/12 oz will be plenty.) Boil the sugar with the juices and simmer for 10 minutes. The jelly is now ready to pour into sterilized, hot jars. Once cold, the jelly will set.

Note: The flavour can be changed slightly with the addition of the grated zest of 1 orange and 2–3 tablespoons of port. This will give you an even richer jelly with an orange tang.

Mango Chutney

This is a chutney I love to spoon on to a good spicy curry. Curries have become a way of British life, so I thought I would include this recipe. Normally, the mango chutney is the thing you buy and quite often the curry is the thing that you make. Next time you order a take-away, at least part of it will be home-made!

Makes about 1.75 kg (4 lb)

6 mangoes, not too ripe
450 g (1 lb) soft light-brown sugar
2 teaspoons ground mixed spice
A good pinch of ground turmeric
½ teaspoon cayenne pepper

3 cooking apples, peeled, cored and chopped
2 onions, finely chopped
4 garlic cloves, finely crushed with 1 teaspoon salt
750 ml (1¼ pints) malt vinegar
50 g (2 oz) finely grated fresh ginger

Peel the mangoes and then cut either side of the stone, giving you two thick slices of the fruit. Cut the opposite ends of the mango away from the edge of the stones. Any remaining fruit should be scraped off into a bowl. Cut the large fruit slices into thick strips.

Stir the sugar, mixed spice, turmeric and cayenne into the mango. This is now best left for a good few hours to 'marinate'.

Next place all the ingredients together in a large saucepan. Bring to the simmer and cook for 1½ hours, stirring from time to time, for even cooking and to prevent it from sticking. The mango will have become soft and cooked through, leaving a thick syrup. If the chutney seems to be too thin, simply increase the heat, reduce and stir to a 'drier' consistency. Leave to rest for 20–30 minutes, before ladling into sterilized preserving jars.

These can now be cooled and kept in a cool area. The chutney can be eaten just days after cooking, but is best left for several weeks to mature.

Pear Chutney

A chutney that can be served with a variety of cold foods, this is at its best with a plate of cheese.

**Makes 900 g–1.25 kg
(2–2½ lb)**

1 kg (2 lb) pears, peeled, cored and
   cut into 1 cm (½ in) dice
1 complete head of celery, peeled
   and cut into 1 cm (½ in) dice
275 g (10 oz) soft light-brown or
   white sugar

1 onion, diced
1 teaspoon finely grated fresh ginger
   or ½ teaspoon ground ginger
1 teaspoon coriander seeds
2 garlic cloves, crushed
300 ml (10 fl oz) cider vinegar

Cook all the ingredients together for 20–25 minutes or until tender but still retaining their shape. Strain off the liquor and reduce to a syrup consistency (10–15 minutes). Pour the syrup back on to the pears and celery. Mix well, spoon into warm, sterilized jars and cover.

Note: This chutney will eat well after just 24 hours but obviously improves with time.

Apple and Mustard Chutney

This is a combination of flavours that goes particularly well with slices of good ham or cold roast pork; apples are the classic accompaniment to pork, and mustard puts fire in the combination.

**Makes 450–750 g
(1–1½ lb)**

10 green apples
4 tablespoons yellow or black
   mustard seeds

250 ml (8 fl oz) white-wine vinegar
225 g (8 oz) caster sugar
The finely grated zest of 1 lemon
2 onions, finely chopped
A pinch of salt

Peel, core and dice the apples. Place all the ingredients together in a pan and cook until the apples have become tender, about an hour. The liquor can now be drained and reduced to a syrupy consistency and then poured over the apple mixture and transferred to air-tight jars. This will give you a chunky chutney. Or just continue to cook to a more 'mashed' texture, cooking all the ingredients to a thick consistency.

Apple, Prune and Lime Chutney

This is a very quick and easy chutney recipe. It eats well with pâtés, terrines and cold meats.

**Makes 450–750 g
(1–1½ lb)**

6 Granny Smith apples, peeled,
    cored and cut into eighths
2 limes, peeled and segmented
½ onion, finely chopped

50 g (2 oz) prunes, chopped
4 tablespoons red-wine vinegar
1 glass of red wine
50 g (2 oz) preserving sugar
¼ teaspoon ground mixed spice
Salt and pepper

Place all the ingredients in a saucepan, bring to the simmer, cover and cook to a thick pickle consistency, about 30 minutes. Season with salt and pepper and the pickle is ready. Place in warm, sterilized jars and seal.

Note: The preserving sugar gives the chutney a longer life and helps it to hold a better consistency. The apple will break down to a chunky purée during the cooking.

index

INDEX

INDEX

INDEX